MACHETE SQUAD

WRITTEN BY

BRENT DULAK

KEVIN KNODELL

AND DAVID AXE

ILLUSTRATED BY

PER DARWIN BERG

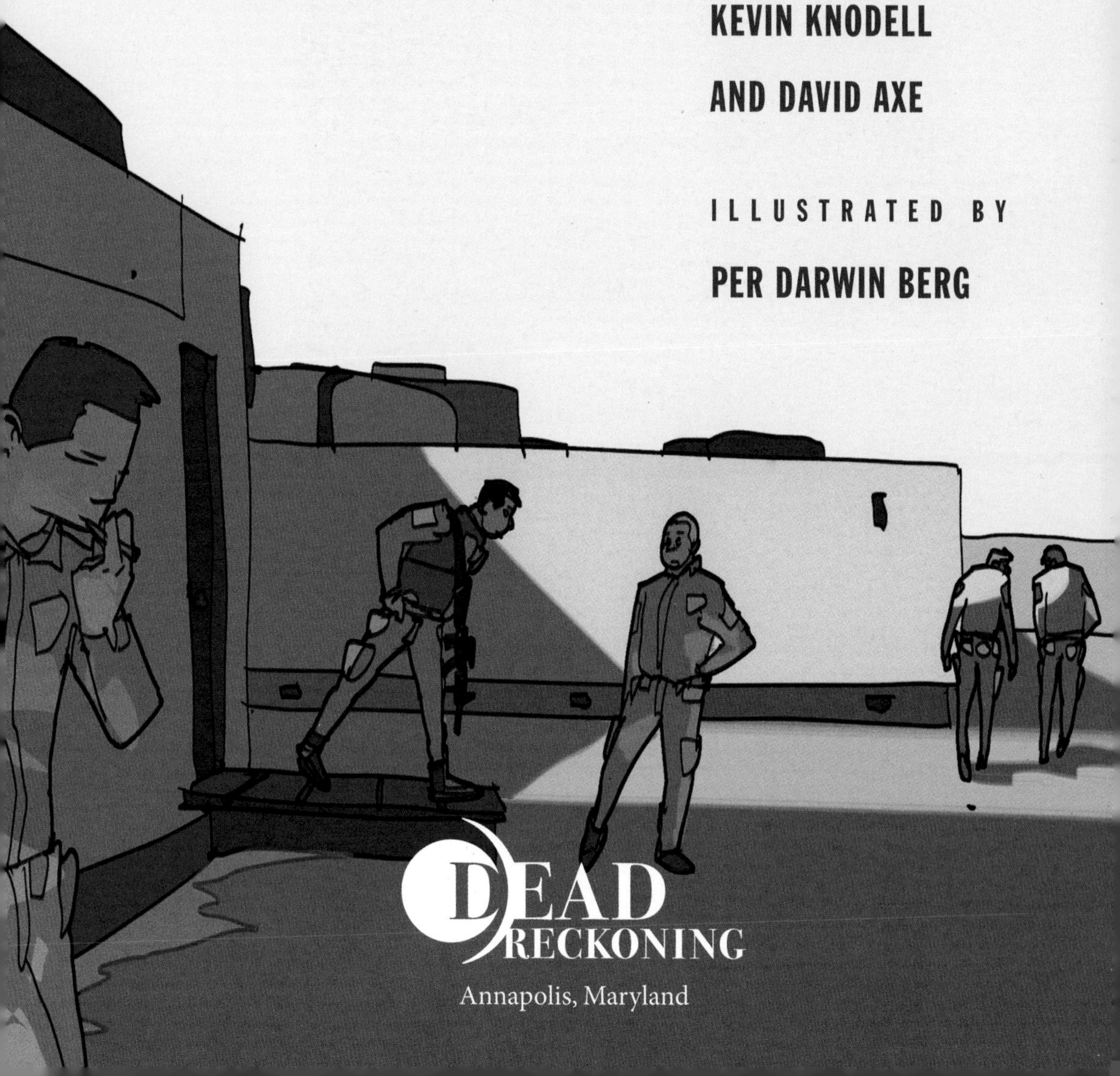

DEAD RECKONING

Annapolis, Maryland

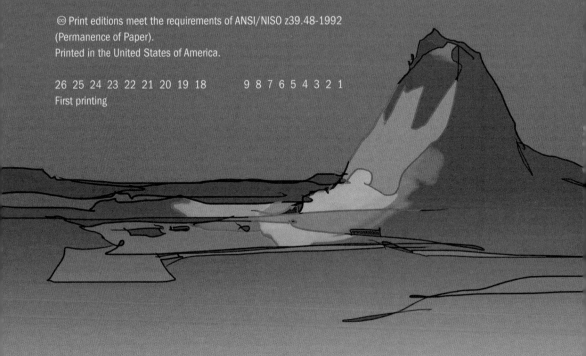

Naval Institute Press
291 Wood Road
Annapolis, MD 21402

Library of Congress Cataloging-in-Publication Data is available.
978-1-68247-100-5 (paperback)
978-1-68247-101-2 (eBook)

♾ Print editions meet the requirements of ANSI/NISO z39.48-1992
(Permanence of Paper).
Printed in the United States of America.

26 25 24 23 22 21 20 19 18   9 8 7 6 5 4 3 2 1
First printing

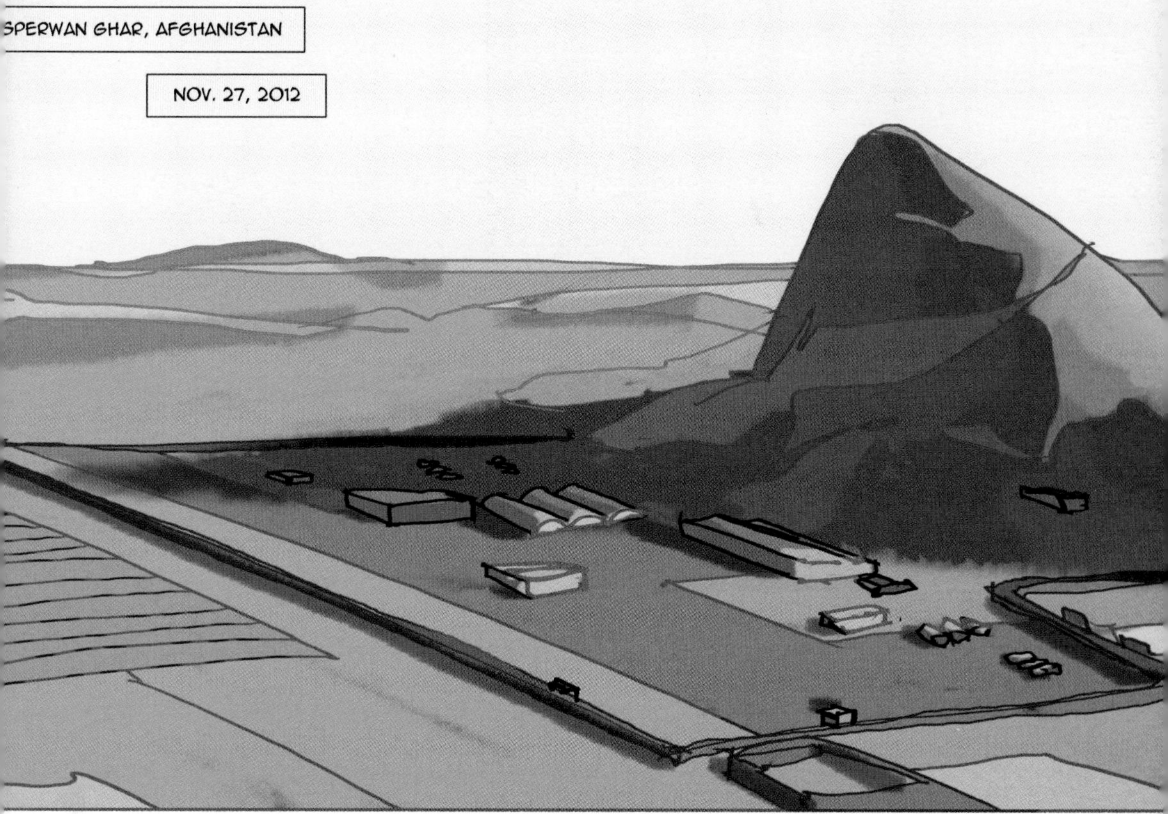
SPERWAN GHAR, AFGHANISTAN
NOV. 27, 2012

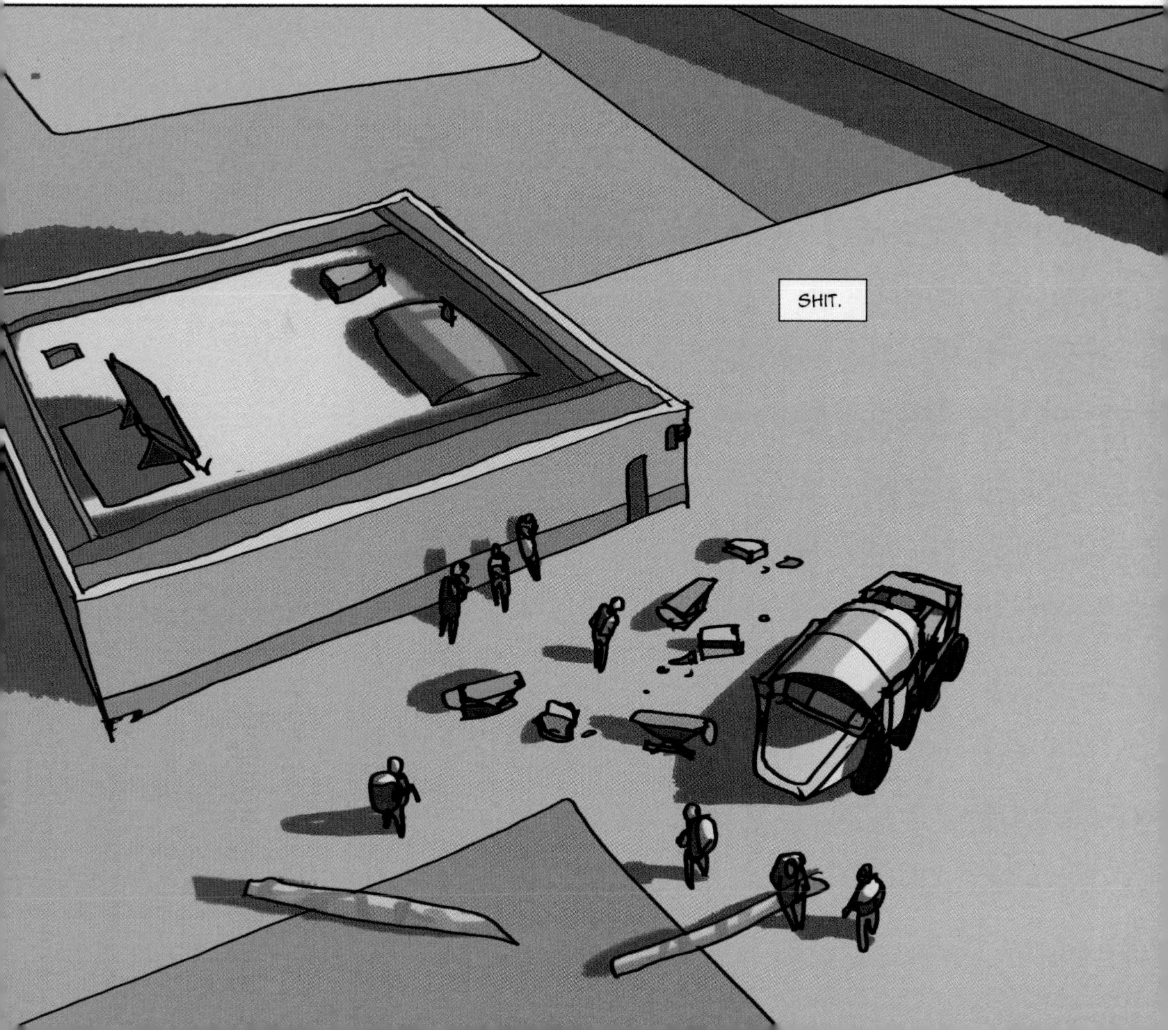
SHIT.

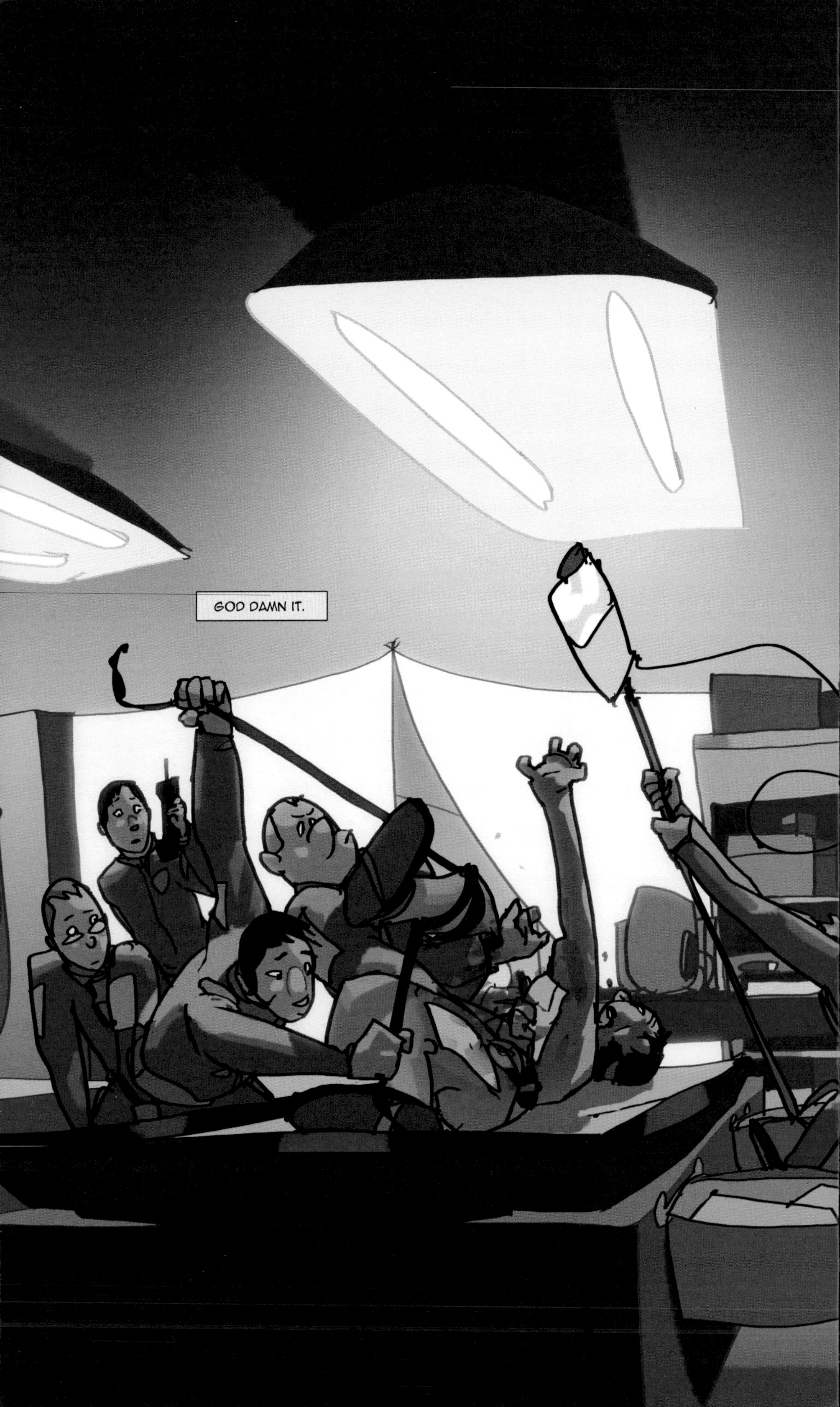
GOD DAMN IT.

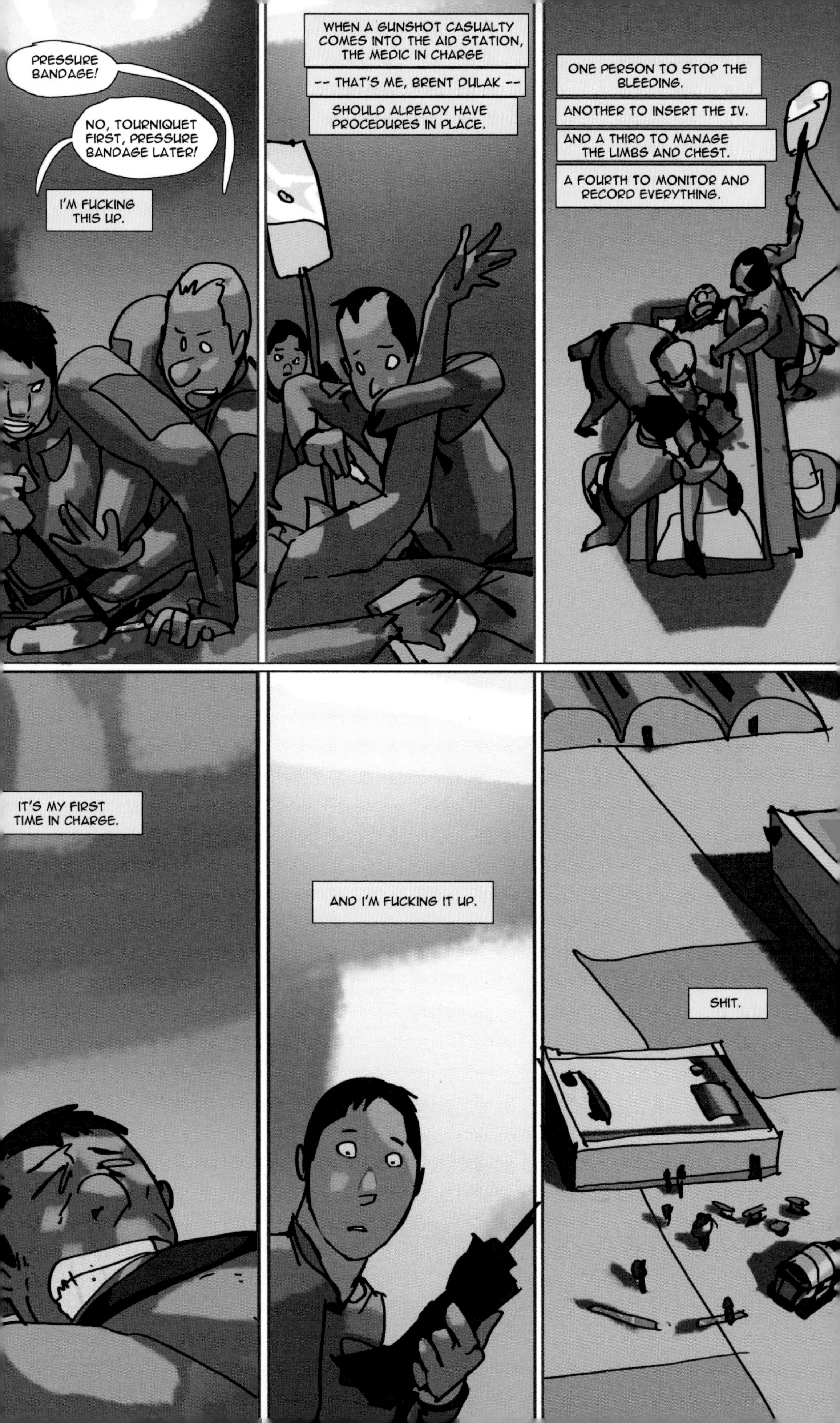
PRESSURE BANDAGE!
NO, TOURNIQUET FIRST, PRESSURE BANDAGE LATER!
I'M FUCKING THIS UP.
WHEN A GUNSHOT CASUALTY COMES INTO THE AID STATION, THE MEDIC IN CHARGE
-- THAT'S ME, BRENT DULAK --
SHOULD ALREADY HAVE PROCEDURES IN PLACE.
ONE PERSON TO STOP THE BLEEDING.
ANOTHER TO INSERT THE IV.
AND A THIRD TO MANAGE THE LIMBS AND CHEST.
A FOURTH TO MONITOR AND RECORD EVERYTHING.
IT'S MY FIRST TIME IN CHARGE.
AND I'M FUCKING IT UP.
SHIT.

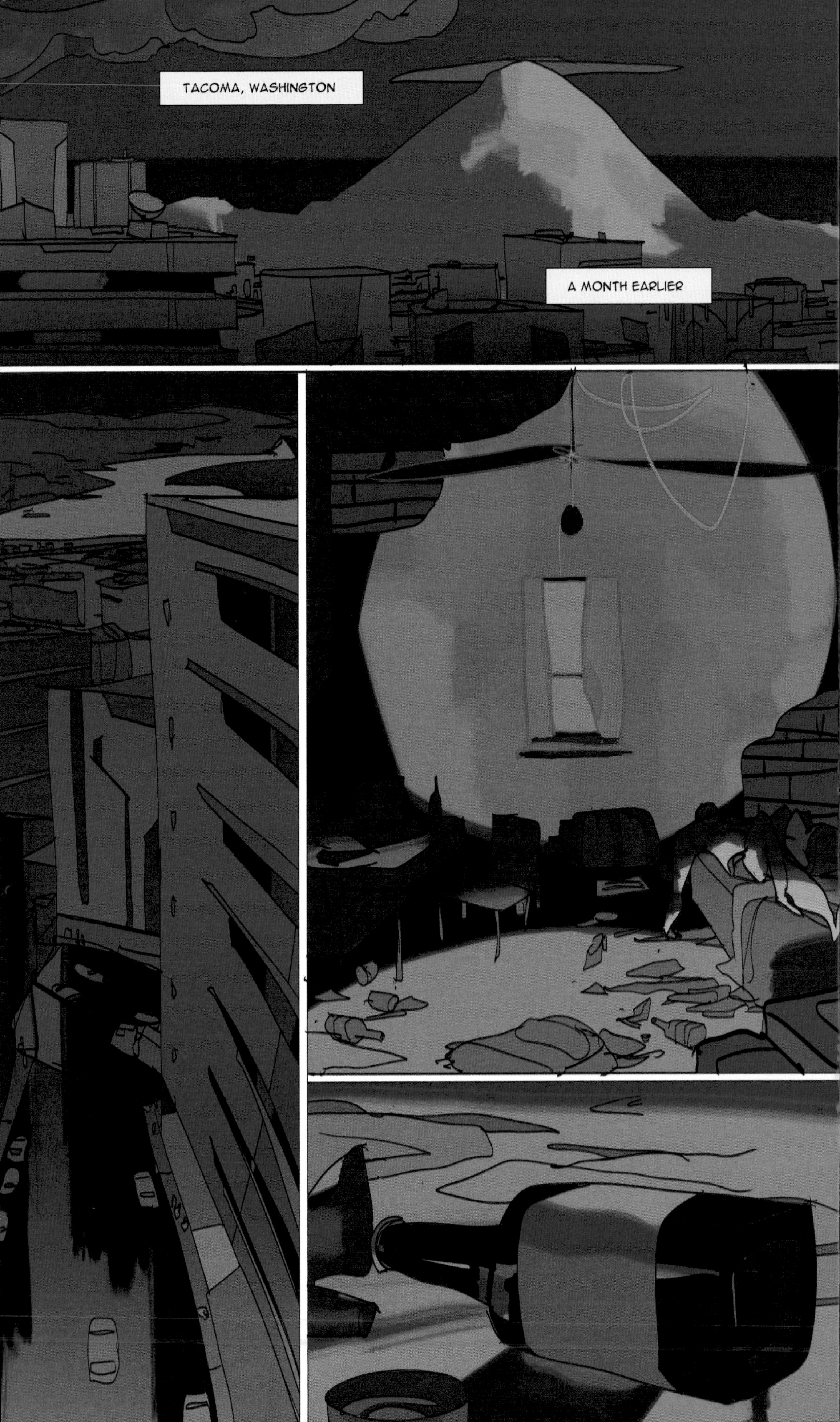
TACOMA, WASHINGTON
A MONTH EARLIER

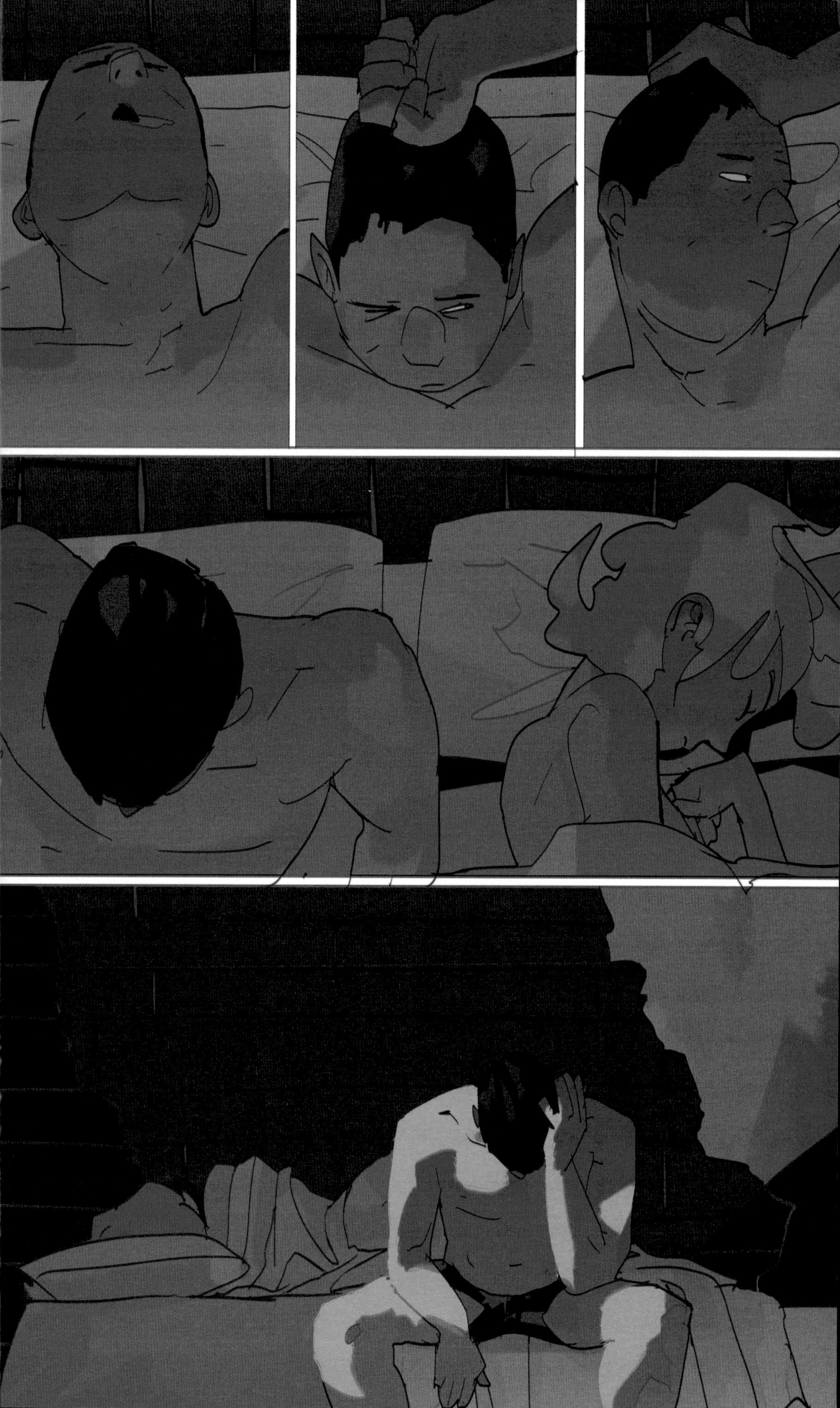

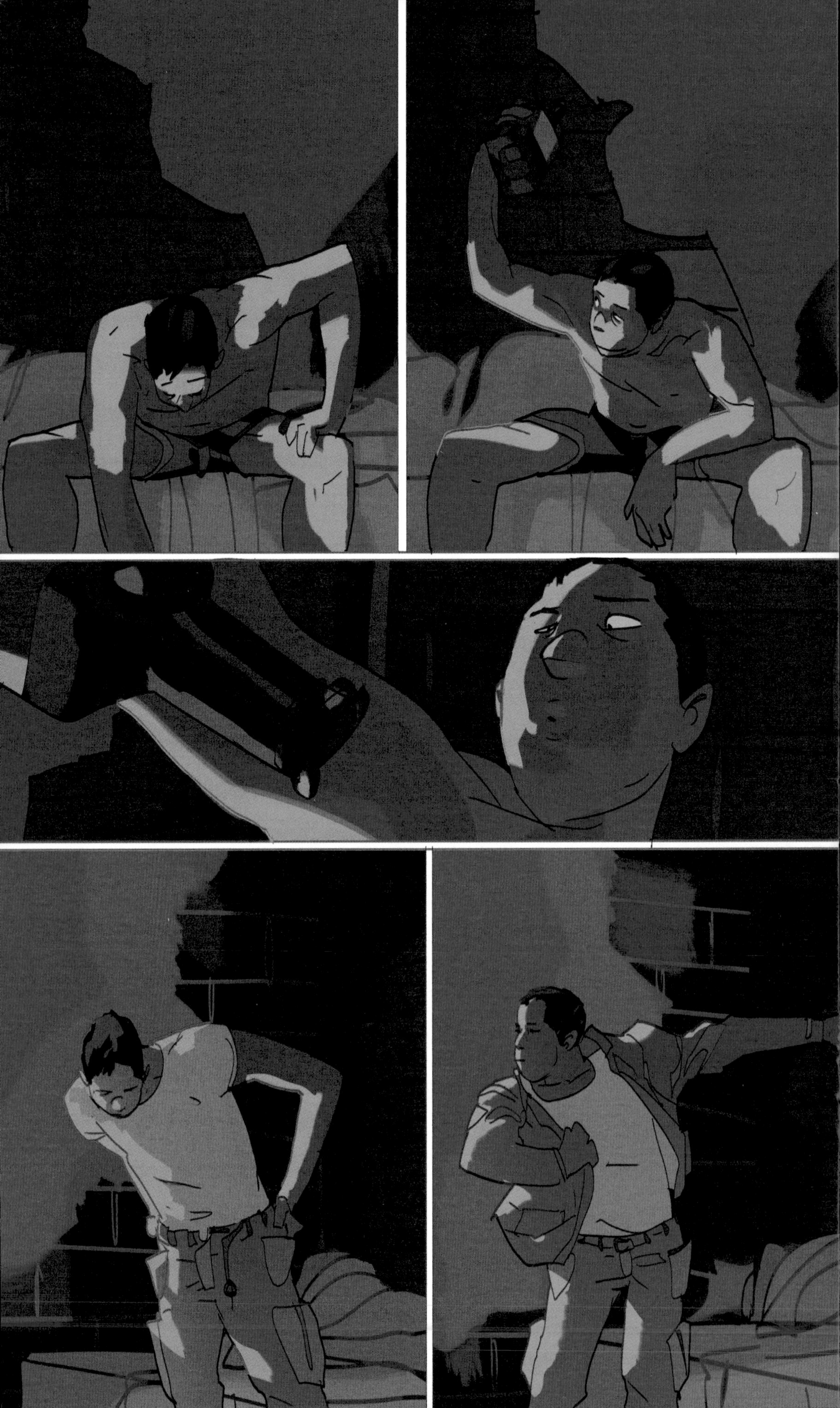

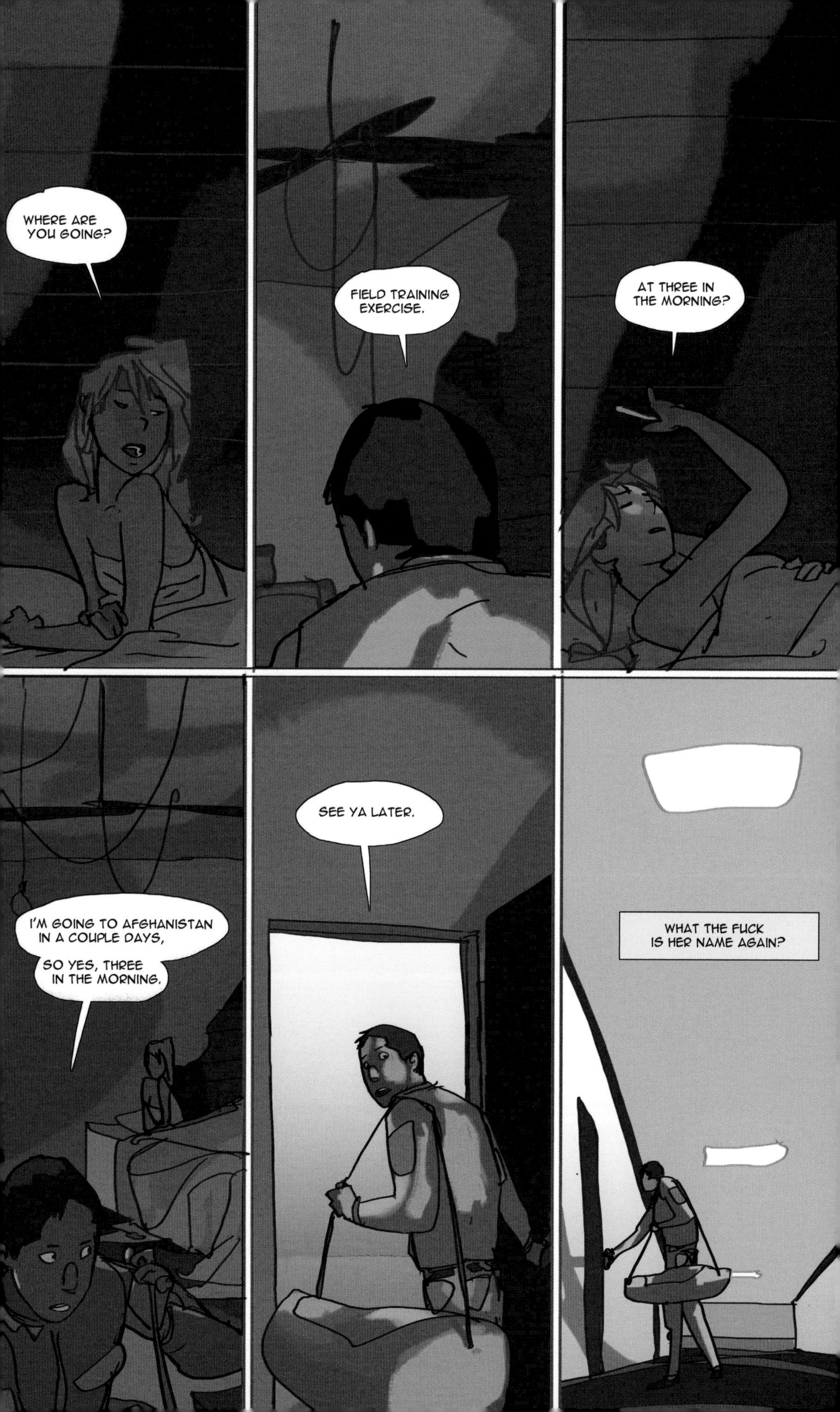
WHERE ARE YOU GOING?
FIELD TRAINING EXERCISE.
AT THREE IN THE MORNING?
I'M GOING TO AFGHANISTAN IN A COUPLE DAYS,
SO YES, THREE IN THE MORNING.
SEE YA LATER.
WHAT THE FUCK IS HER NAME AGAIN?

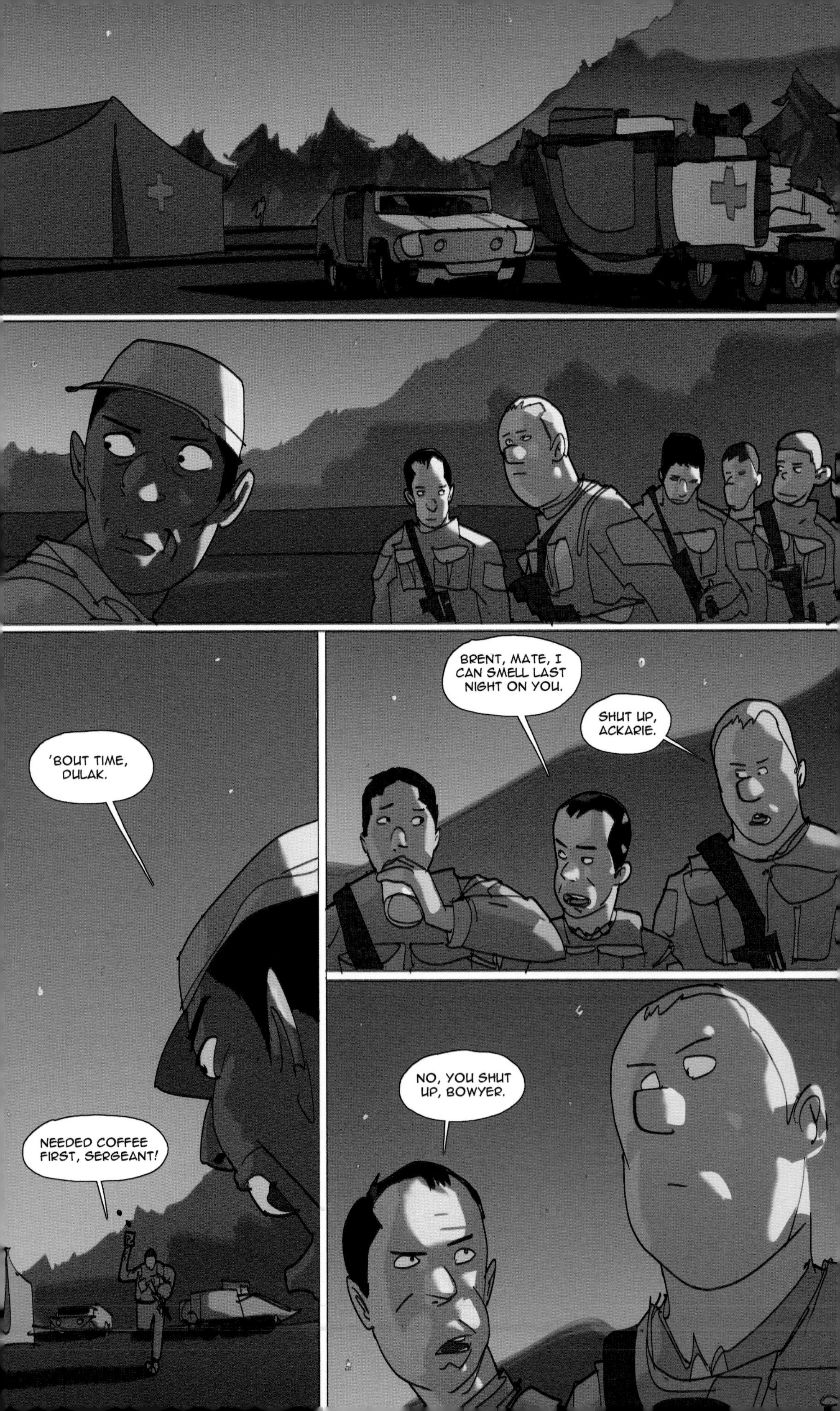
'BOUT TIME, DULAK.
NEEDED COFFEE FIRST, SERGEANT!
BRENT, MATE, I CAN SMELL LAST NIGHT ON YOU.
SHUT UP, ACKARIE.
NO, YOU SHUT UP, BOWYER.

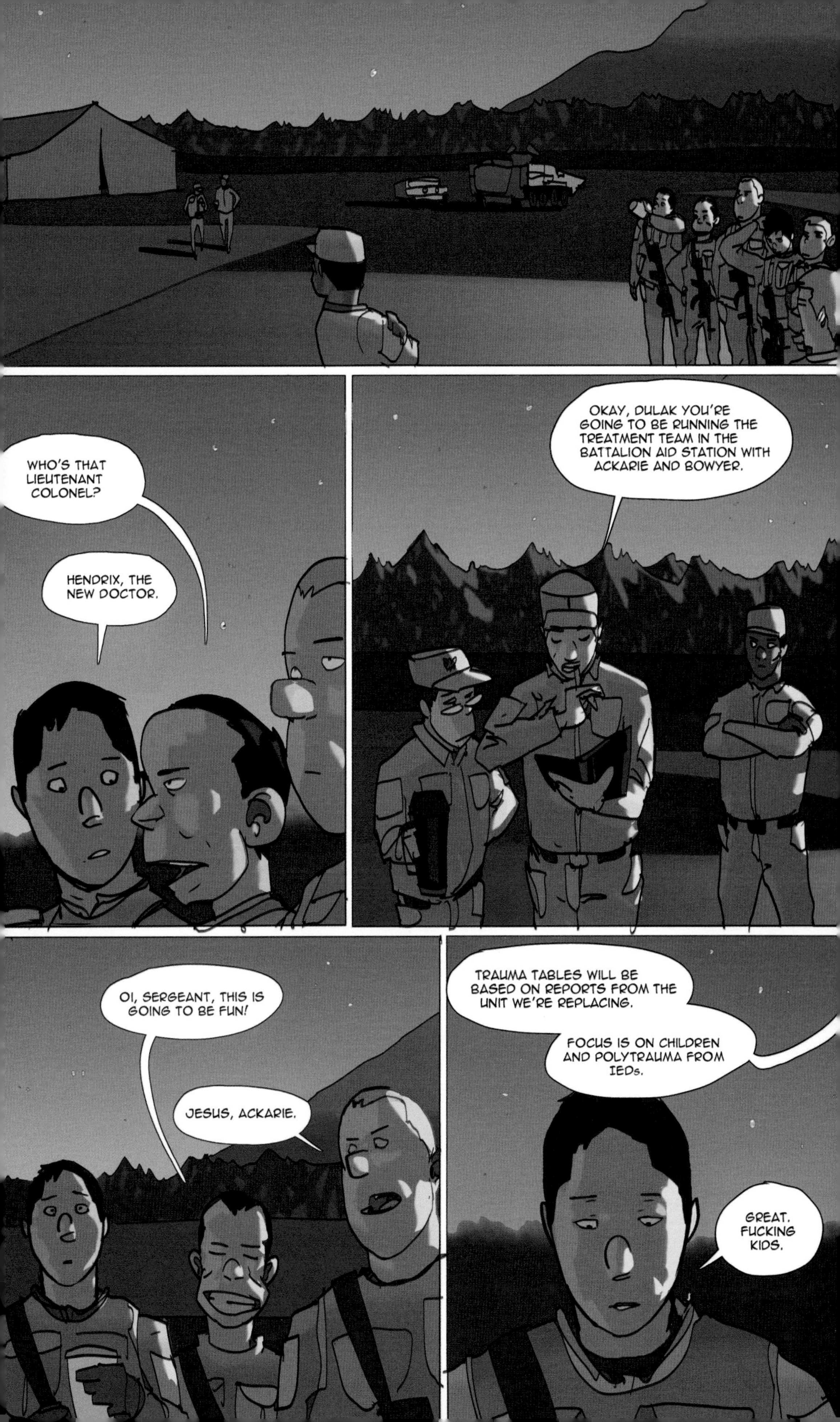
WHO'S THAT LIEUTENANT COLONEL?
HENDRIX, THE NEW DOCTOR.
OKAY, DULAK YOU'RE GOING TO BE RUNNING THE TREATMENT TEAM IN THE BATTALION AID STATION WITH ACKARIE AND BOWYER.
OI, SERGEANT, THIS IS GOING TO BE FUN!
JESUS, ACKARIE.
TRAUMA TABLES WILL BE BASED ON REPORTS FROM THE UNIT WE'RE REPLACING.
FOCUS IS ON CHILDREN AND POLYTRAUMA FROM IEDs.
GREAT. FUCKING KIDS.

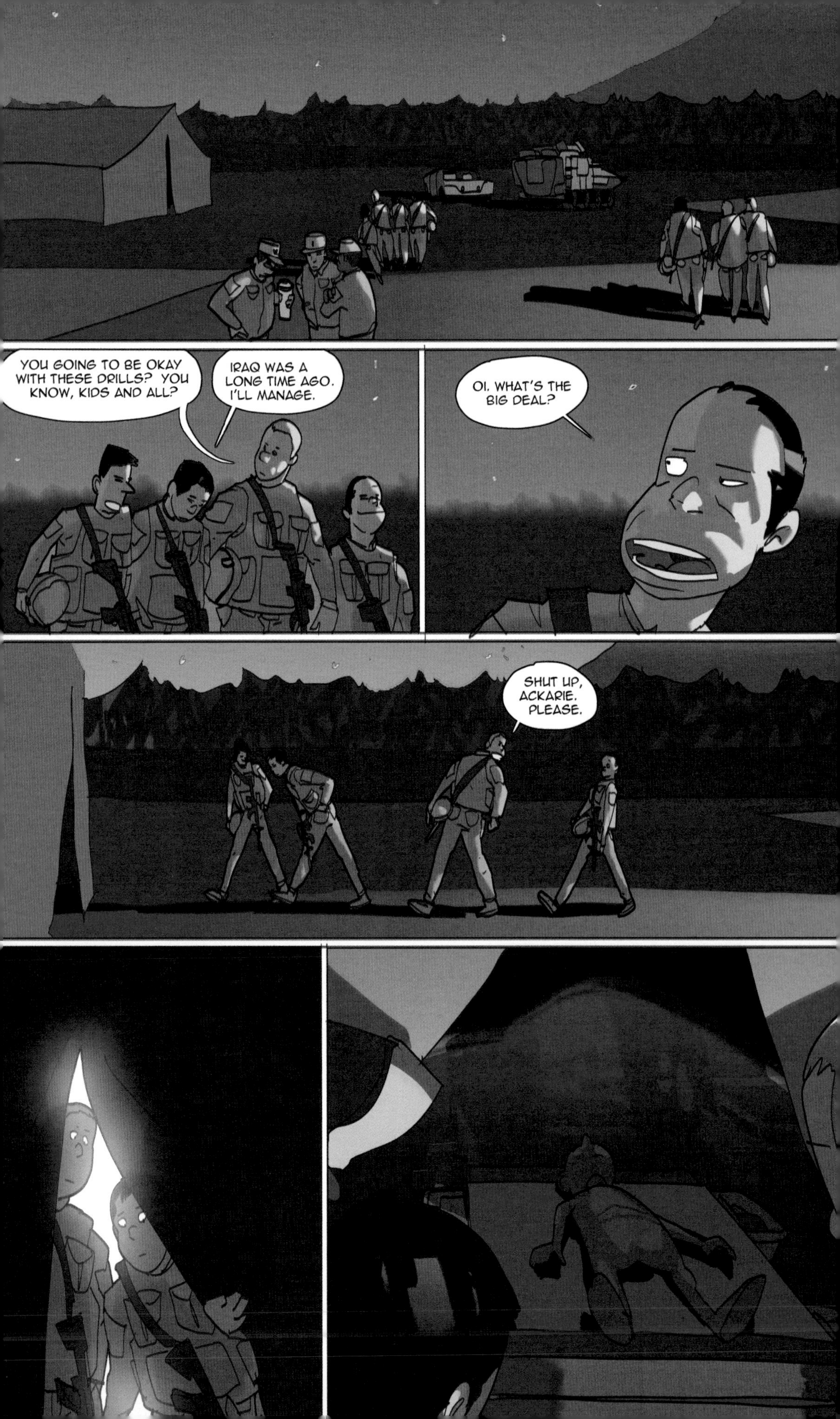

YOU GOING TO BE OKAY WITH THESE DRILLS? YOU KNOW, KIDS AND ALL?
IRAQ WAS A LONG TIME AGO. I'LL MANAGE.
OI. WHAT'S THE BIG DEAL?
SHUT UP, ACKARIE. PLEASE.

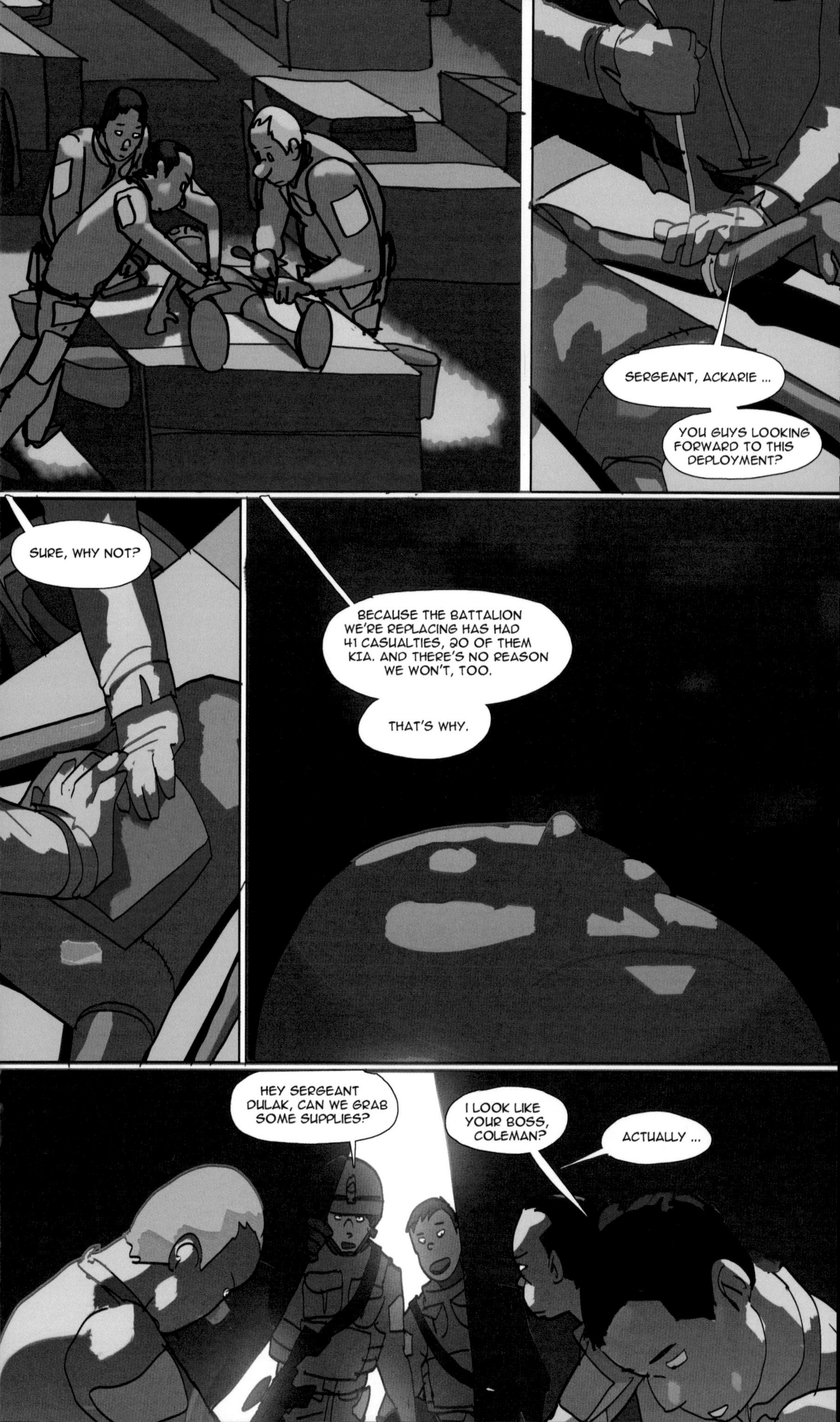
SERGEANT, ACKARIE ...
YOU GUYS LOOKING FORWARD TO THIS DEPLOYMENT?
SURE, WHY NOT?
BECAUSE THE BATTALION WE'RE REPLACING HAS HAD 41 CASUALTIES, 20 OF THEM KIA. AND THERE'S NO REASON WE WON'T, TOO.
THAT'S WHY.
HEY SERGEANT DULAK, CAN WE GRAB SOME SUPPLIES?
I LOOK LIKE YOUR BOSS, COLEMAN?
ACTUALLY ...

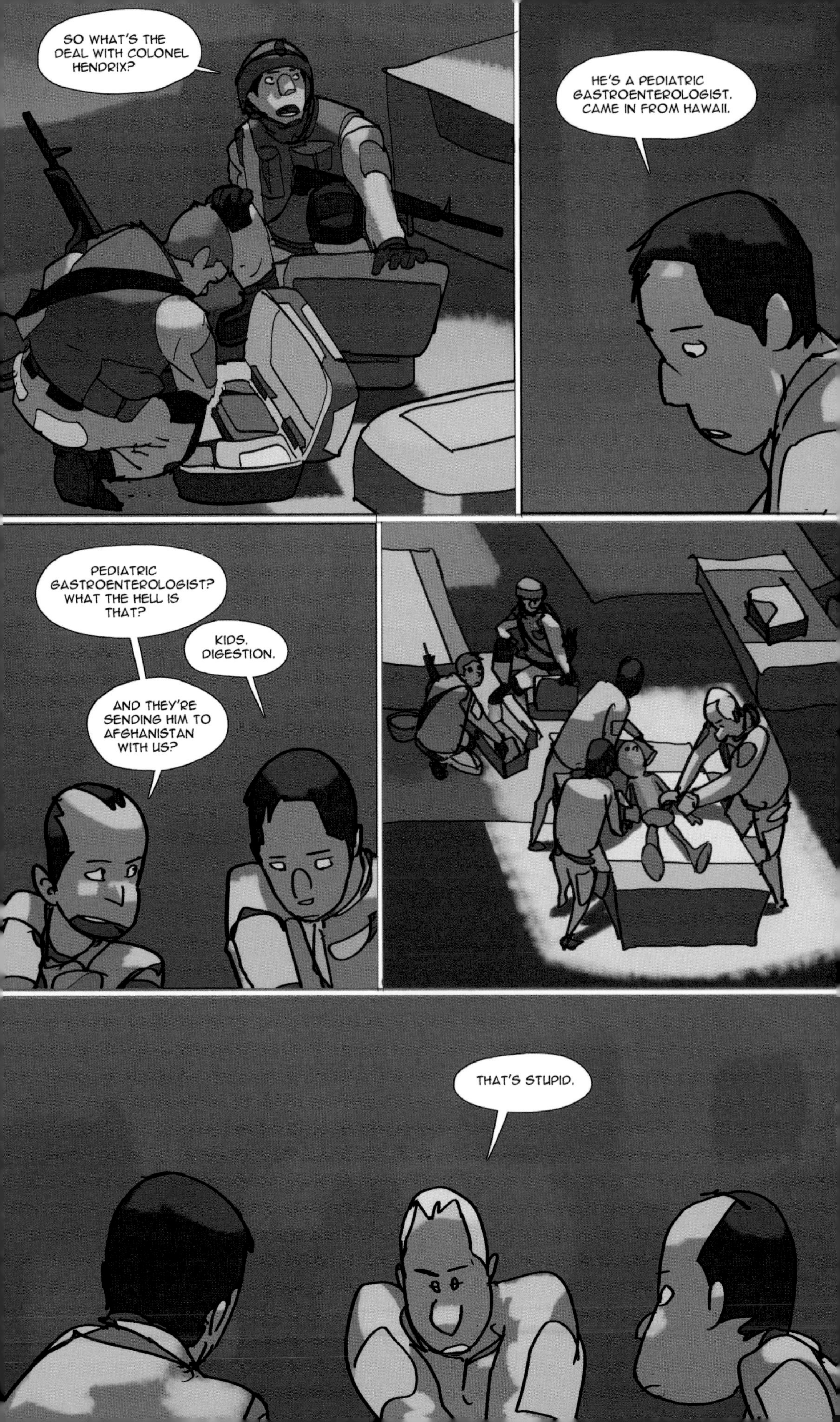
SO WHAT'S THE DEAL WITH COLONEL HENDRIX?
HE'S A PEDIATRIC GASTROENTEROLOGIST. CAME IN FROM HAWAII.
PEDIATRIC GASTROENTEROLOGIST? WHAT THE HELL IS THAT?
KIDS. DIGESTION.
AND THEY'RE SENDING HIM TO AFGHANISTAN WITH US?
THAT'S STUPID.

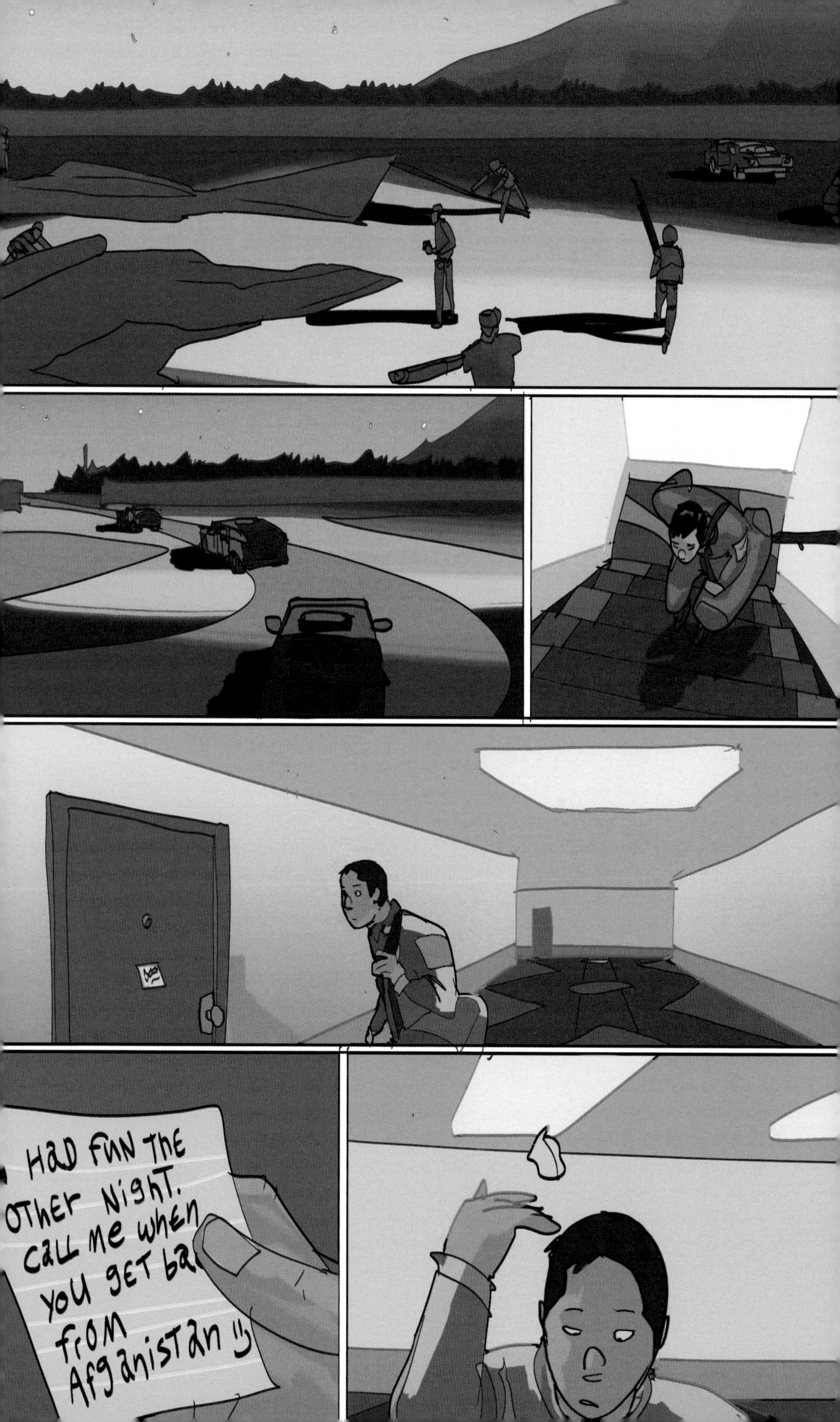
HAD FUN THE
OTHER NIGHT.
CALL ME WHEN
YOU GET BA
FROM
AFGANISTAN

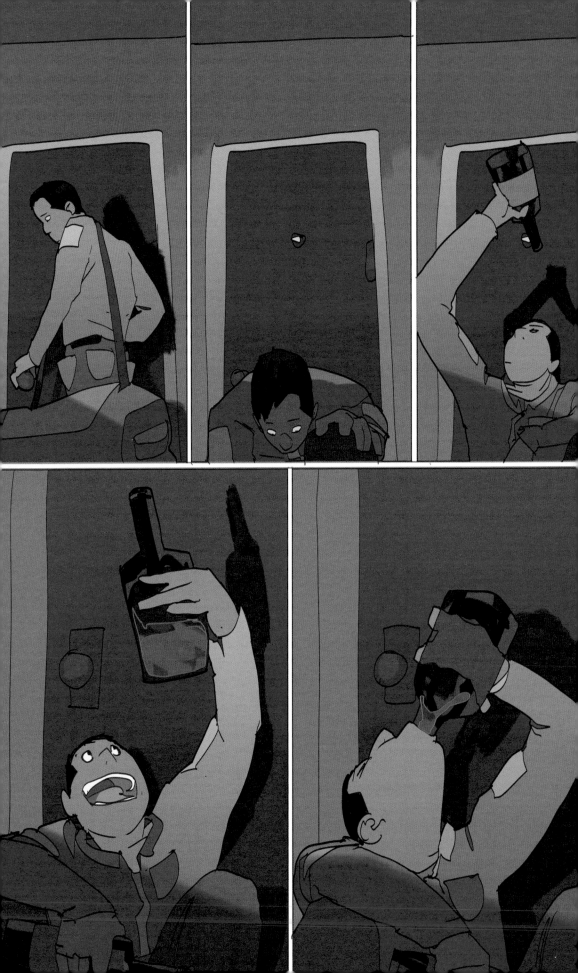

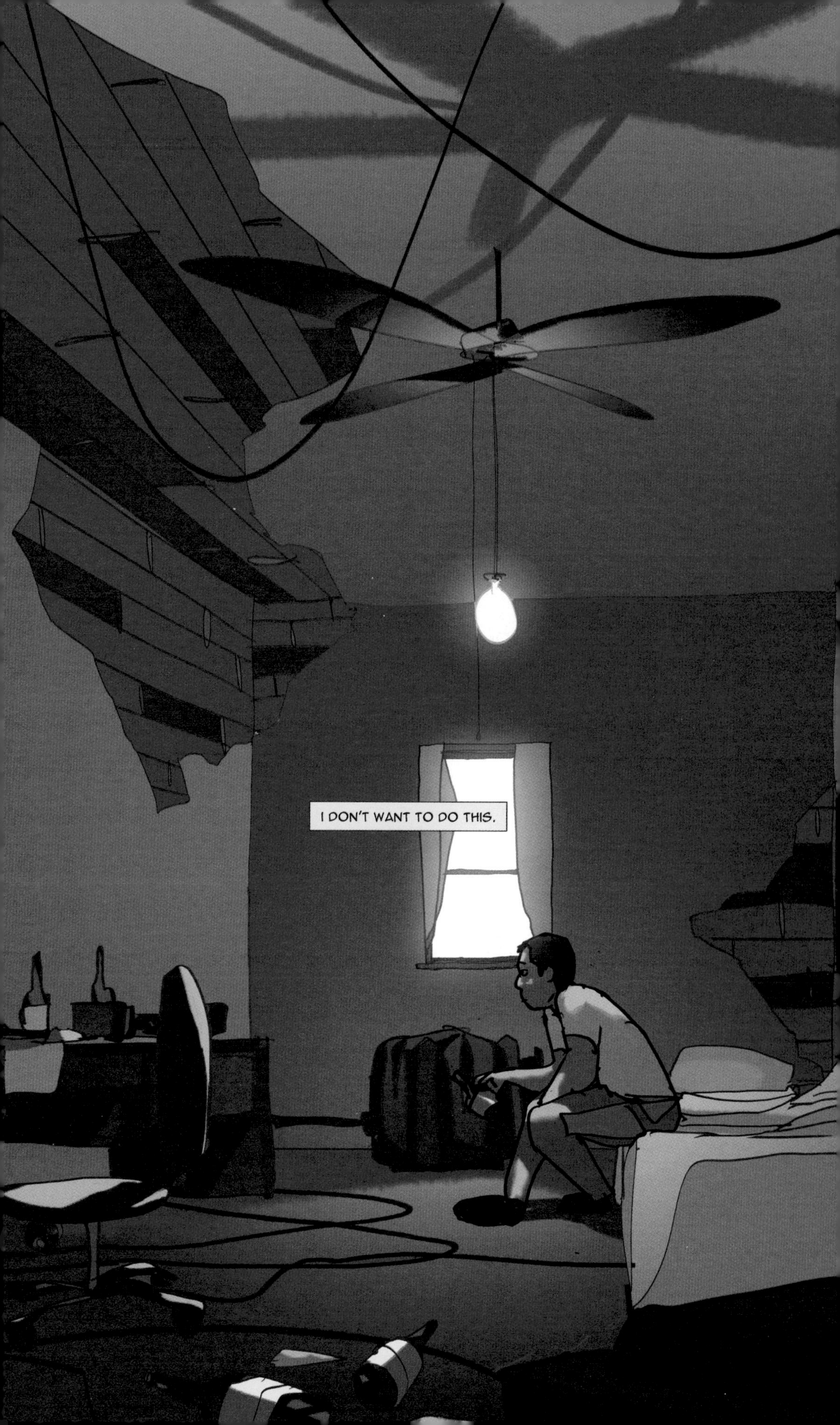
I DON'T WANT TO DO THIS.

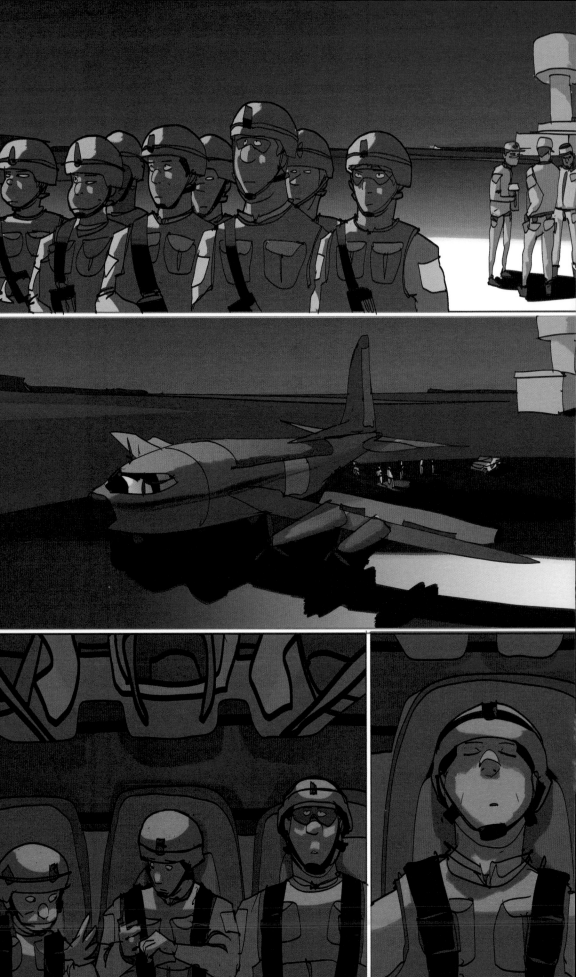

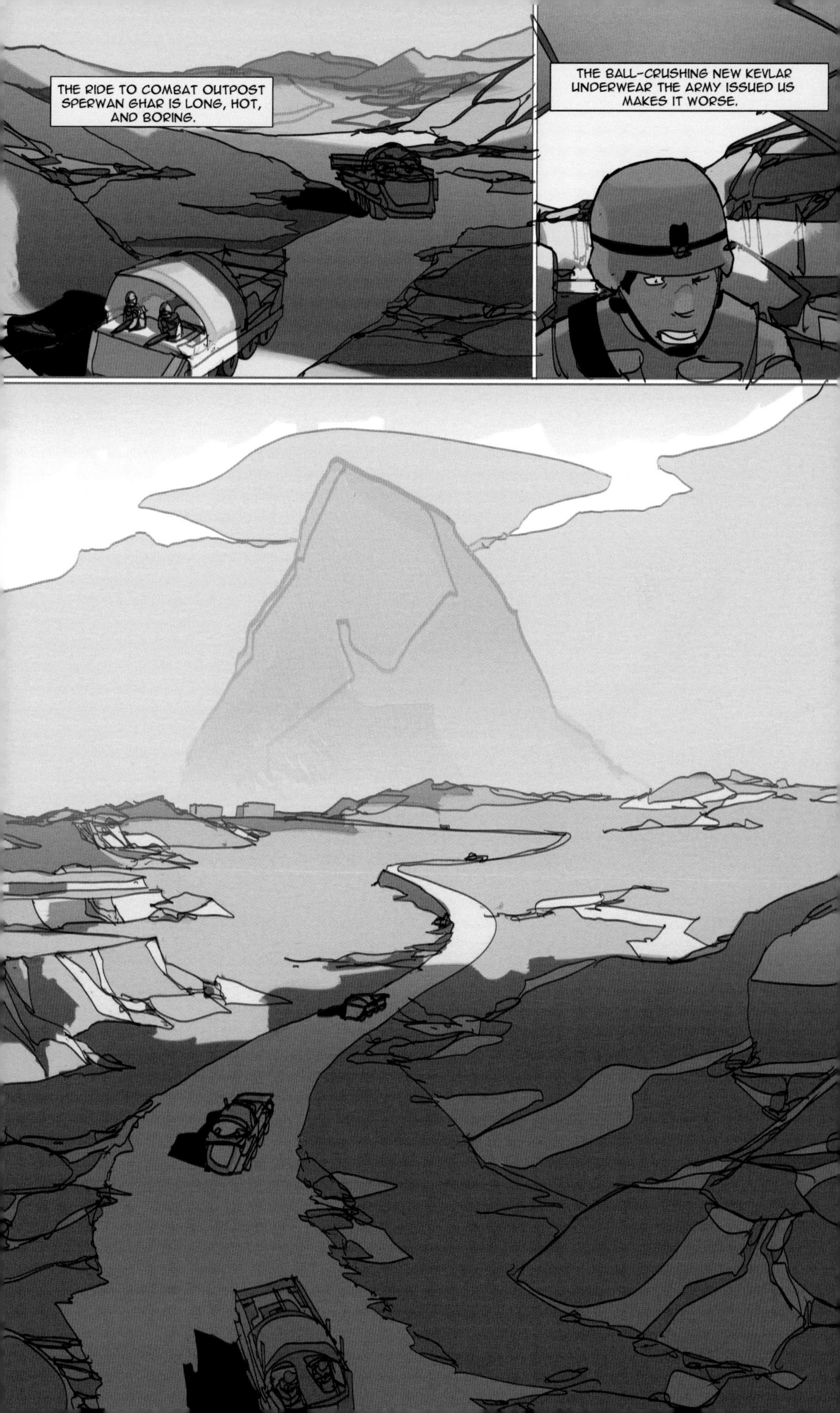
THE RIDE TO COMBAT OUTPOST SPERWAN GHAR IS LONG, HOT, AND BORING.
THE BALL-CRUSHING NEW KEVLAR UNDERWEAR THE ARMY ISSUED US MAKES IT WORSE.

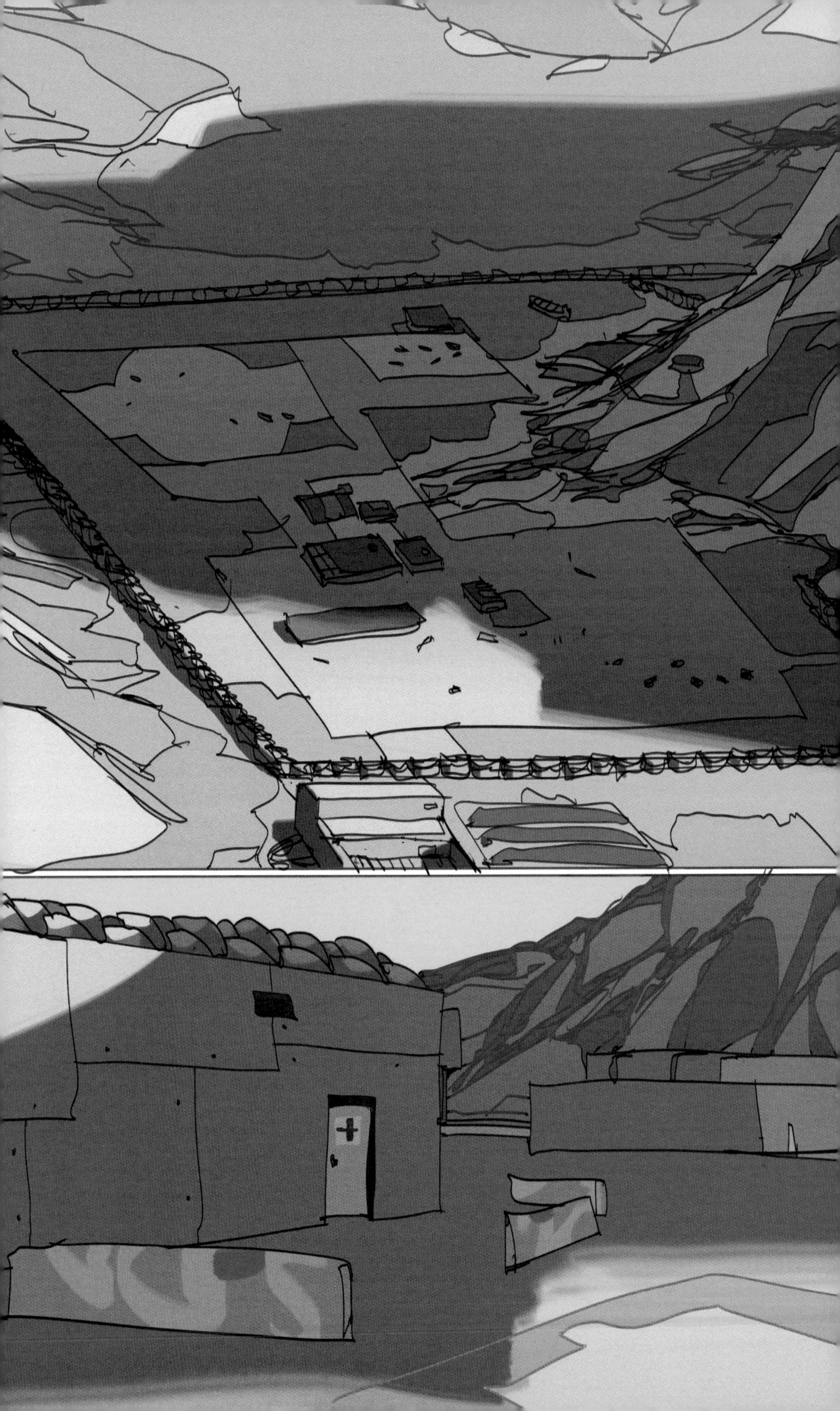

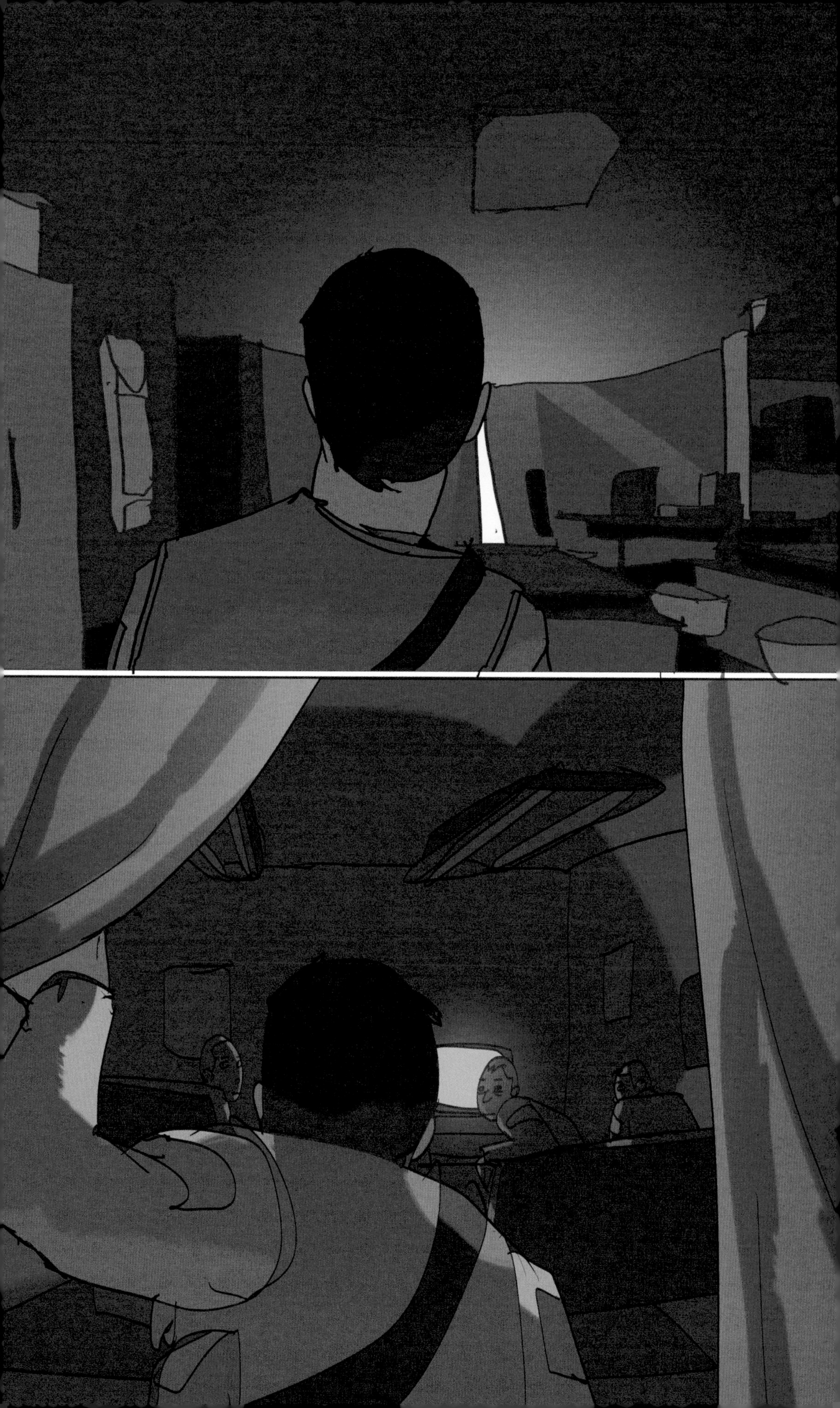

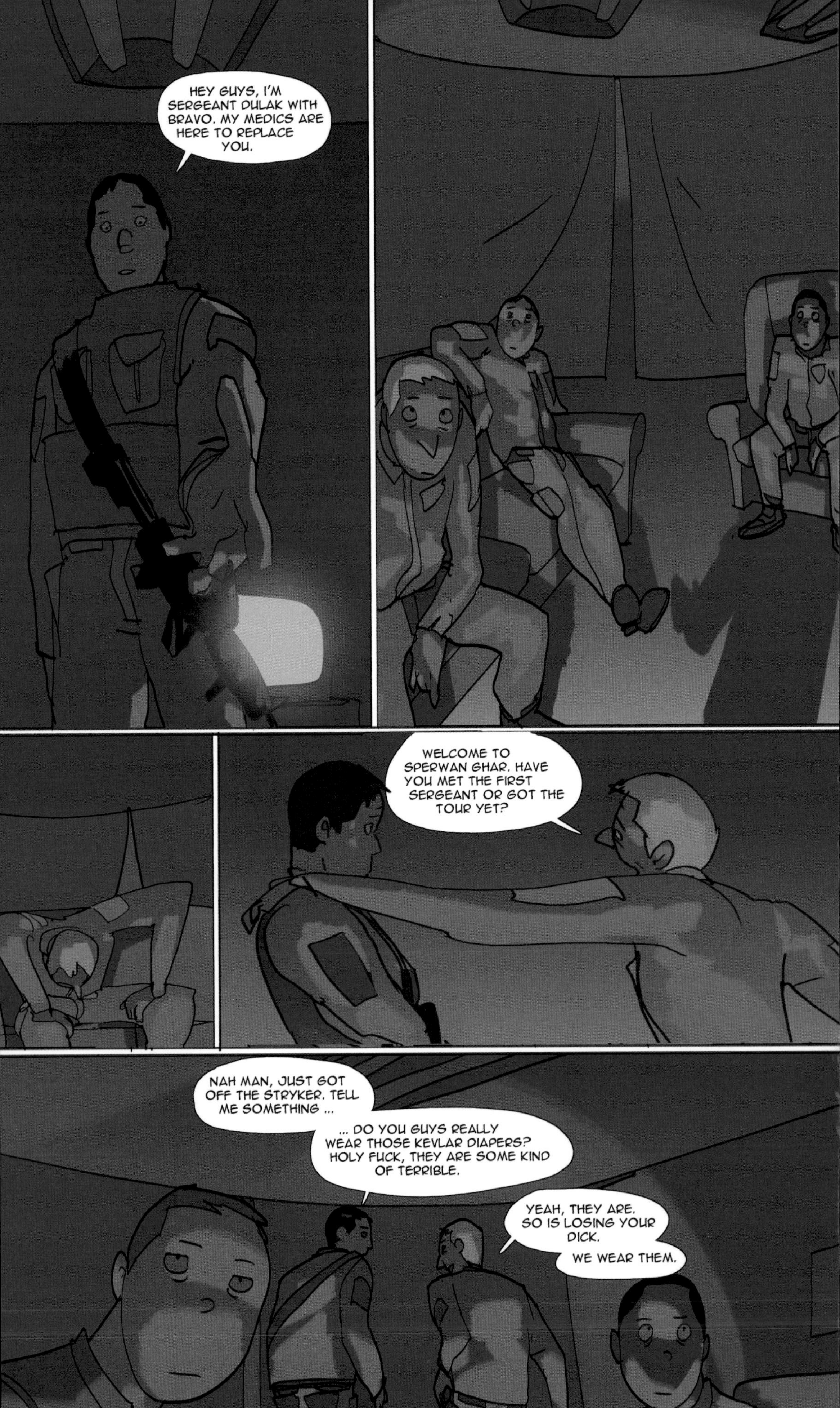
HEY GUYS, I'M SERGEANT DULAK WITH BRAVO. MY MEDICS ARE HERE TO REPLACE YOU.
WELCOME TO SPERWAN GHAR. HAVE YOU MET THE FIRST SERGEANT OR GOT THE TOUR YET?
NAH MAN, JUST GOT OFF THE STRYKER. TELL ME SOMETHING ...
... DO YOU GUYS REALLY WEAR THOSE KEVLAR DIAPERS? HOLY FUCK, THEY ARE SOME KIND OF TERRIBLE.
YEAH, THEY ARE. SO IS LOSING YOUR DICK.
WE WEAR THEM.

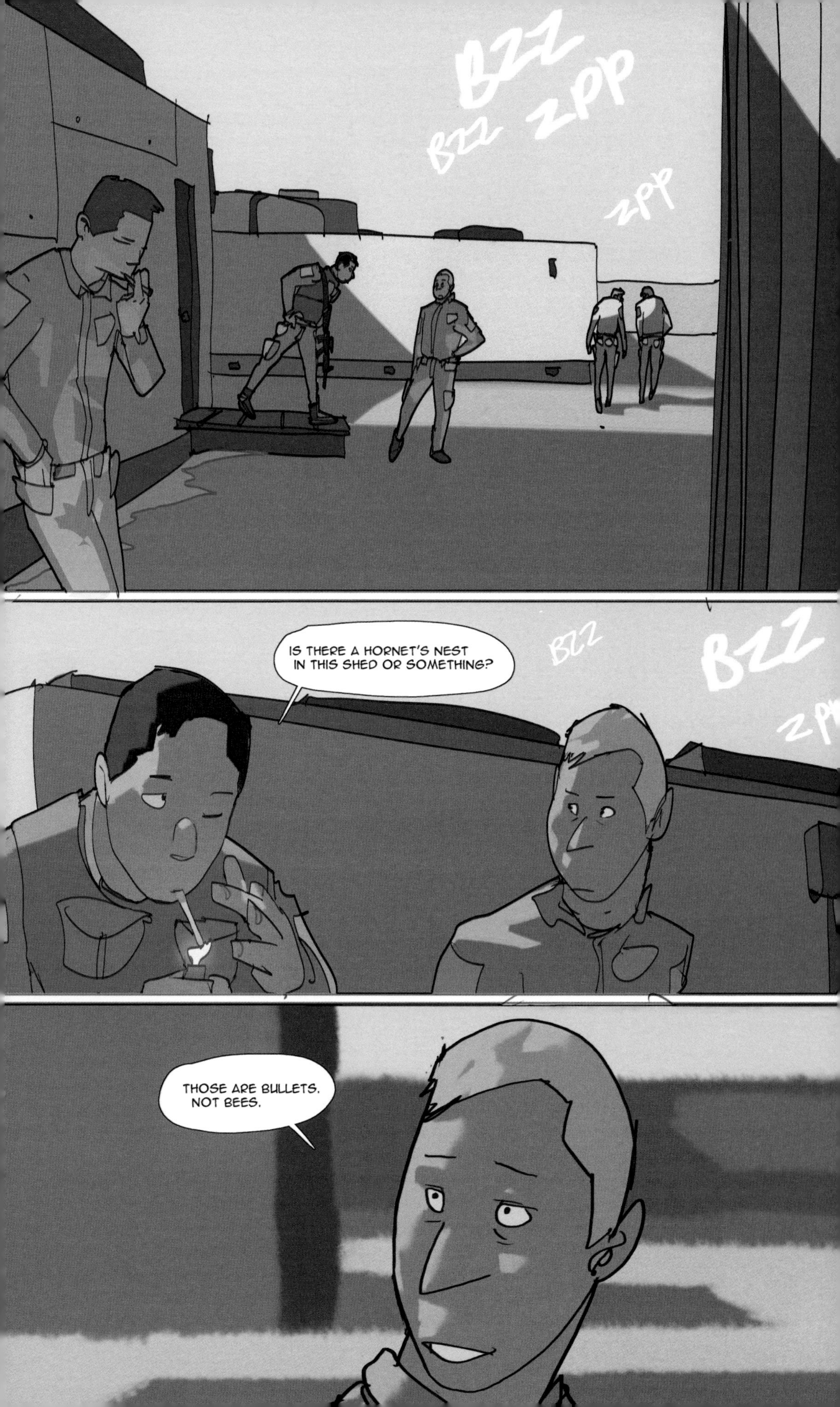
BZZ
BZZ ZPP
ZPP
IS THERE A HORNET'S NEST IN THIS SHED OR SOMETHING?
BZZ
BZZ
THOSE ARE BULLETS. NOT BEES.

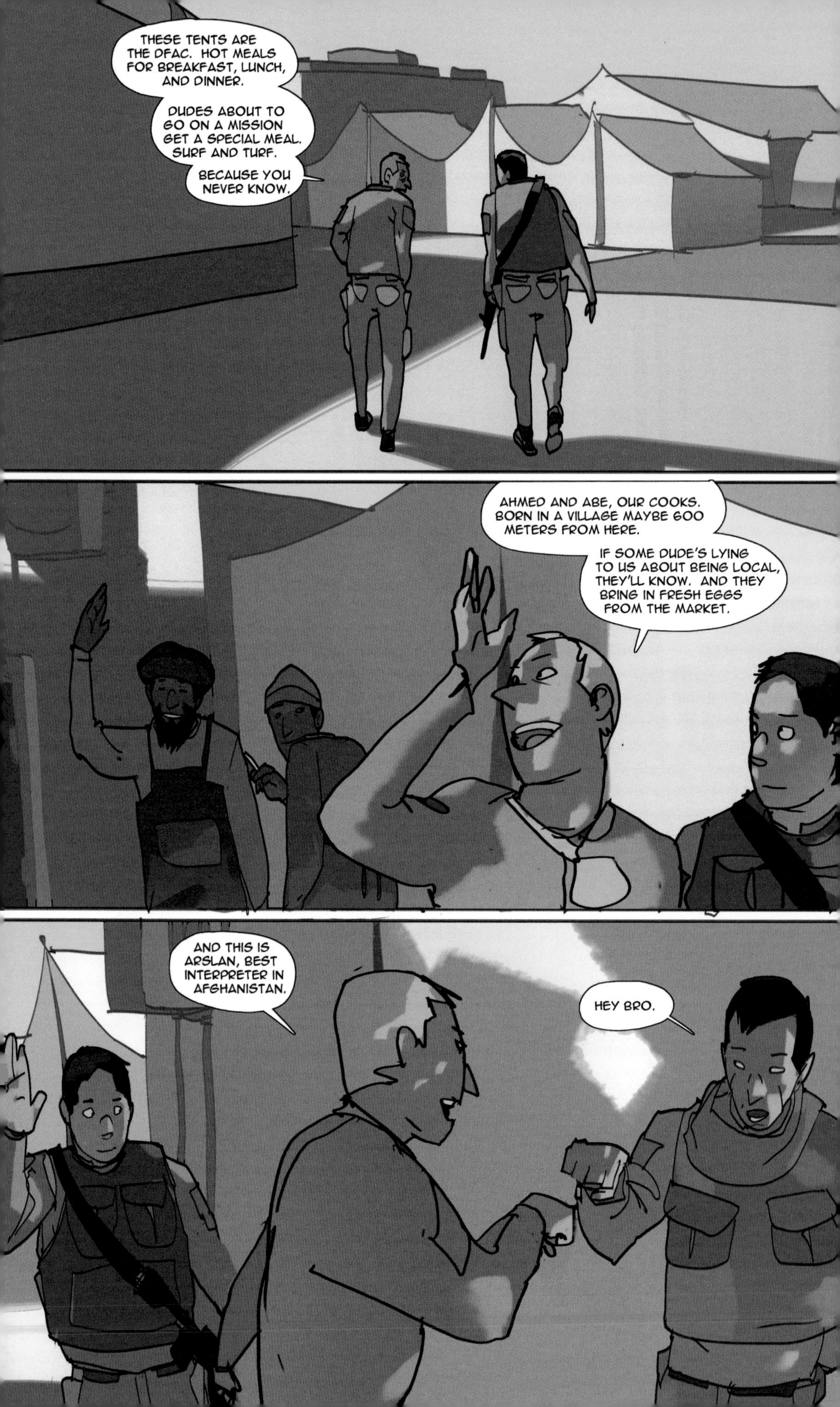
THESE TENTS ARE THE DFAC. HOT MEALS FOR BREAKFAST, LUNCH, AND DINNER.
DUDES ABOUT TO GO ON A MISSION GET A SPECIAL MEAL. SURF AND TURF.
BECAUSE YOU NEVER KNOW.
AHMED AND ABE, OUR COOKS. BORN IN A VILLAGE MAYBE 600 METERS FROM HERE.
IF SOME DUDE'S LYING TO US ABOUT BEING LOCAL, THEY'LL KNOW. AND THEY BRING IN FRESH EGGS FROM THE MARKET.
AND THIS IS ARSLAN, BEST INTERPRETER IN AFGHANISTAN.
HEY BRO.

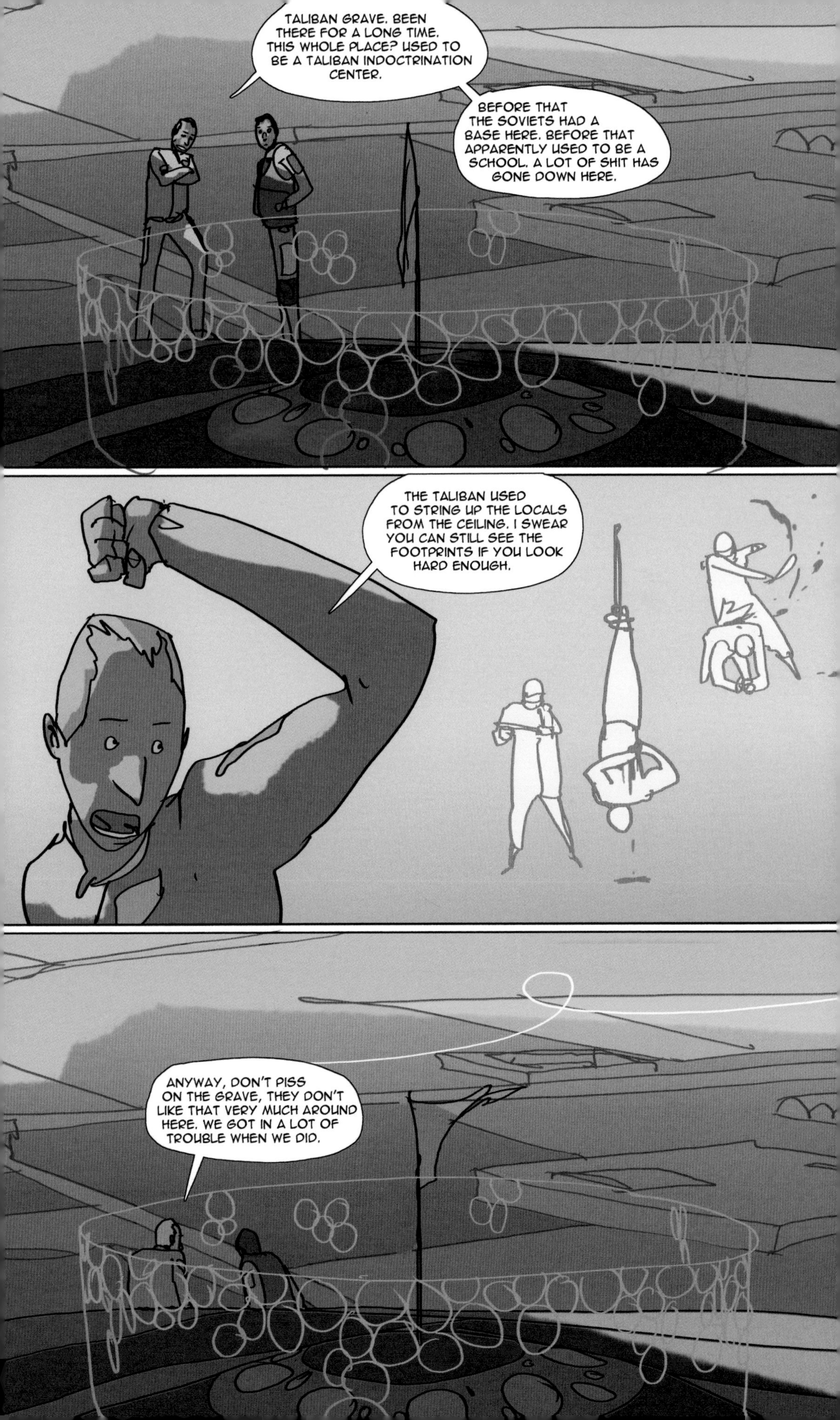
TALIBAN GRAVE. BEEN THERE FOR A LONG TIME. THIS WHOLE PLACE? USED TO BE A TALIBAN INDOCTRINATION CENTER.
BEFORE THAT THE SOVIETS HAD A BASE HERE. BEFORE THAT APPARENTLY USED TO BE A SCHOOL. A LOT OF SHIT HAS GONE DOWN HERE.
THE TALIBAN USED TO STRING UP THE LOCALS FROM THE CEILING. I SWEAR YOU CAN STILL SEE THE FOOTPRINTS IF YOU LOOK HARD ENOUGH.
ANYWAY, DON'T PISS ON THE GRAVE, THEY DON'T LIKE THAT VERY MUCH AROUND HERE. WE GOT IN A LOT OF TROUBLE WHEN WE DID.

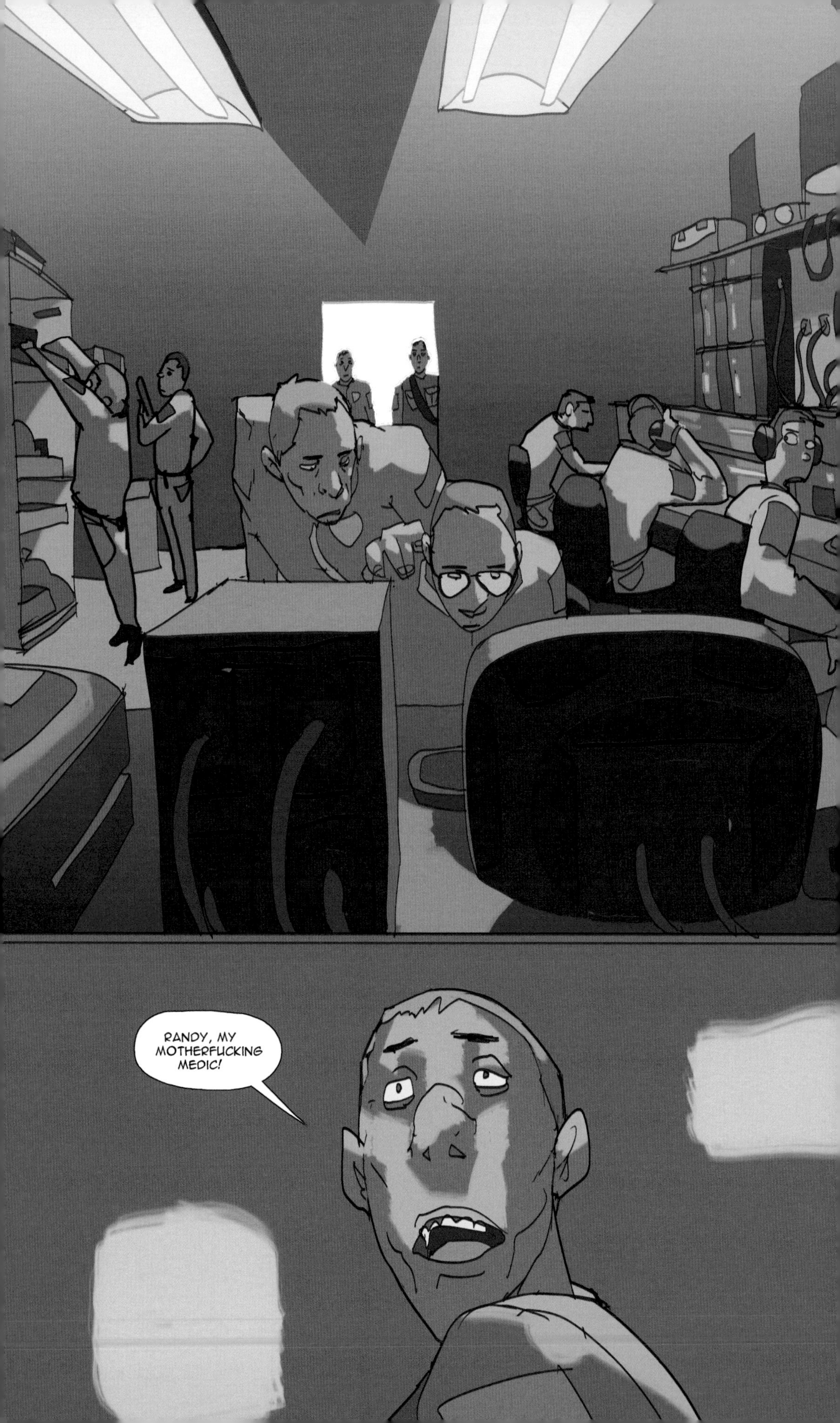
RANDY, MY MOTHERFUCKING MEDIC!

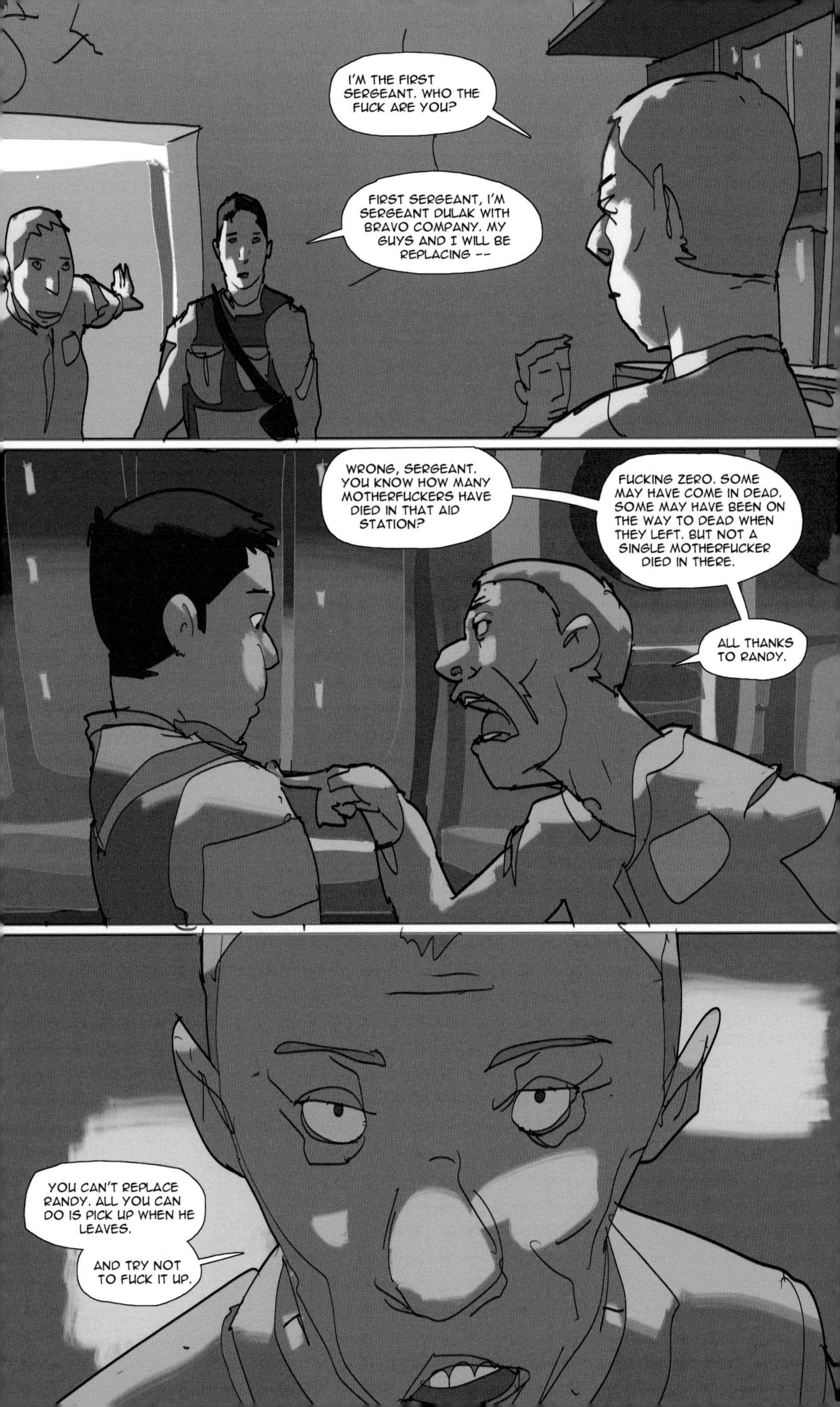
I'M THE FIRST SERGEANT. WHO THE FUCK ARE YOU?
FIRST SERGEANT, I'M SERGEANT DULAK WITH BRAVO COMPANY. MY GUYS AND I WILL BE REPLACING --
WRONG, SERGEANT. YOU KNOW HOW MANY MOTHERFUCKERS HAVE DIED IN THAT AID STATION?
FUCKING ZERO. SOME MAY HAVE COME IN DEAD. SOME MAY HAVE BEEN ON THE WAY TO DEAD WHEN THEY LEFT. BUT NOT A SINGLE MOTHERFUCKER DIED IN THERE.
ALL THANKS TO RANDY.
YOU CAN'T REPLACE RANDY. ALL YOU CAN DO IS PICK UP WHEN HE LEAVES.
AND TRY NOT TO FUCK IT UP.

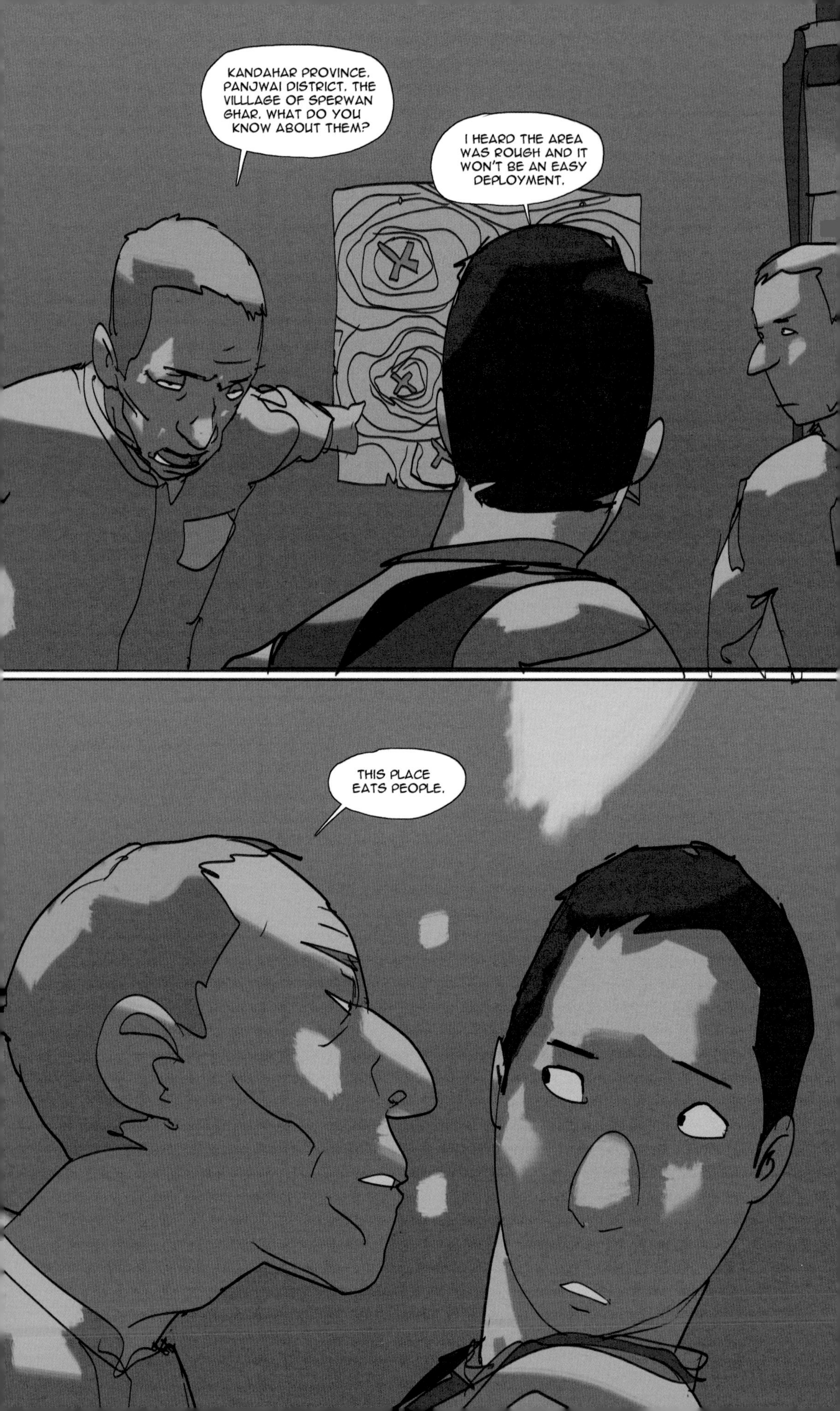
KANDAHAR PROVINCE. PANJWAI DISTRICT. THE VILLLAGE OF SPERWAN GHAR. WHAT DO YOU KNOW ABOUT THEM?
I HEARD THE AREA WAS ROUGH AND IT WON'T BE AN EASY DEPLOYMENT.
THIS PLACE EATS PEOPLE.

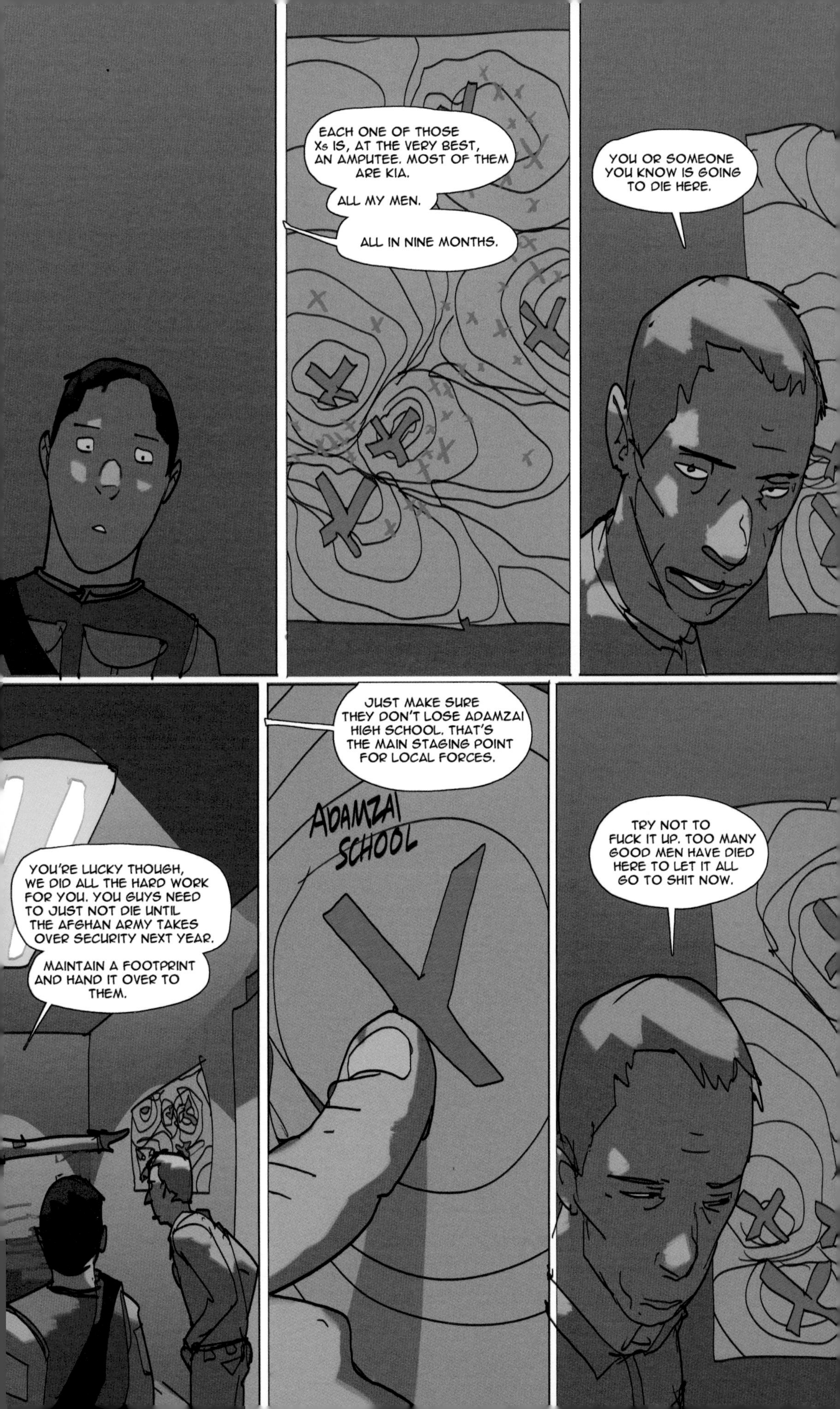

EACH ONE OF THOSE Xs IS, AT THE VERY BEST, AN AMPUTEE. MOST OF THEM ARE KIA.
ALL MY MEN.
ALL IN NINE MONTHS.
YOU OR SOMEONE YOU KNOW IS GOING TO DIE HERE.
YOU'RE LUCKY THOUGH, WE DID ALL THE HARD WORK FOR YOU. YOU GUYS NEED TO JUST NOT DIE UNTIL THE AFGHAN ARMY TAKES OVER SECURITY NEXT YEAR.
MAINTAIN A FOOTPRINT AND HAND IT OVER TO THEM.
JUST MAKE SURE THEY DON'T LOSE ADAMZAI HIGH SCHOOL. THAT'S THE MAIN STAGING POINT FOR LOCAL FORCES.
ADAMZAI SCHOOL
TRY NOT TO FUCK IT UP. TOO MANY GOOD MEN HAVE DIED HERE TO LET IT ALL GO TO SHIT NOW.

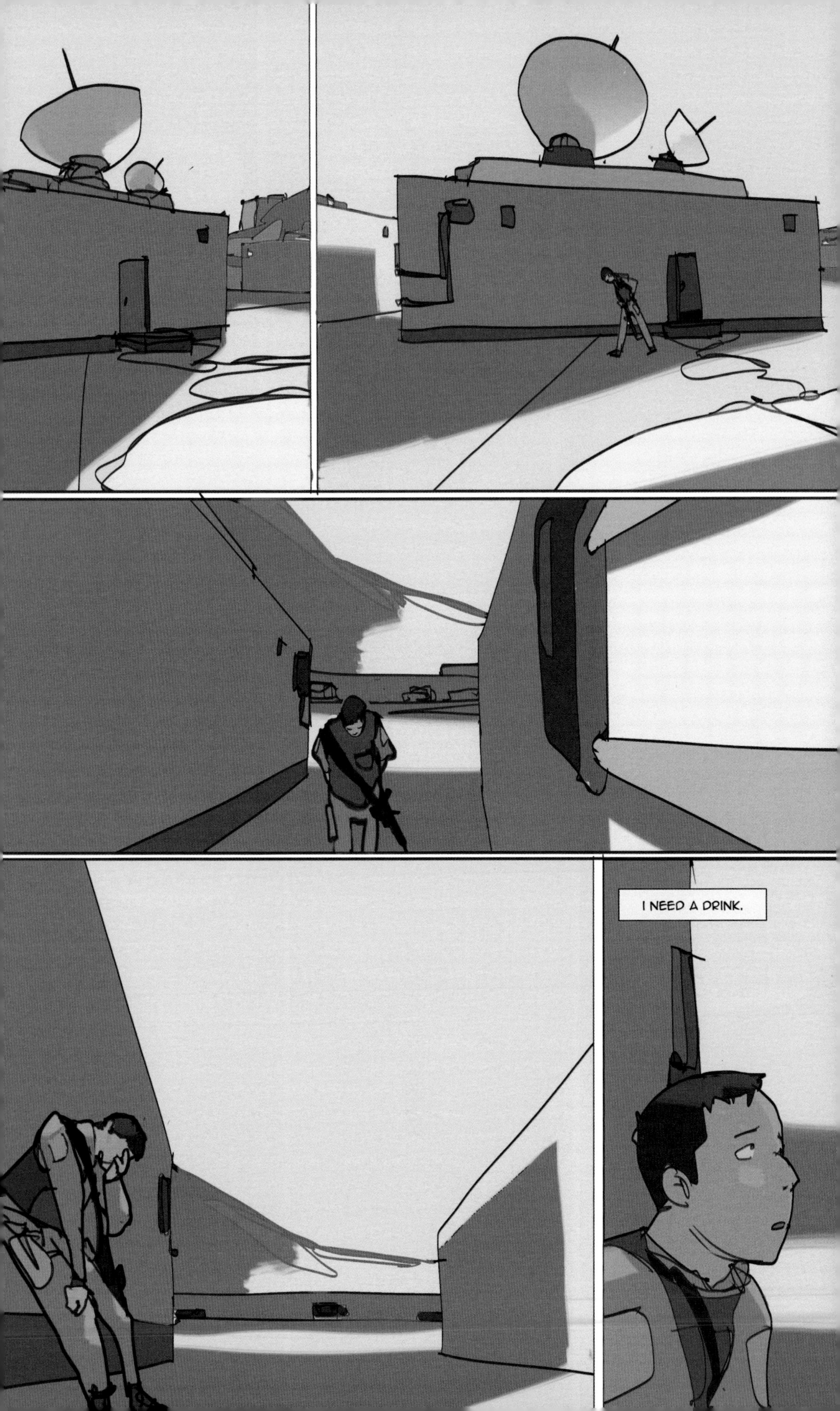
I NEED A DRINK.

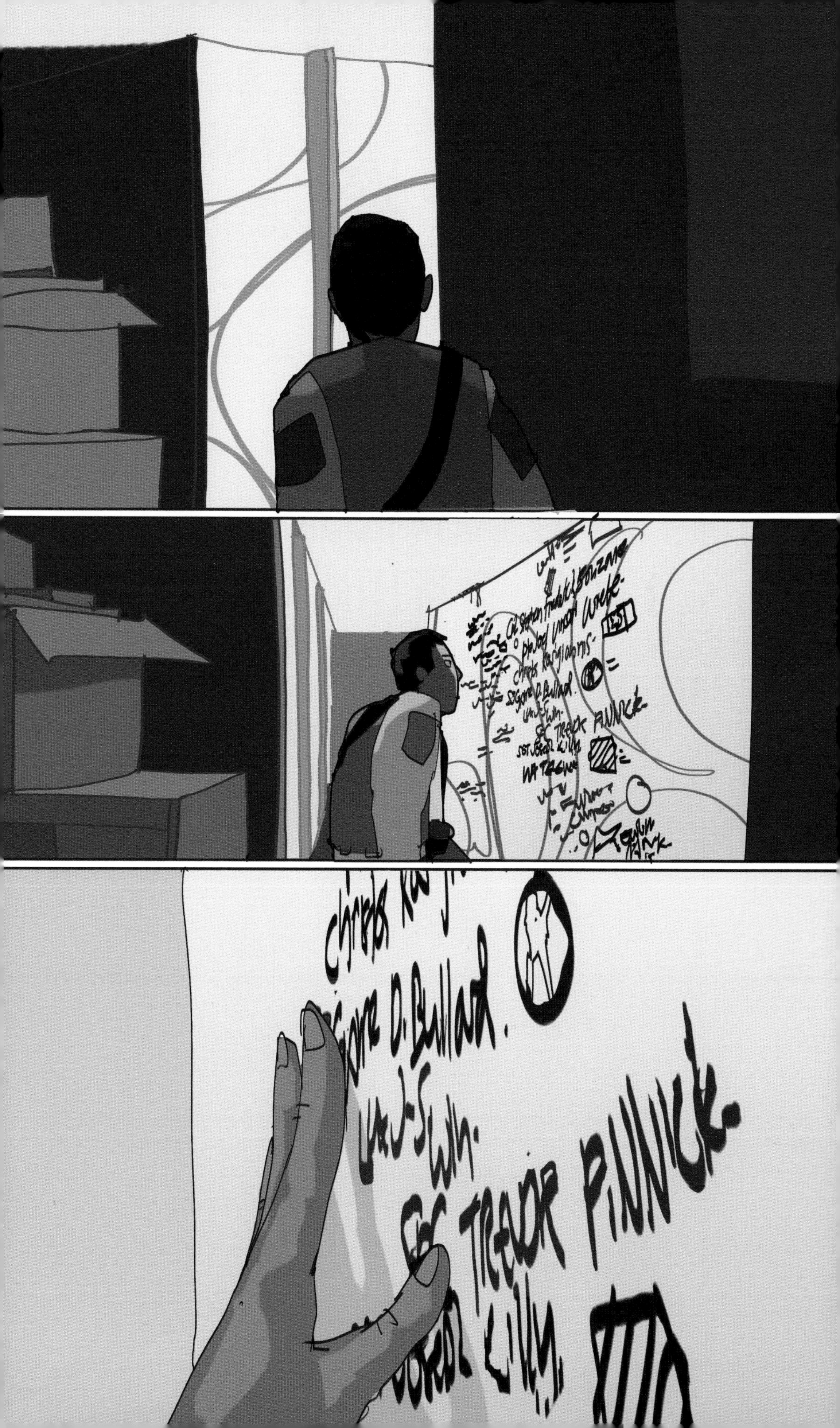
SPC TREVOR PINNICK.

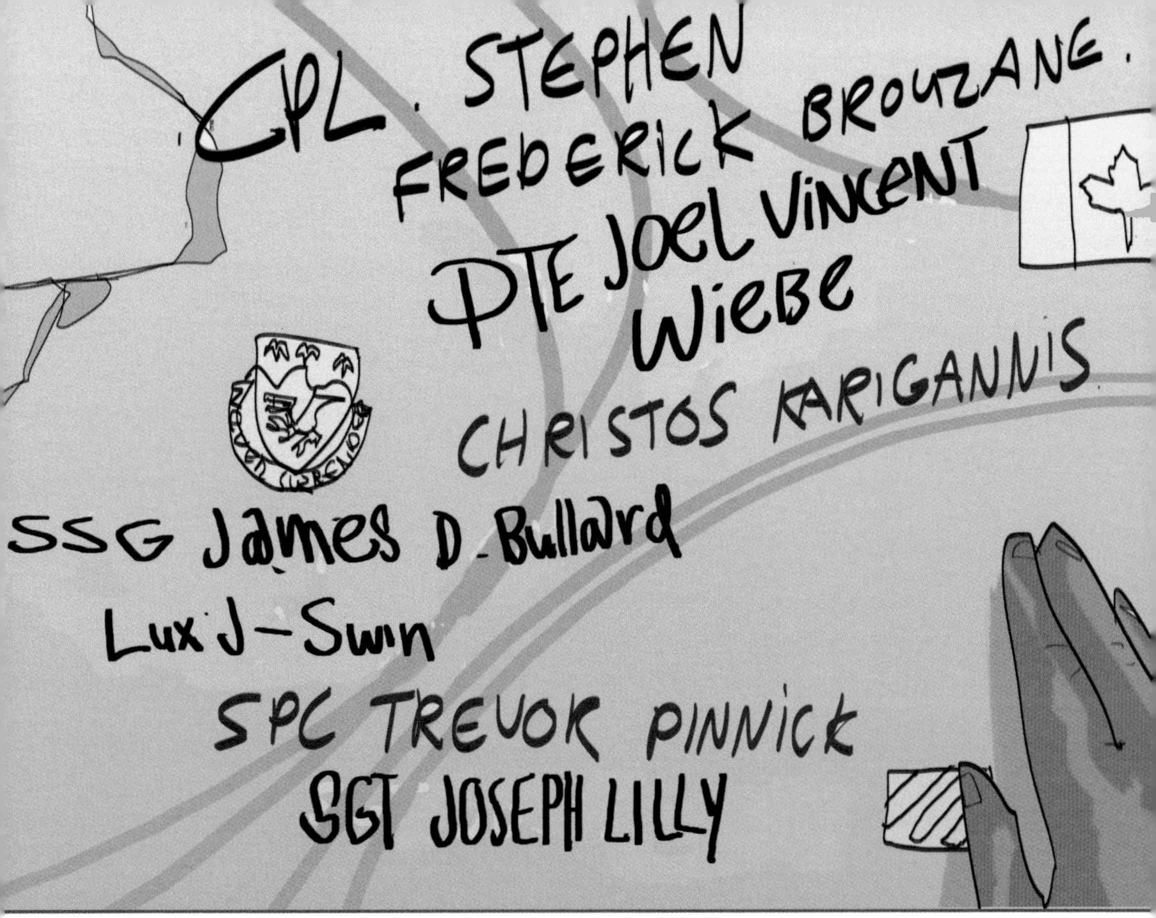
CPL. STEPHEN FREDERICK BROUZANE.
PTE JOEL VINCENT WIEBE
CHRISTOS KARIGANNIS
SSG James D. Bullard
Lux J-Swin
SPC TREVOR PINNICK
SGT JOSEPH LILLY

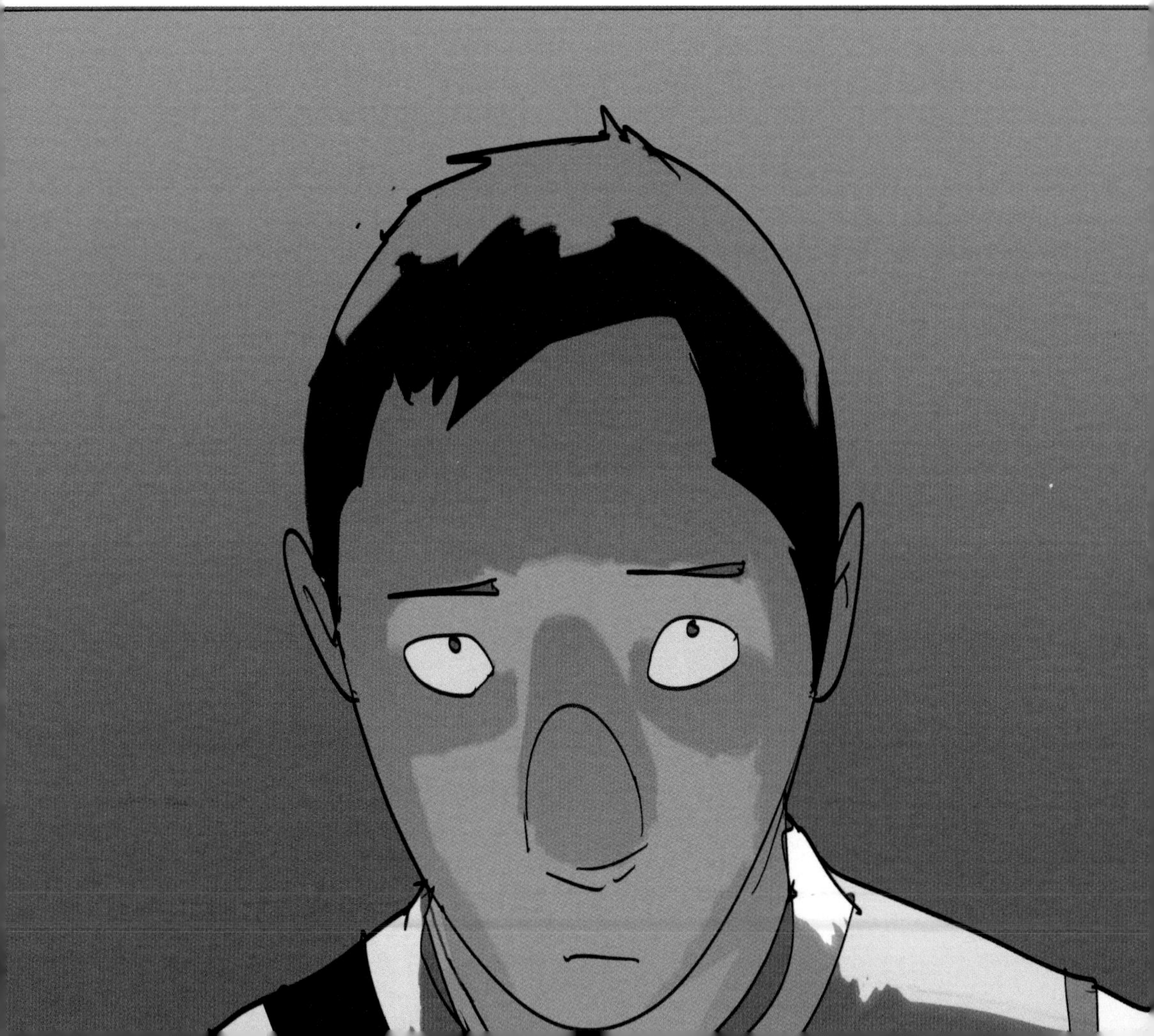

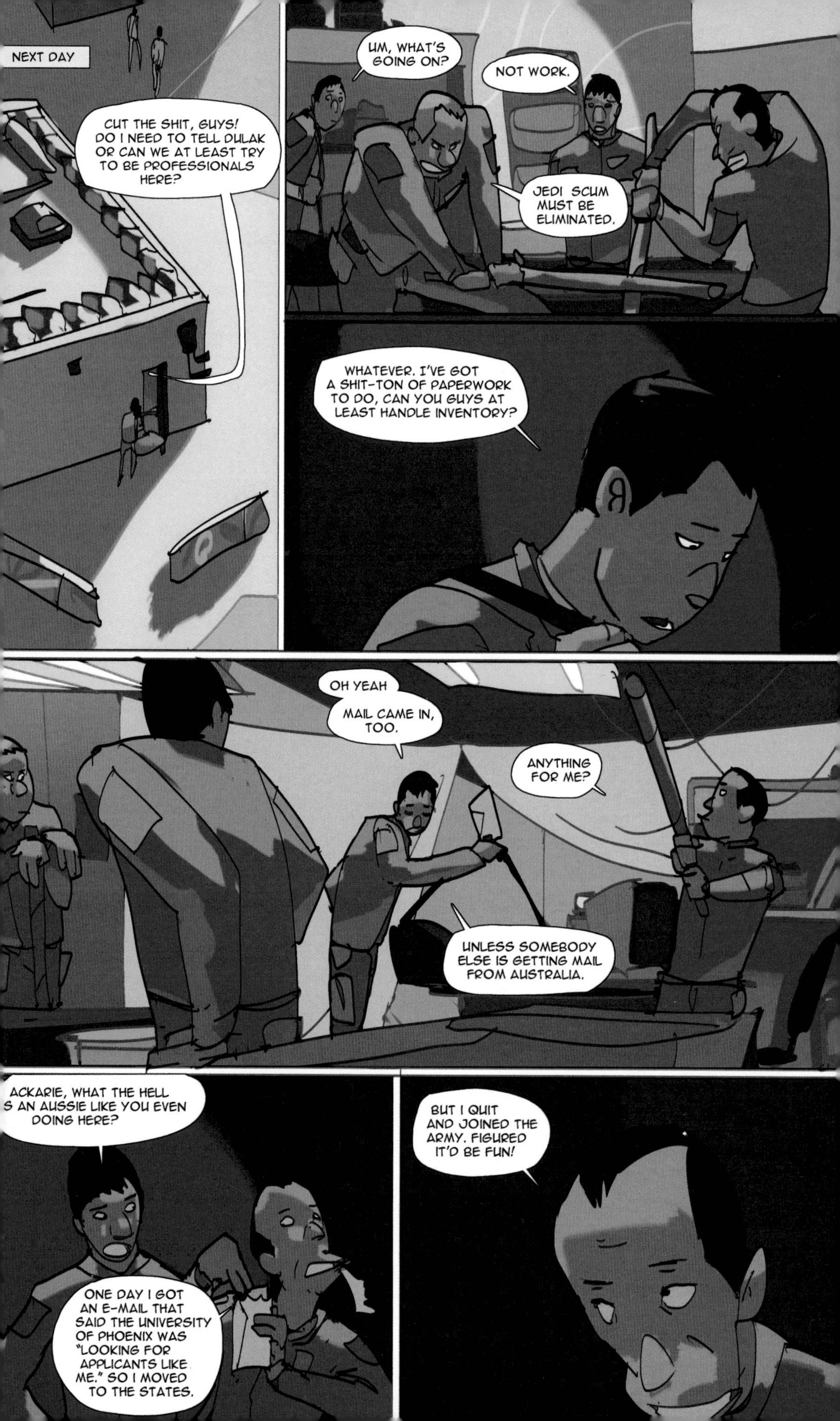
NEXT DAY
CUT THE SHIT, GUYS! DO I NEED TO TELL DULAK OR CAN WE AT LEAST TRY TO BE PROFESSIONALS HERE?
UM, WHAT'S GOING ON?
NOT WORK.
JEDI SCUM MUST BE ELIMINATED.
WHATEVER. I'VE GOT A SHIT-TON OF PAPERWORK TO DO, CAN YOU GUYS AT LEAST HANDLE INVENTORY?
OH YEAH
MAIL CAME IN, TOO.
ANYTHING FOR ME?
UNLESS SOMEBODY ELSE IS GETTING MAIL FROM AUSTRALIA.
ACKARIE, WHAT THE HELL S AN AUSSIE LIKE YOU EVEN DOING HERE?
ONE DAY I GOT AN E-MAIL THAT SAID THE UNIVERSITY OF PHOENIX WAS "LOOKING FOR APPLICANTS LIKE ME." SO I MOVED TO THE STATES.
BUT I QUIT AND JOINED THE ARMY. FIGURED IT'D BE FUN!

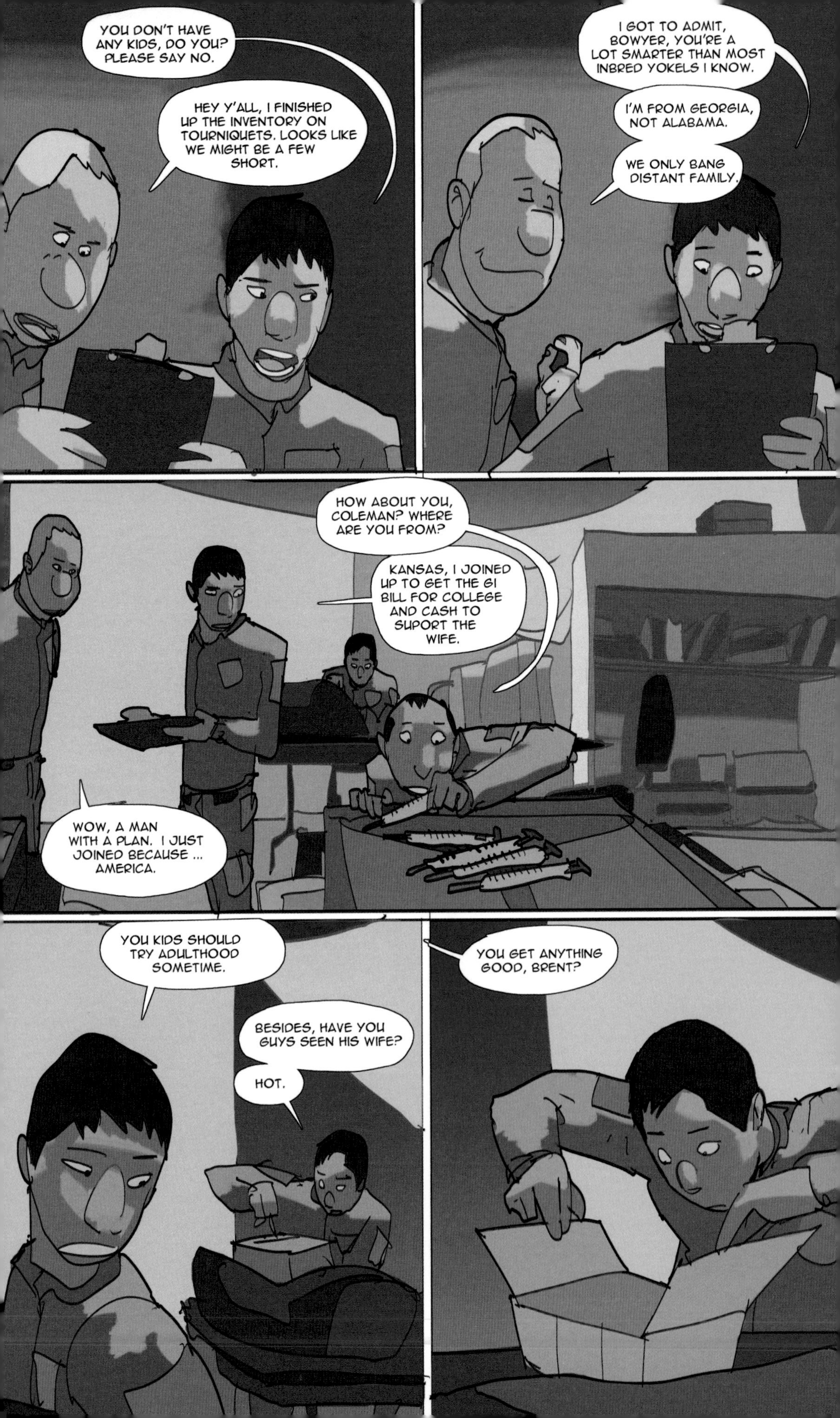
YOU DON'T HAVE ANY KIDS, DO YOU? PLEASE SAY NO.
HEY Y'ALL, I FINISHED UP THE INVENTORY ON TOURNIQUETS. LOOKS LIKE WE MIGHT BE A FEW SHORT.
I GOT TO ADMIT, BOWYER, YOU'RE A LOT SMARTER THAN MOST INBRED YOKELS I KNOW.
I'M FROM GEORGIA, NOT ALABAMA.
WE ONLY BANG DISTANT FAMILY.
HOW ABOUT YOU, COLEMAN? WHERE ARE YOU FROM?
KANSAS, I JOINED UP TO GET THE GI BILL FOR COLLEGE AND CASH TO SUPORT THE WIFE.
WOW, A MAN WITH A PLAN. I JUST JOINED BECAUSE ... AMERICA.
YOU KIDS SHOULD TRY ADULTHOOD SOMETIME.
BESIDES, HAVE YOU GUYS SEEN HIS WIFE?
HOT.
YOU GET ANYTHING GOOD, BRENT?

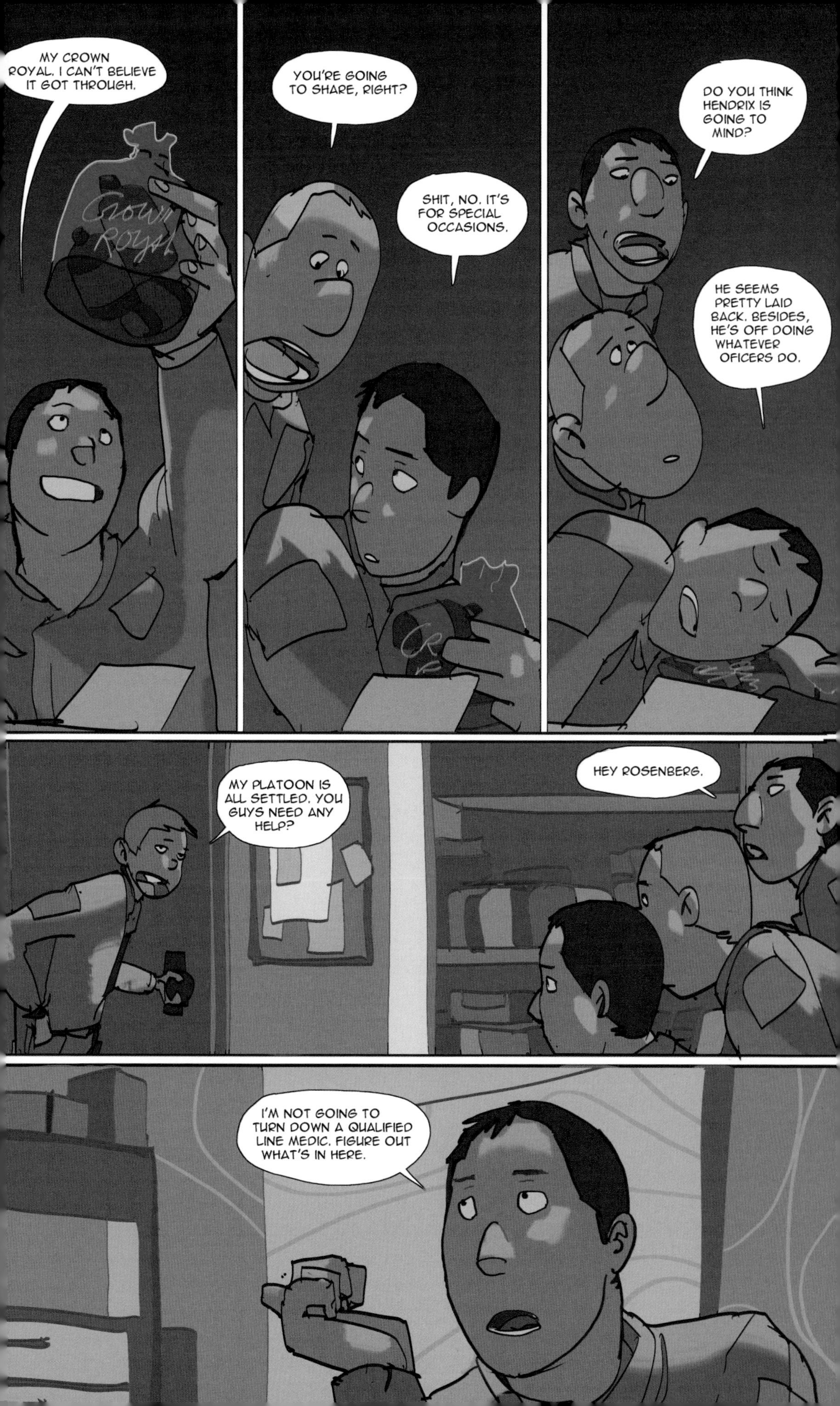
MY CROWN ROYAL. I CAN'T BELIEVE IT GOT THROUGH.
YOU'RE GOING TO SHARE, RIGHT?
SHIT, NO. IT'S FOR SPECIAL OCCASIONS.
DO YOU THINK HENDRIX IS GOING TO MIND?
HE SEEMS PRETTY LAID BACK. BESIDES, HE'S OFF DOING WHATEVER OFICERS DO.
MY PLATOON IS ALL SETTLED. YOU GUYS NEED ANY HELP?
HEY ROSENBERG.
I'M NOT GOING TO TURN DOWN A QUALIFIED LINE MEDIC. FIGURE OUT WHAT'S IN HERE.

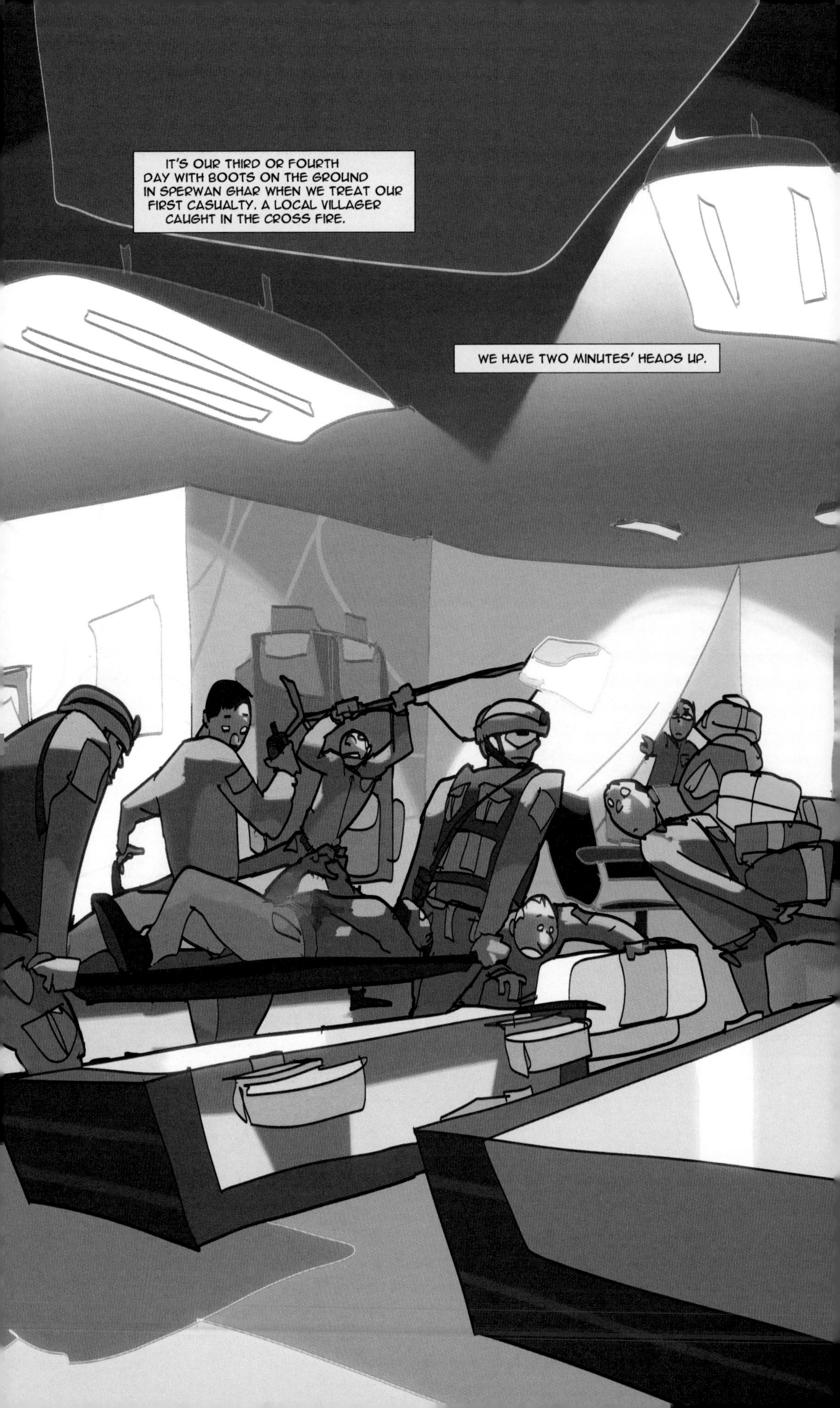
IT'S OUR THIRD OR FOURTH DAY WITH BOOTS ON THE GROUND IN SPERWAN GHAR WHEN WE TREAT OUR FIRST CASUALTY. A LOCAL VILLAGER CAUGHT IN THE CROSS FIRE.
WE HAVE TWO MINUTES' HEADS UP.

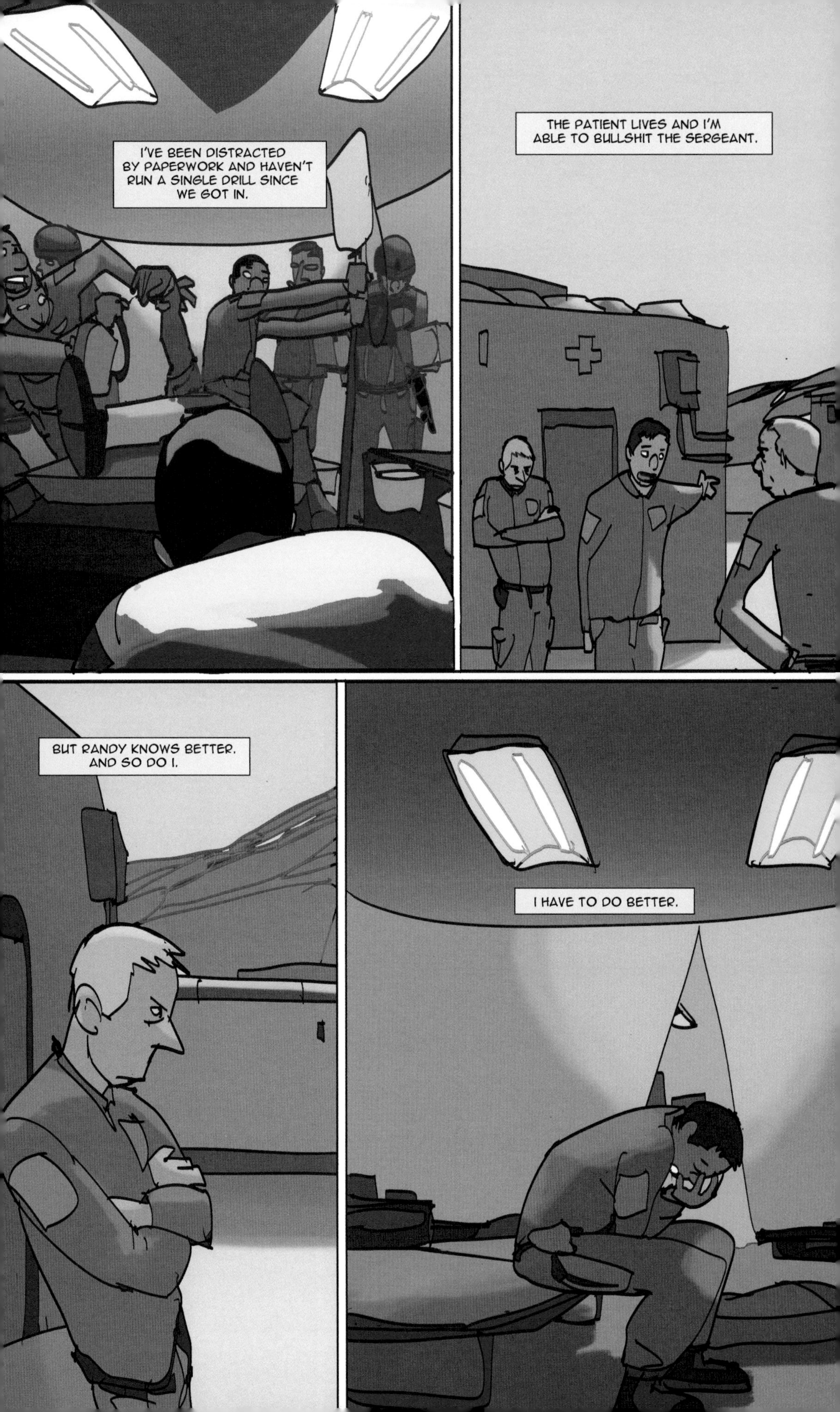
I'VE BEEN DISTRACTED BY PAPERWORK AND HAVEN'T RUN A SINGLE DRILL SINCE WE GOT IN.
THE PATIENT LIVES AND I'M ABLE TO BULLSHIT THE SERGEANT.
BUT RANDY KNOWS BETTER. AND SO DO I.
I HAVE TO DO BETTER.

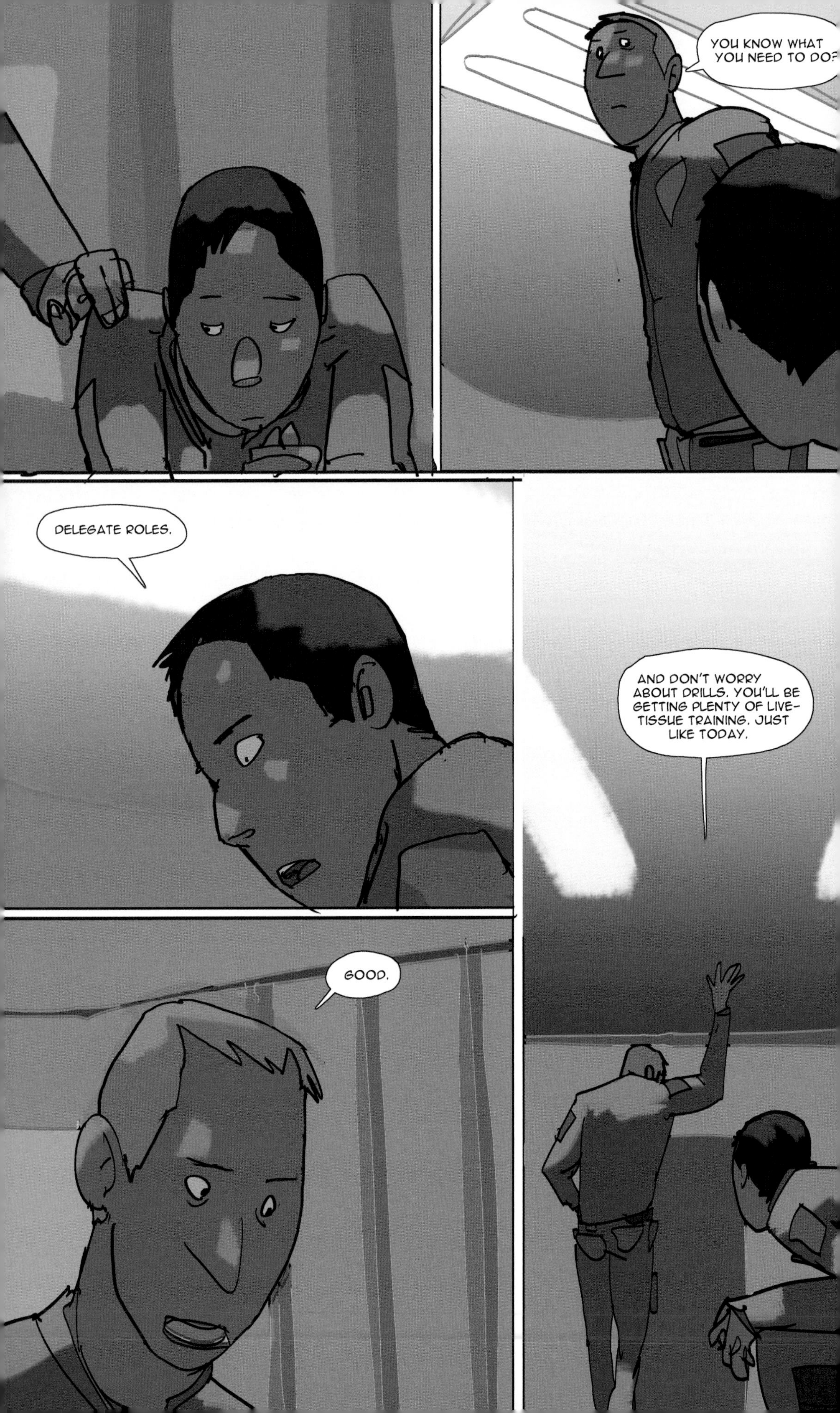
YOU KNOW WHAT YOU NEED TO DO?
DELEGATE ROLES.
AND DON'T WORRY ABOUT DRILLS. YOU'LL BE GETTING PLENTY OF LIVE-TISSUE TRAINING. JUST LIKE TODAY.
GOOD.

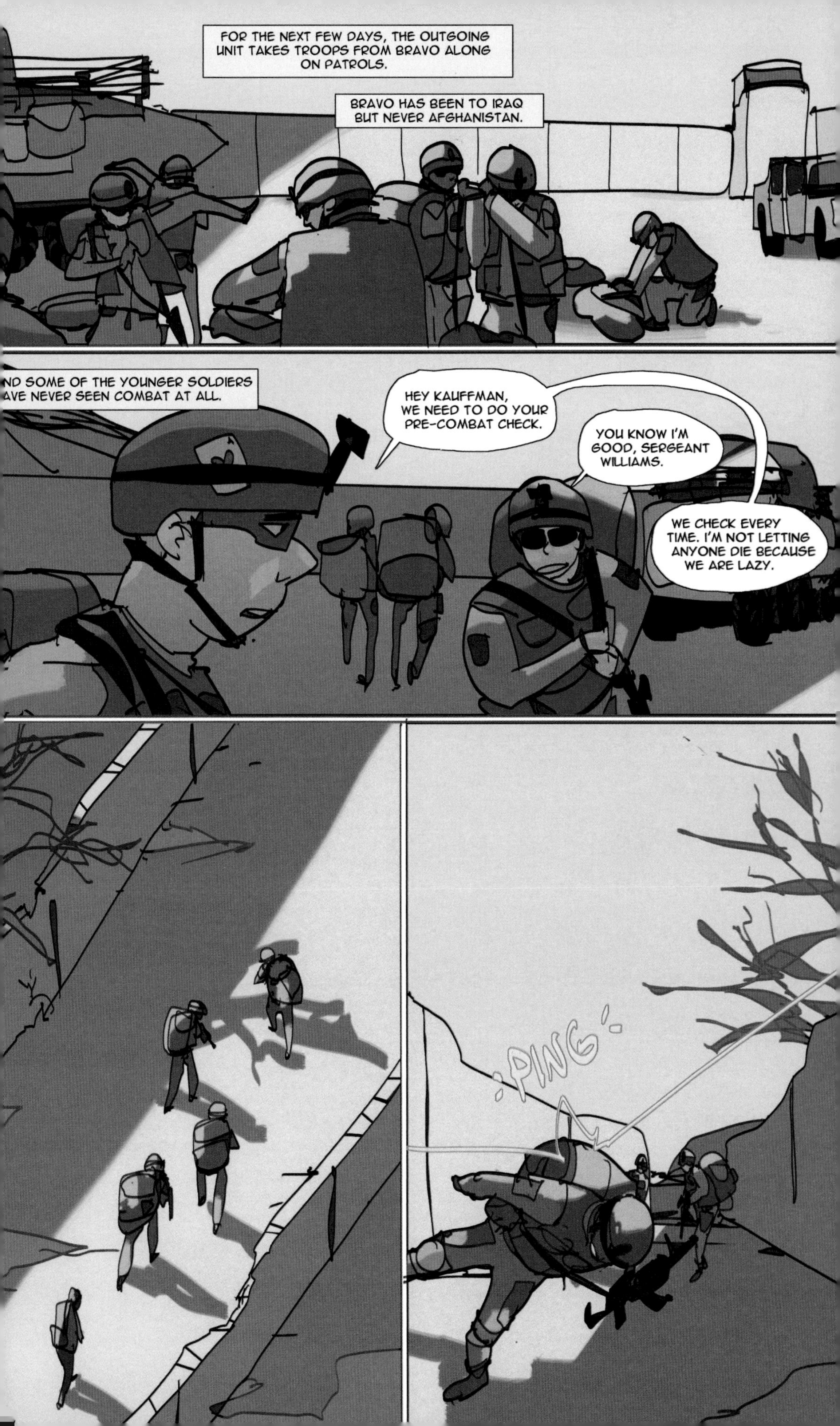

FOR THE NEXT FEW DAYS, THE OUTGOING UNIT TAKES TROOPS FROM BRAVO ALONG ON PATROLS.
BRAVO HAS BEEN TO IRAQ BUT NEVER AFGHANISTAN.
ND SOME OF THE YOUNGER SOLDIERS AVE NEVER SEEN COMBAT AT ALL.
HEY KAUFFMAN, WE NEED TO DO YOUR PRE-COMBAT CHECK.
YOU KNOW I'M GOOD, SERGEANT WILLIAMS.
WE CHECK EVERY TIME. I'M NOT LETTING ANYONE DIE BECAUSE WE ARE LAZY.
PING

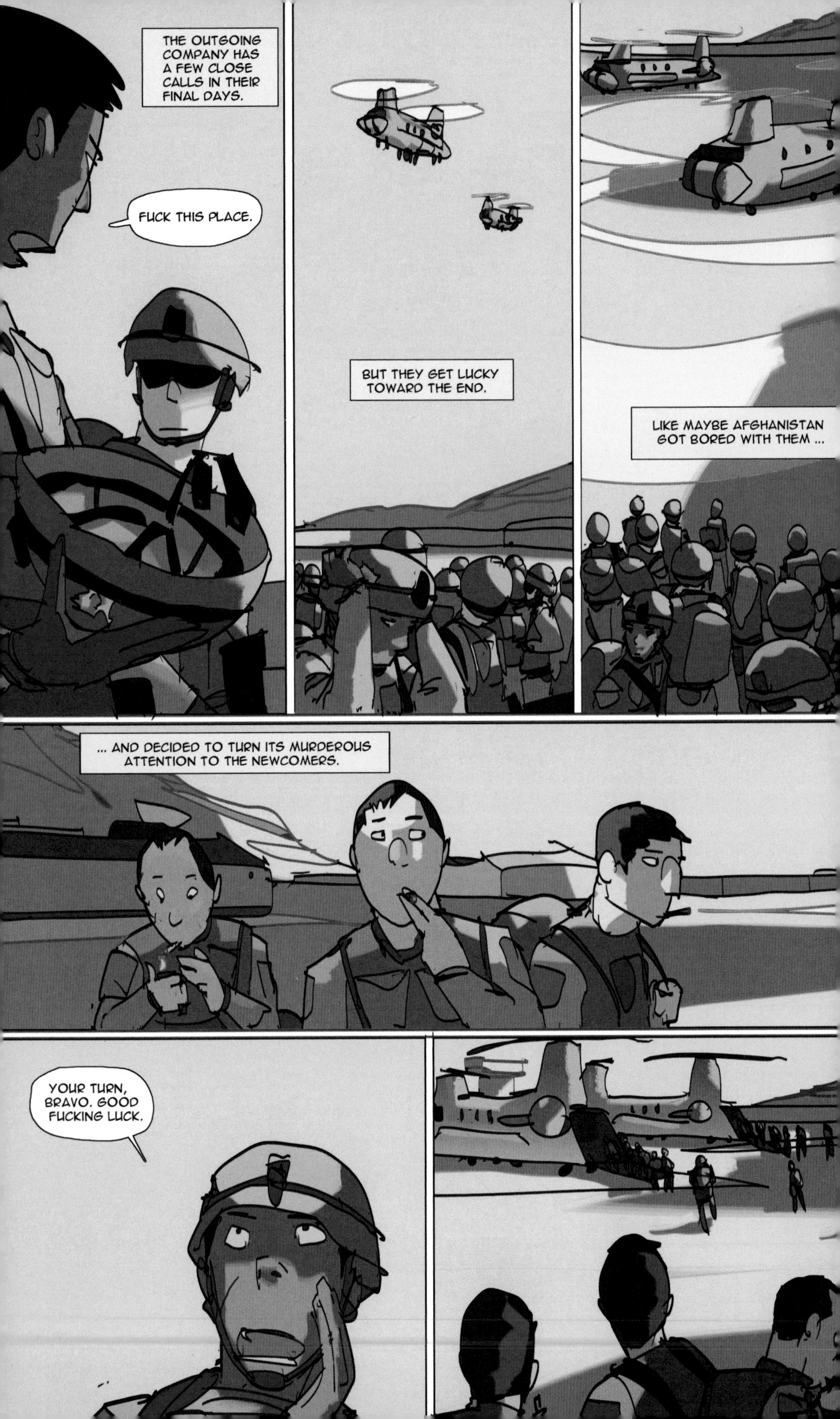
THE OUTGOING COMPANY HAS A FEW CLOSE CALLS IN THEIR FINAL DAYS.
FUCK THIS PLACE.
BUT THEY GET LUCKY TOWARD THE END.
LIKE MAYBE AFGHANISTAN GOT BORED WITH THEM ...
... AND DECIDED TO TURN ITS MURDEROUS ATTENTION TO THE NEWCOMERS.
YOUR TURN, BRAVO. GOOD FUCKING LUCK.

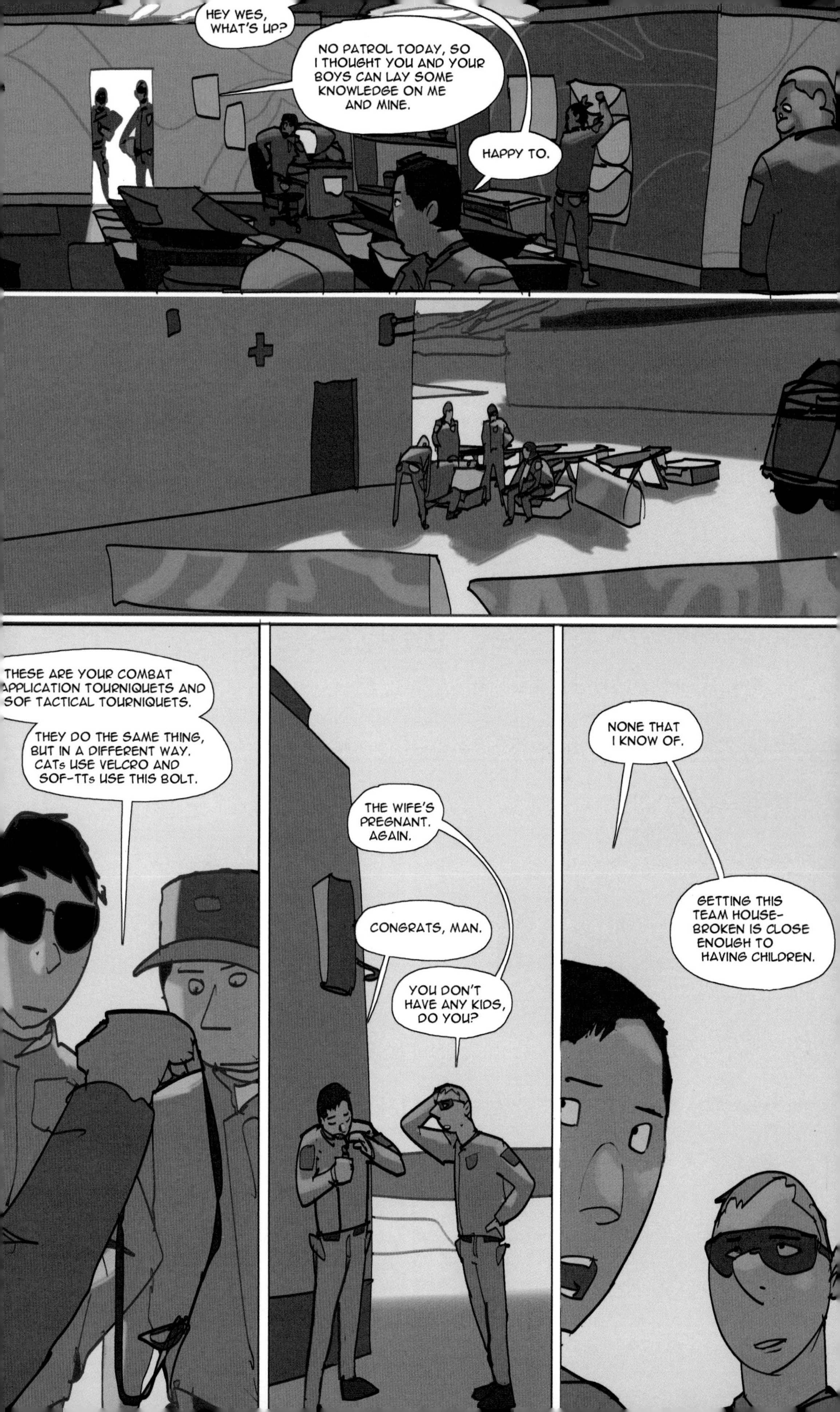
HEY WES,
WHAT'S UP?
NO PATROL TODAY, SO I THOUGHT YOU AND YOUR BOYS CAN LAY SOME KNOWLEDGE ON ME AND MINE.
HAPPY TO.
THESE ARE YOUR COMBAT APPLICATION TOURNIQUETS AND SOF TACTICAL TOURNIQUETS.
THEY DO THE SAME THING, BUT IN A DIFFERENT WAY. CATs USE VELCRO AND SOF-TTs USE THIS BOLT.
THE WIFE'S PREGNANT. AGAIN.
CONGRATS, MAN.
YOU DON'T HAVE ANY KIDS, DO YOU?
NONE THAT I KNOW OF.
GETTING THIS TEAM HOUSE-BROKEN IS CLOSE ENOUGH TO HAVING CHILDREN.

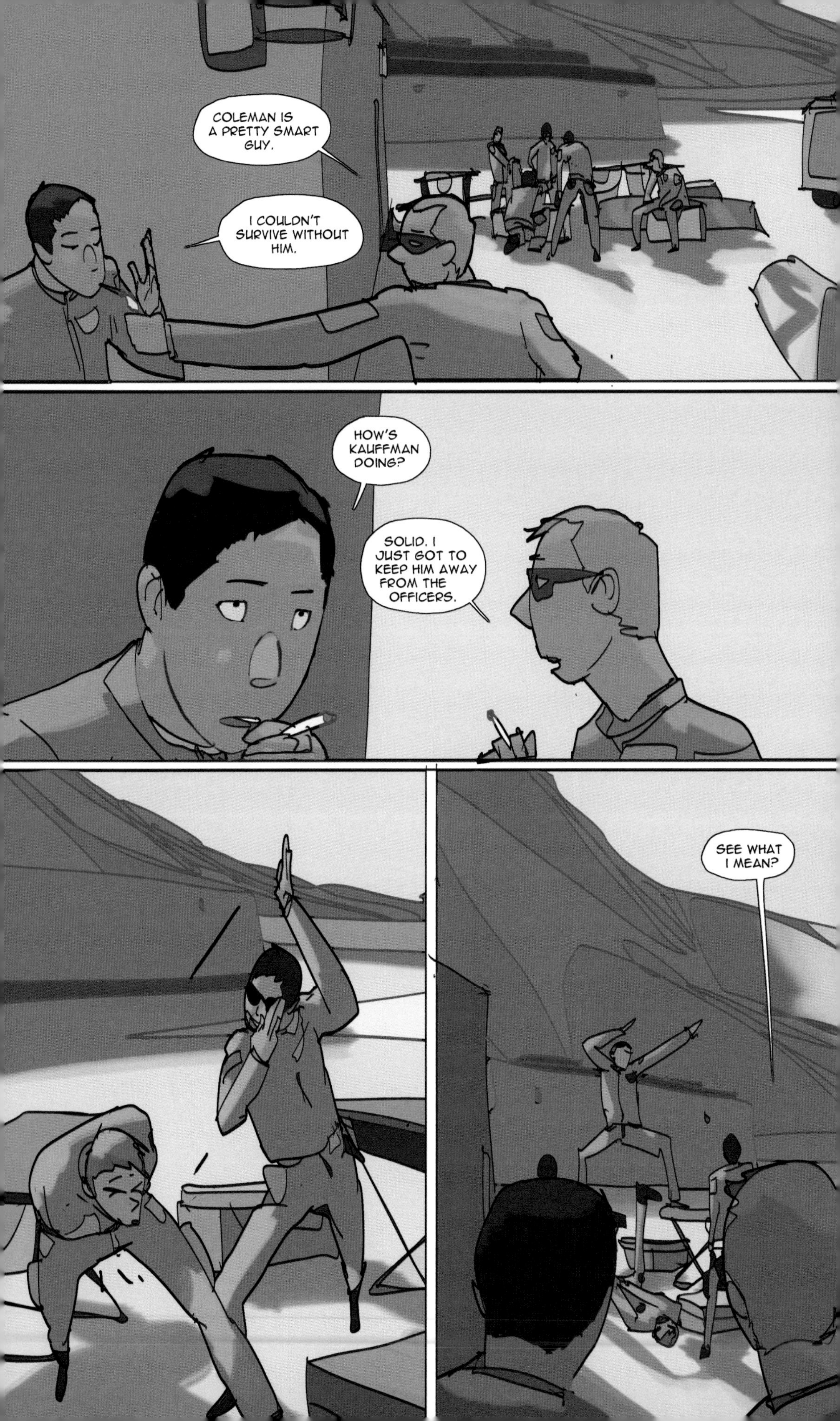
COLEMAN IS A PRETTY SMART GUY.
I COULDN'T SURVIVE WITHOUT HIM.
HOW'S KAUFFMAN DOING?
SOLID. I JUST GOT TO KEEP HIM AWAY FROM THE OFFICERS.
SEE WHAT I MEAN?

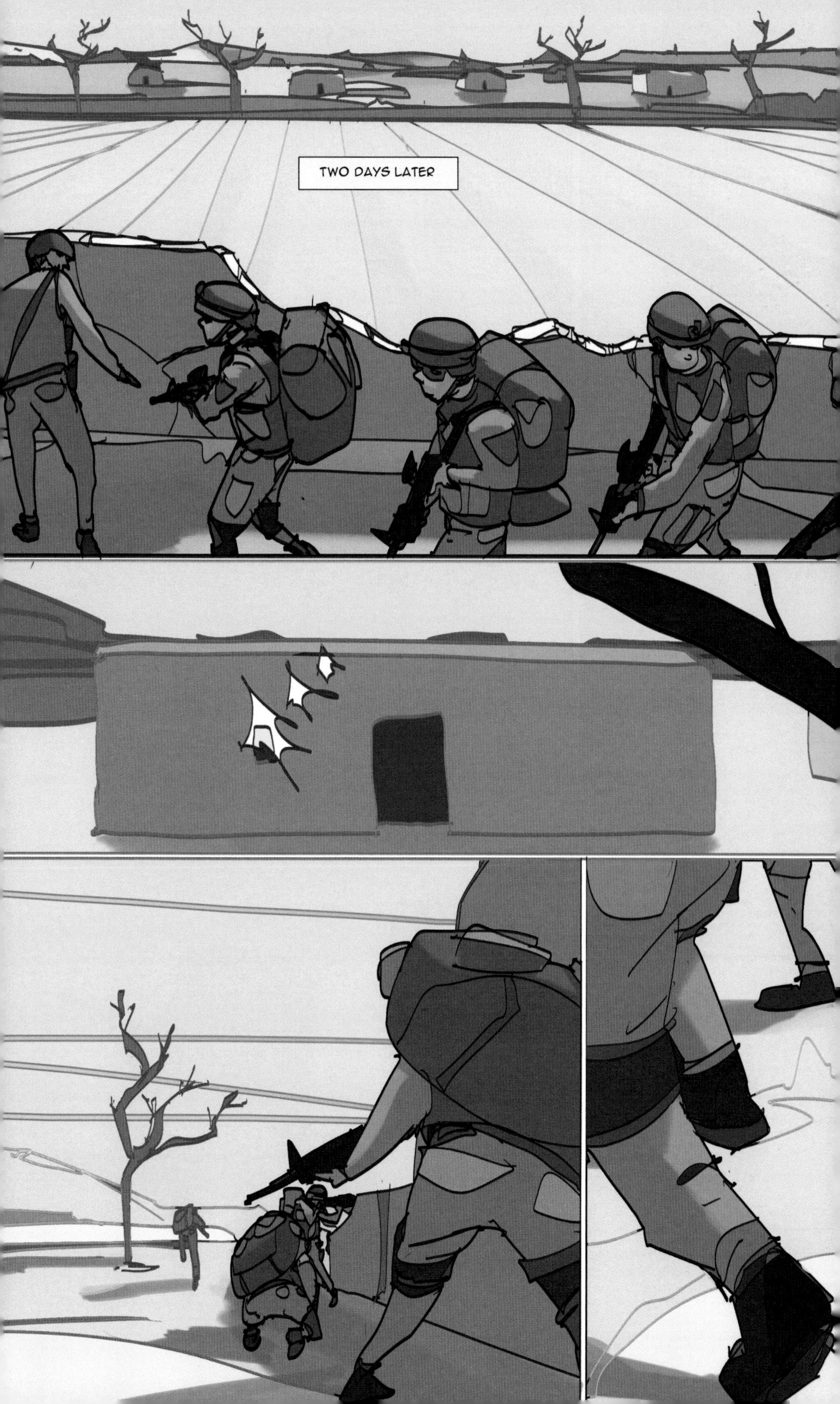

TWO DAYS LATER

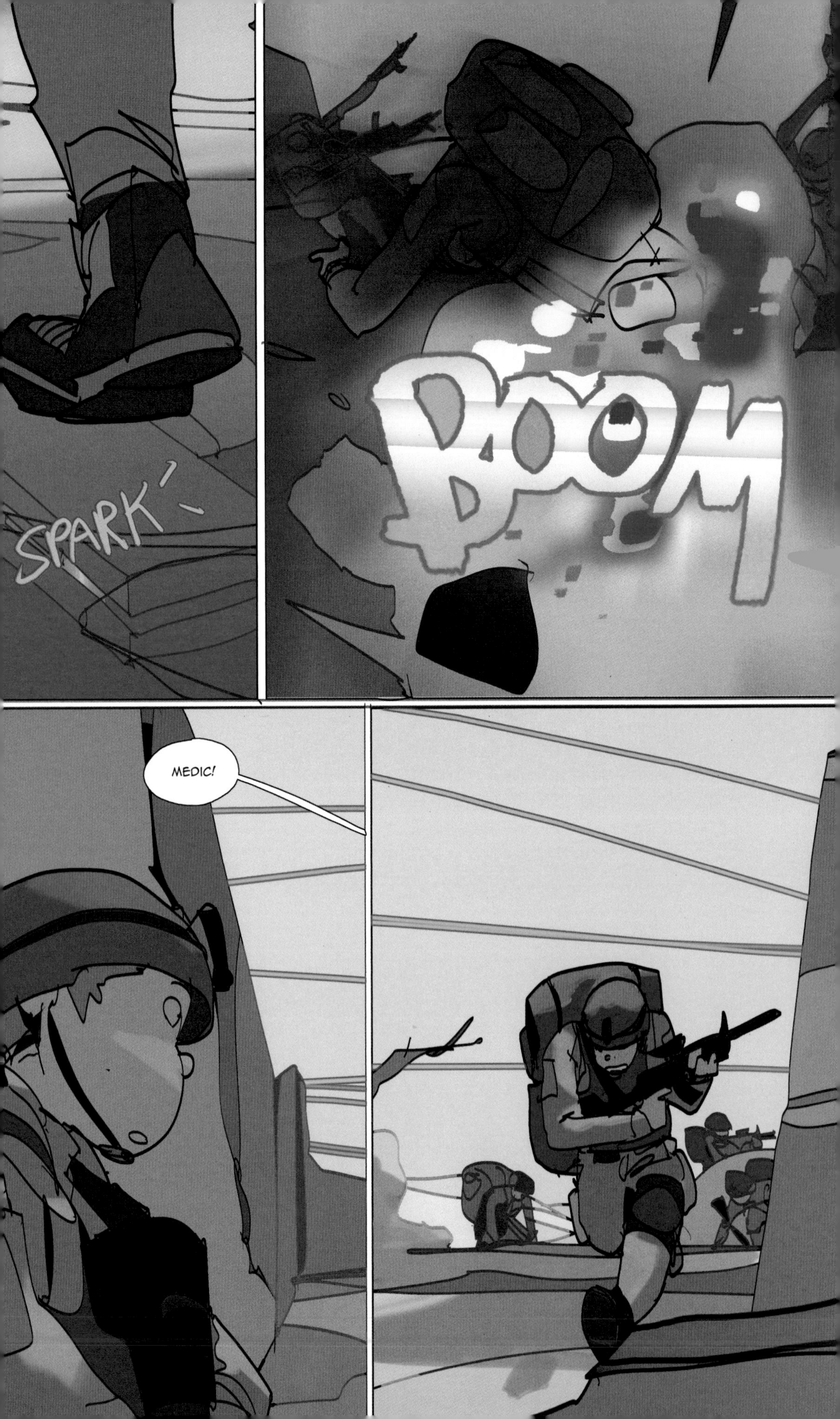
SPARK
BOOM
MEDIC!

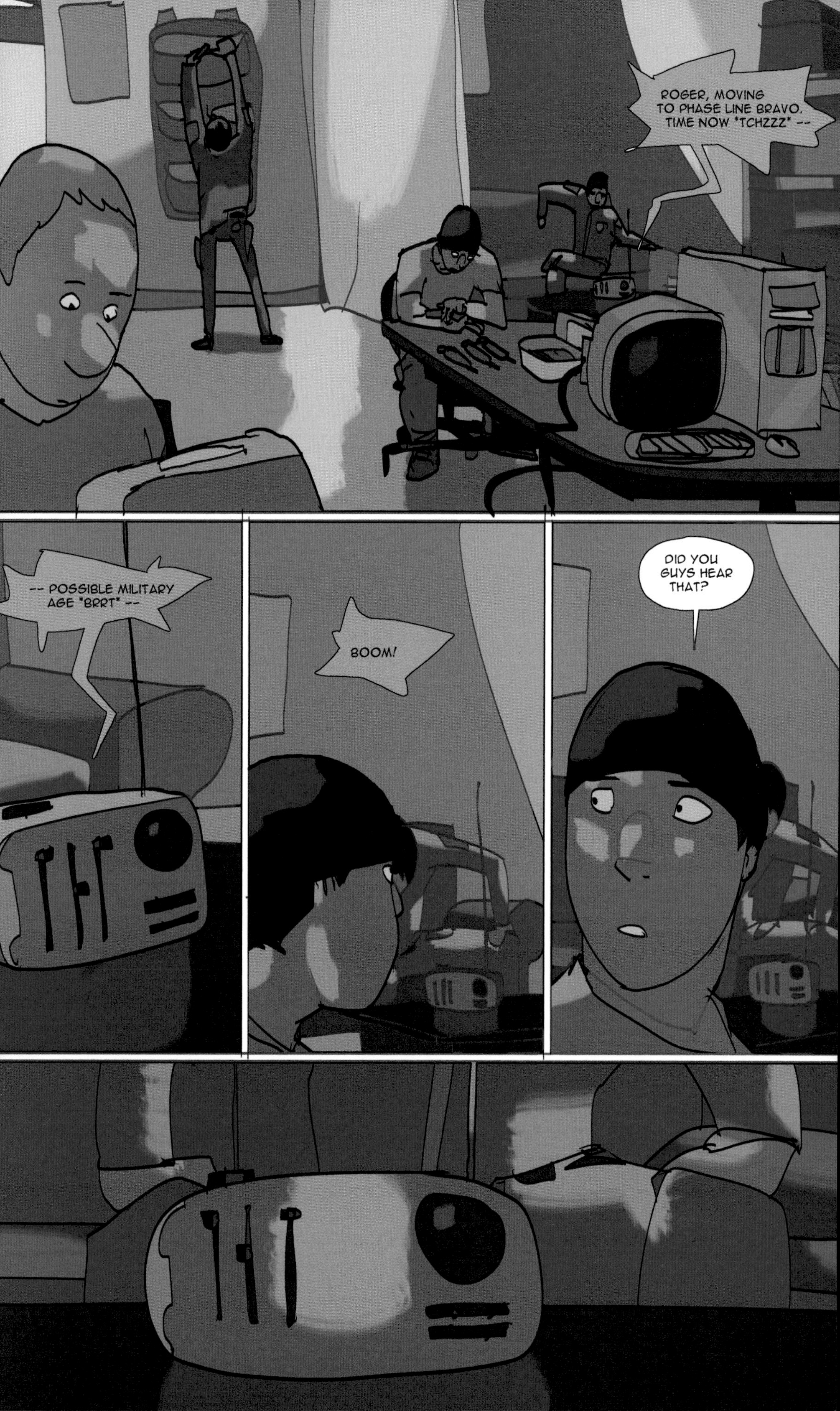
ROGER, MOVING TO PHASE LINE BRAVO. TIME NOW *TCHZZZ* --
-- POSSIBLE MILITARY AGE *BRRT* --
BOOM!
DID YOU GUYS HEAR THAT?

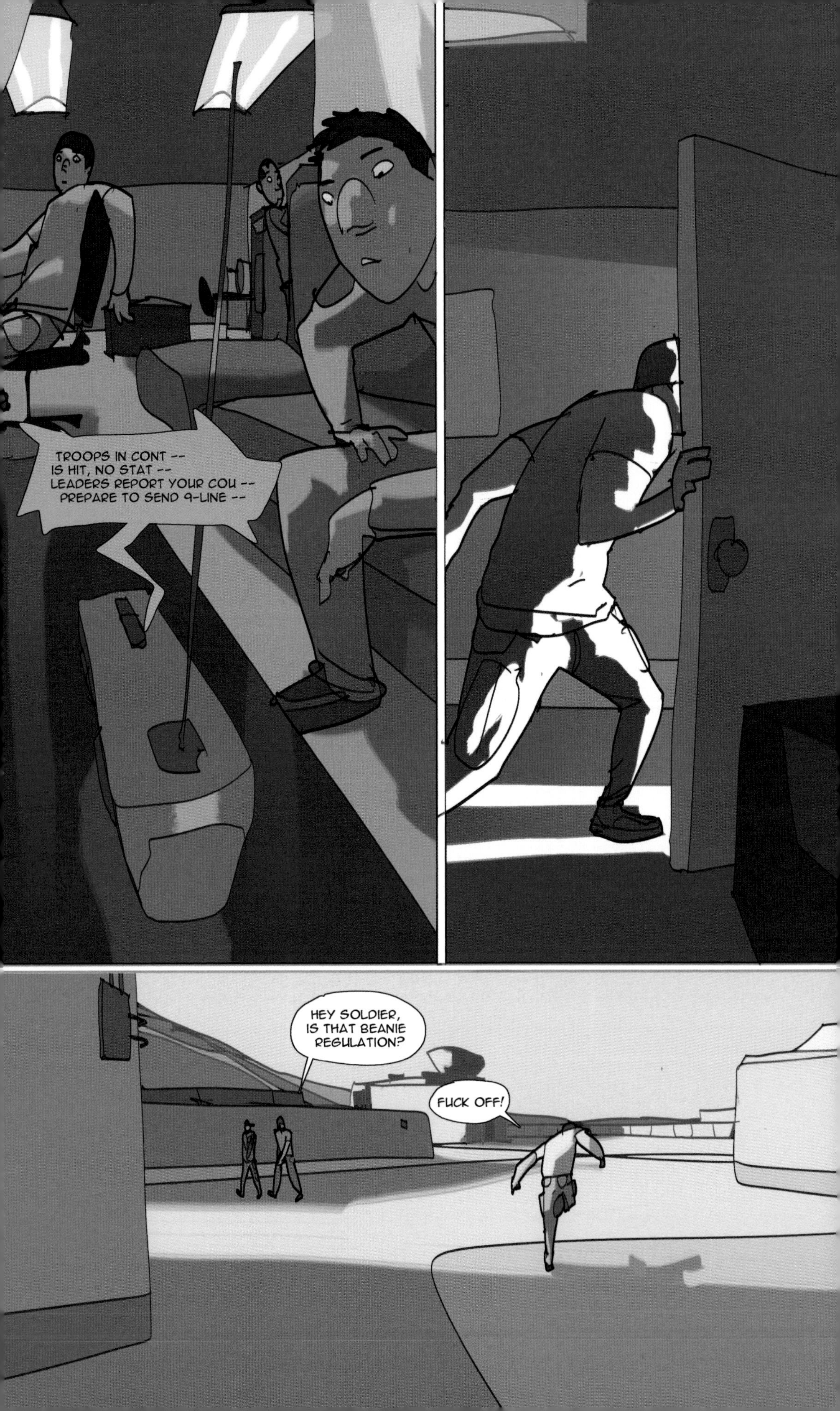
TROOPS IN CONT -- IS HIT, NO STAT -- LEADERS REPORT YOUR COU -- PREPARE TO SEND 9-LINE --
HEY SOLDIER, IS THAT BEANIE REGULATION?
FUCK OFF!

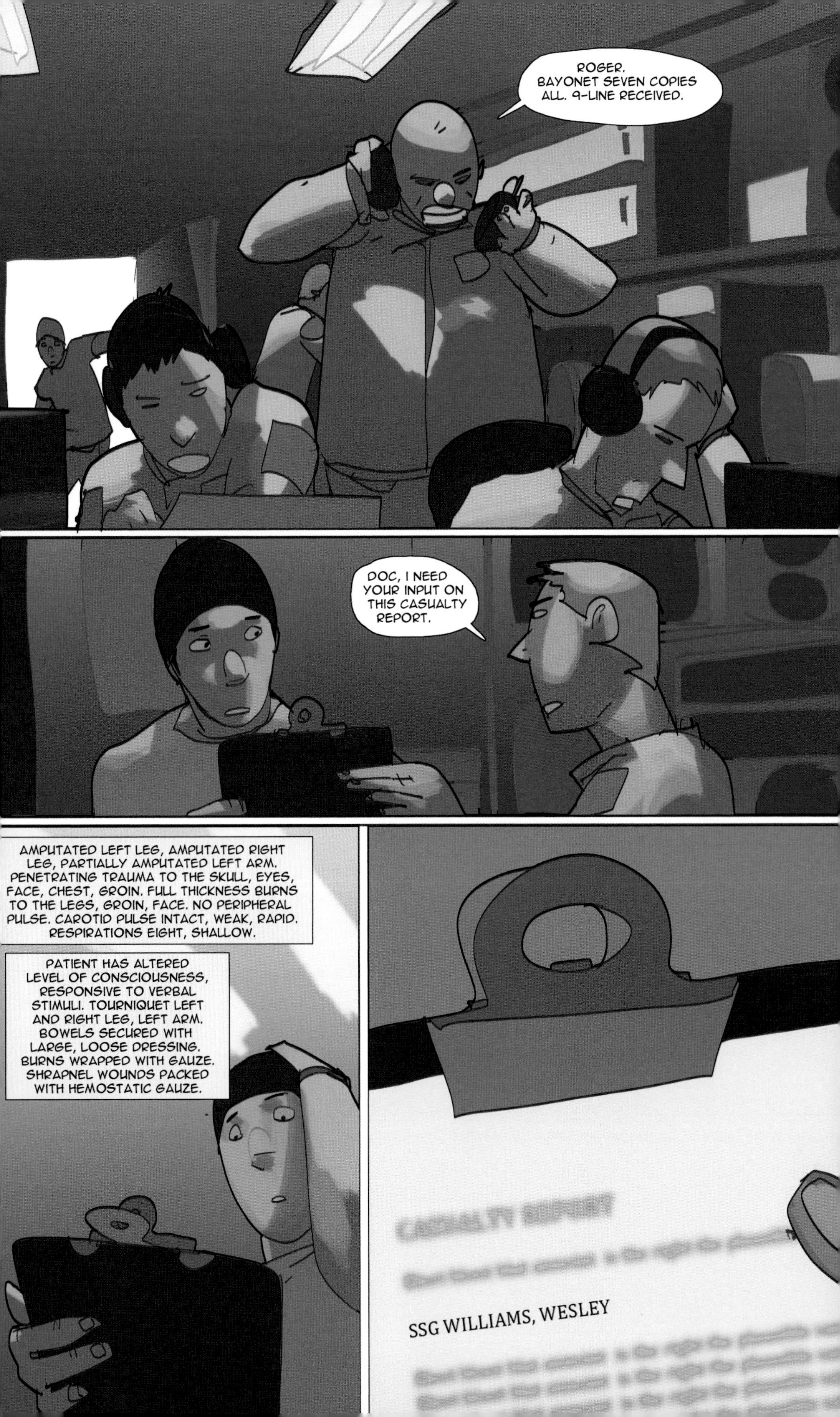

ROGER. BAYONET SEVEN COPIES ALL. 9-LINE RECEIVED.
DOC, I NEED YOUR INPUT ON THIS CASUALTY REPORT.
AMPUTATED LEFT LEG, AMPUTATED RIGHT LEG, PARTIALLY AMPUTATED LEFT ARM. PENETRATING TRAUMA TO THE SKULL, EYES, FACE, CHEST, GROIN. FULL THICKNESS BURNS TO THE LEGS, GROIN, FACE. NO PERIPHERAL PULSE. CAROTID PULSE INTACT, WEAK, RAPID. RESPIRATIONS EIGHT, SHALLOW.
PATIENT HAS ALTERED LEVEL OF CONSCIOUSNESS, RESPONSIVE TO VERBAL STIMULI. TOURNIQUET LEFT AND RIGHT LEG, LEFT ARM. BOWELS SECURED WITH LARGE, LOOSE DRESSING. BURNS WRAPPED WITH GAUZE. SHRAPNEL WOUNDS PACKED WITH HEMOSTATIC GAUZE.
SSG WILLIAMS, WESLEY

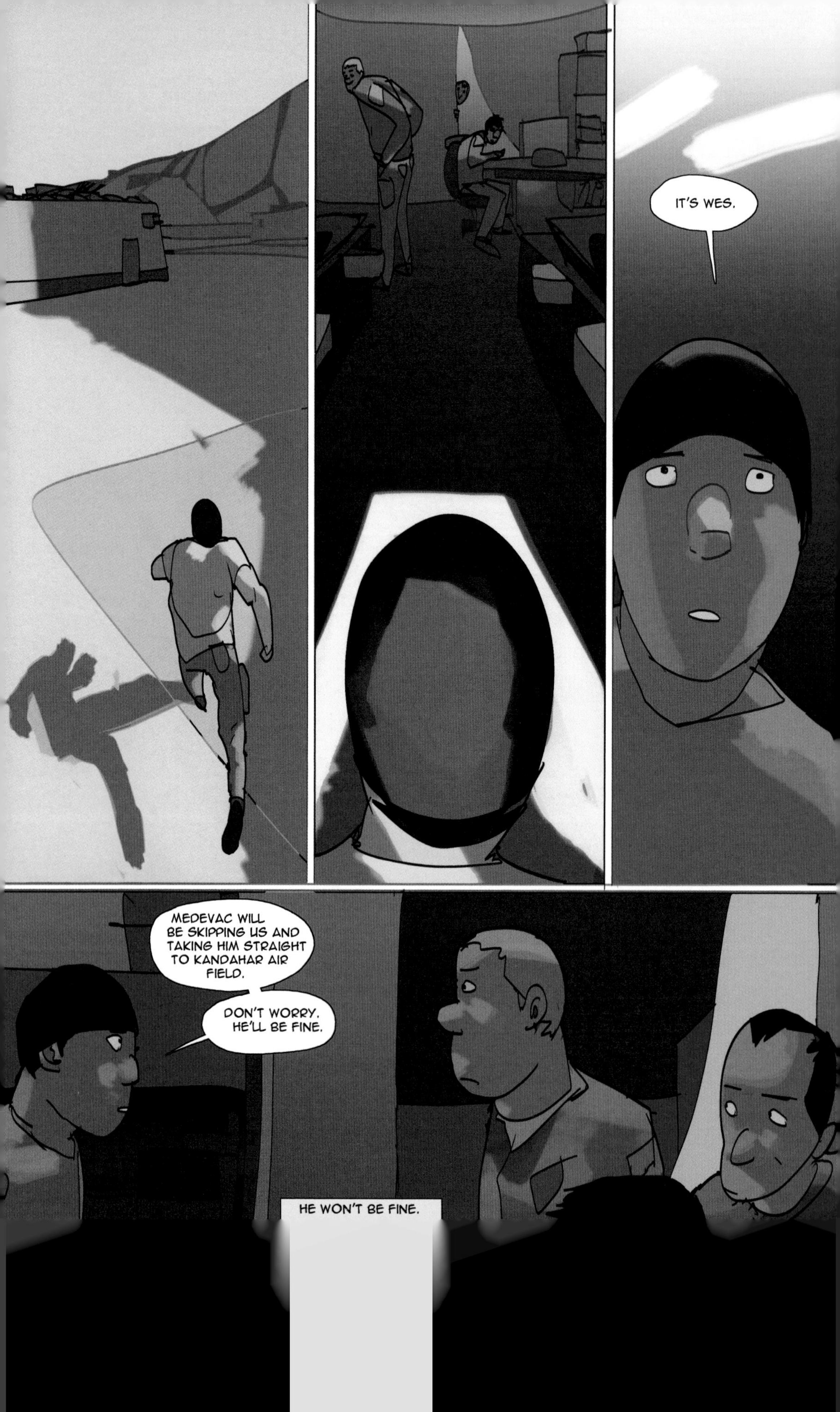
IT'S WES.
MEDEVAC WILL BE SKIPPING US AND TAKING HIM STRAIGHT TO KANDAHAR AIR FIELD.
DON'T WORRY. HE'LL BE FINE.
HE WON'T BE FINE.

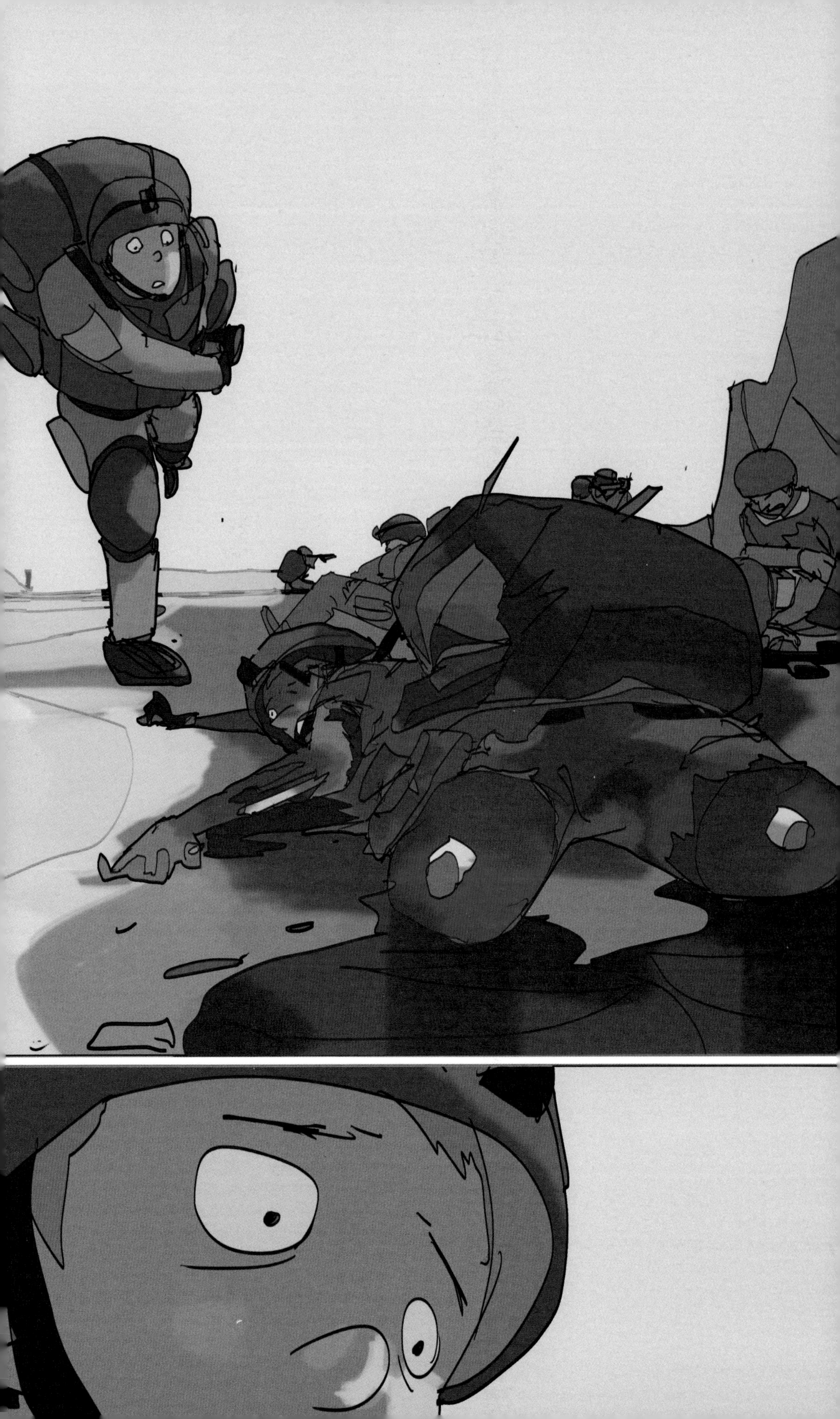

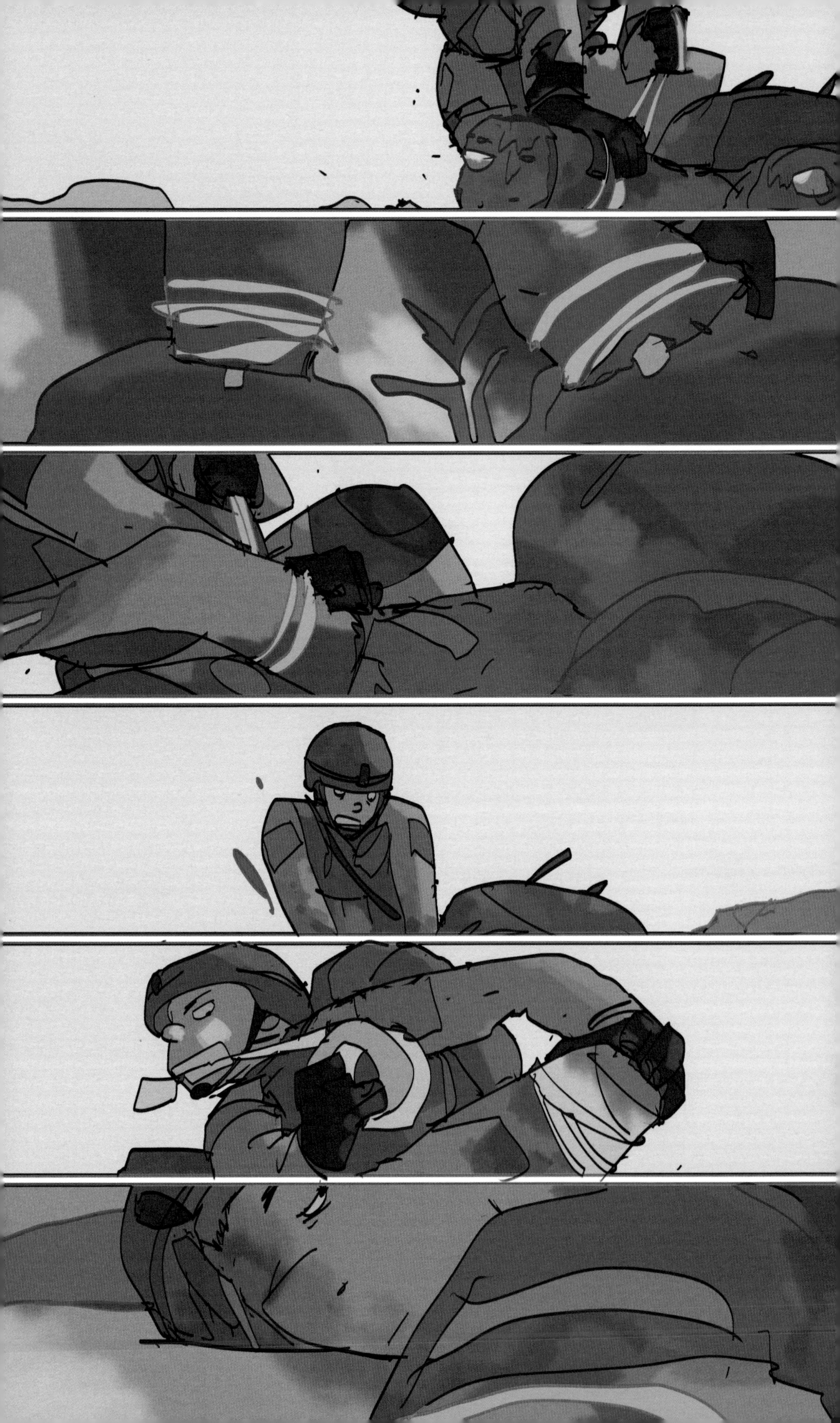

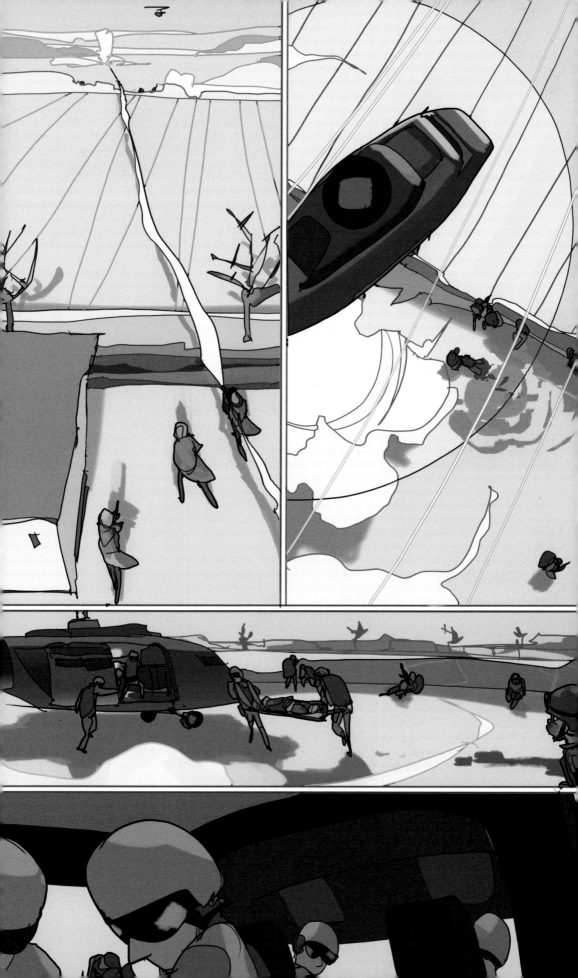

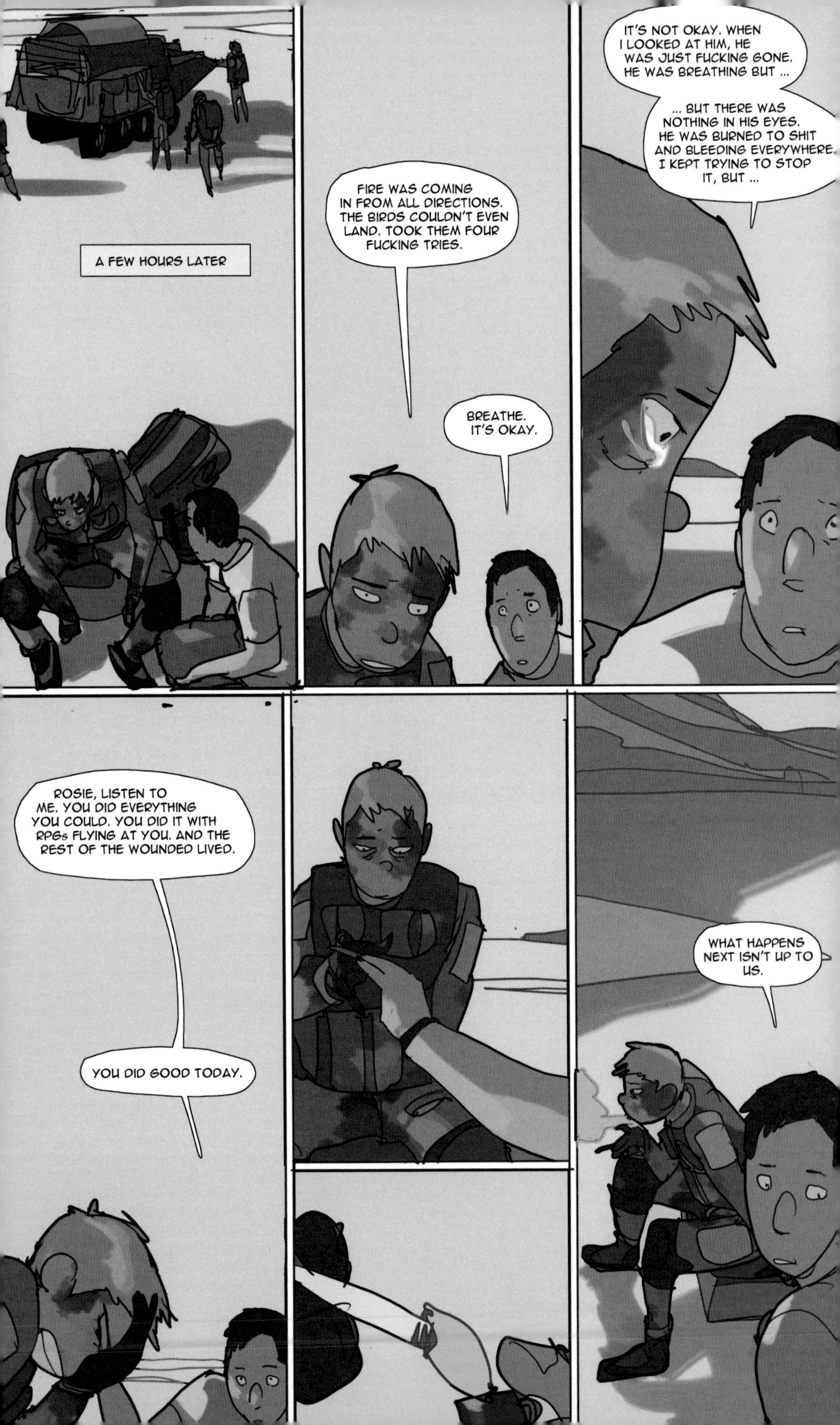
A FEW HOURS LATER
FIRE WAS COMING IN FROM ALL DIRECTIONS. THE BIRDS COULDN'T EVEN LAND. TOOK THEM FOUR FUCKING TRIES.
BREATHE. IT'S OKAY.
IT'S NOT OKAY. WHEN I LOOKED AT HIM, HE WAS JUST FUCKING GONE. HE WAS BREATHING BUT ...
... BUT THERE WAS NOTHING IN HIS EYES. HE WAS BURNED TO SHIT AND BLEEDING EVERYWHERE. I KEPT TRYING TO STOP IT, BUT ...
ROSIE, LISTEN TO ME. YOU DID EVERYTHING YOU COULD. YOU DID IT WITH RPGs FLYING AT YOU. AND THE REST OF THE WOUNDED LIVED.
YOU DID GOOD TODAY.
WHAT HAPPENS NEXT ISN'T UP TO US.

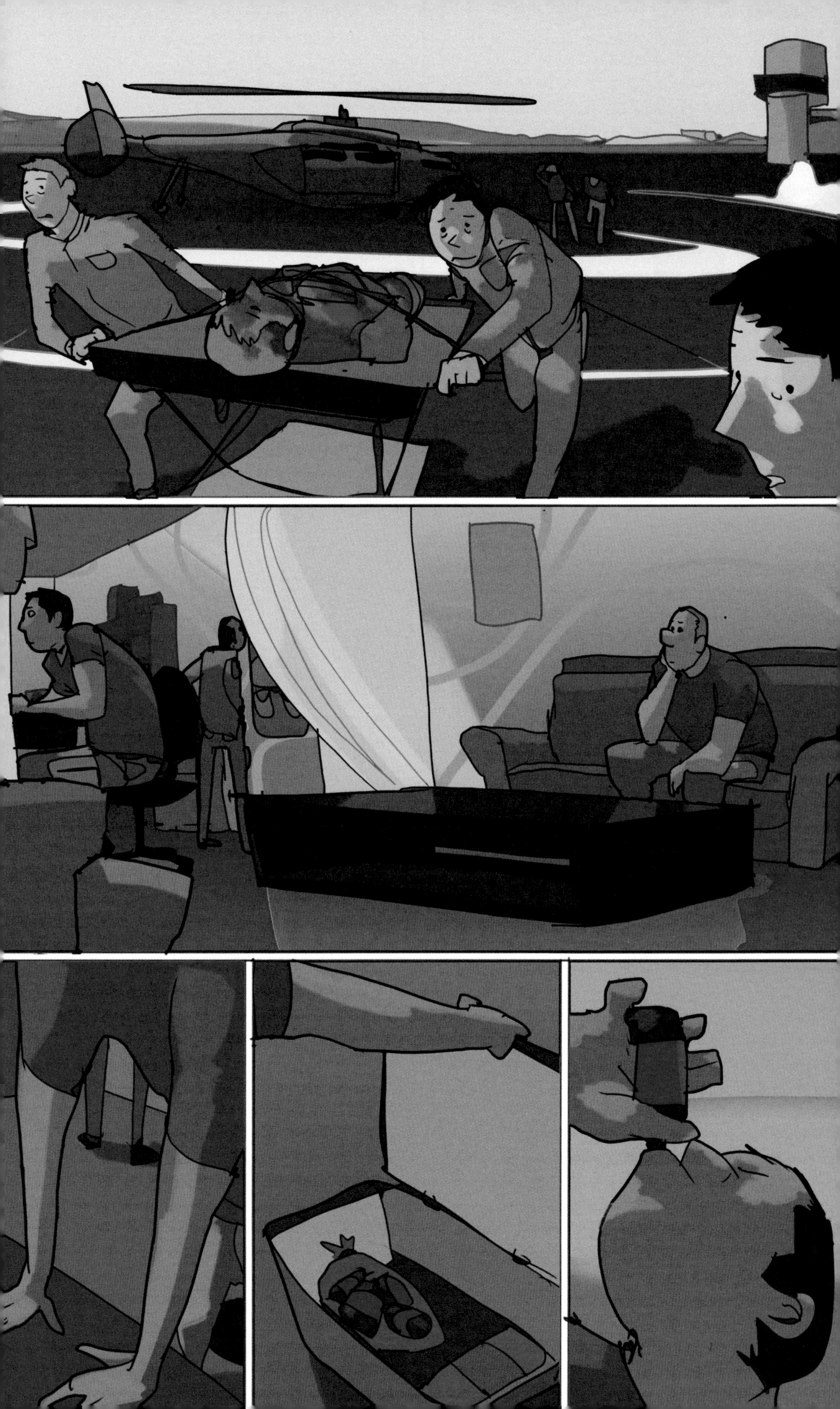

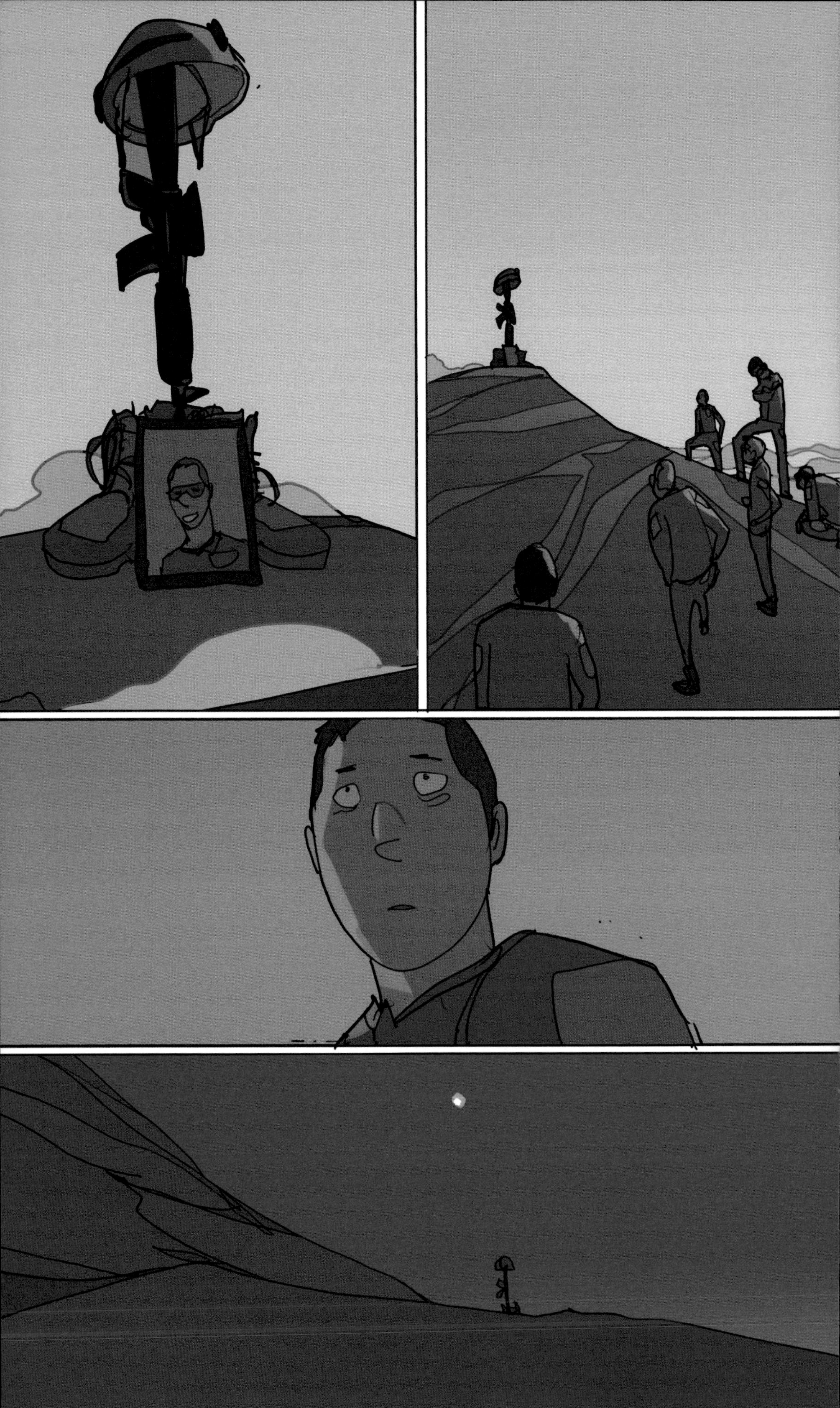

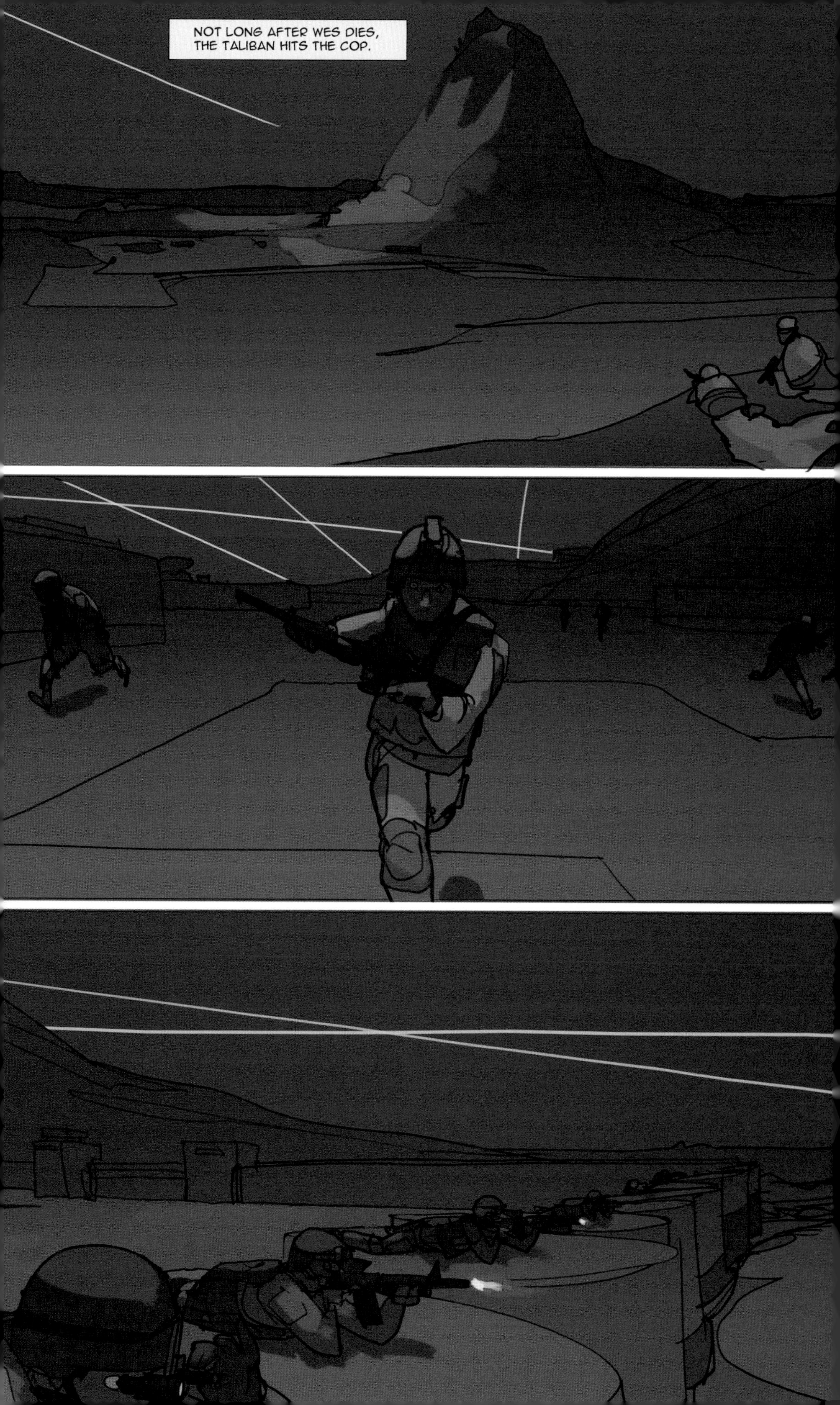
NOT LONG AFTER WES DIES,
THE TALIBAN HITS THE COP.

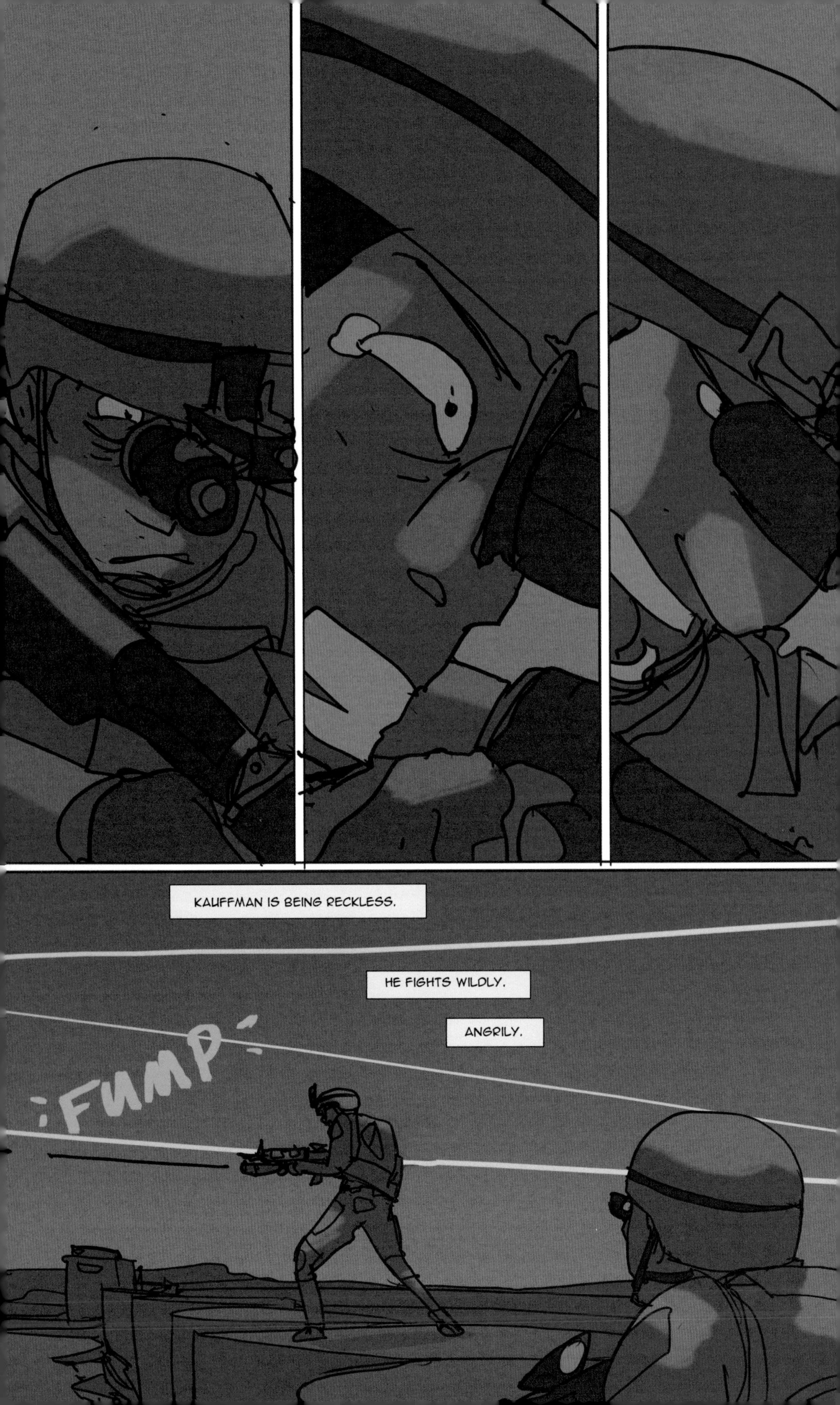
KAUFFMAN IS BEING RECKLESS.
HE FIGHTS WILDLY.
ANGRILY.
FUMP

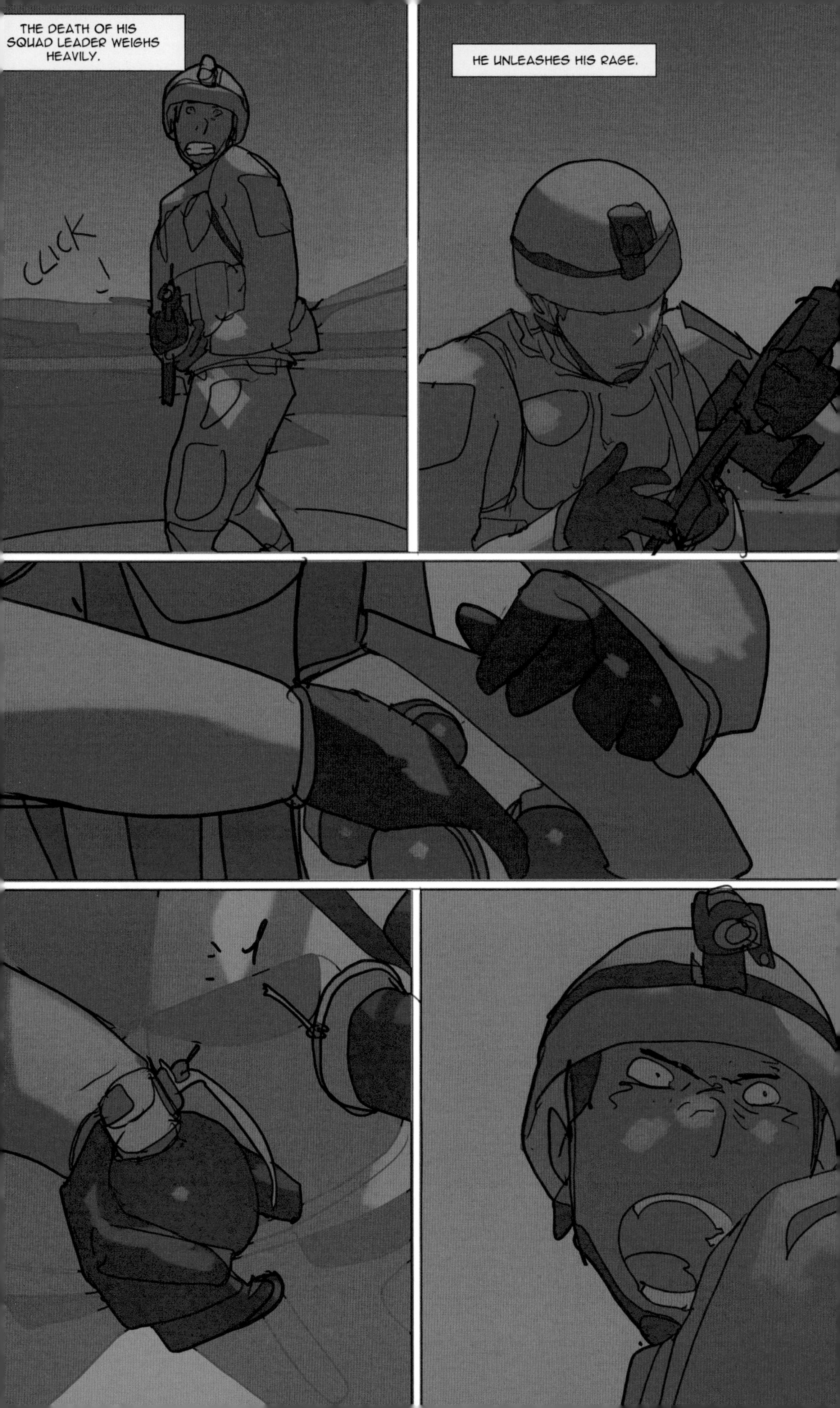
THE DEATH OF HIS SQUAD LEADER WEIGHS HEAVILY.
CLICK
HE UNLEASHES HIS RAGE.

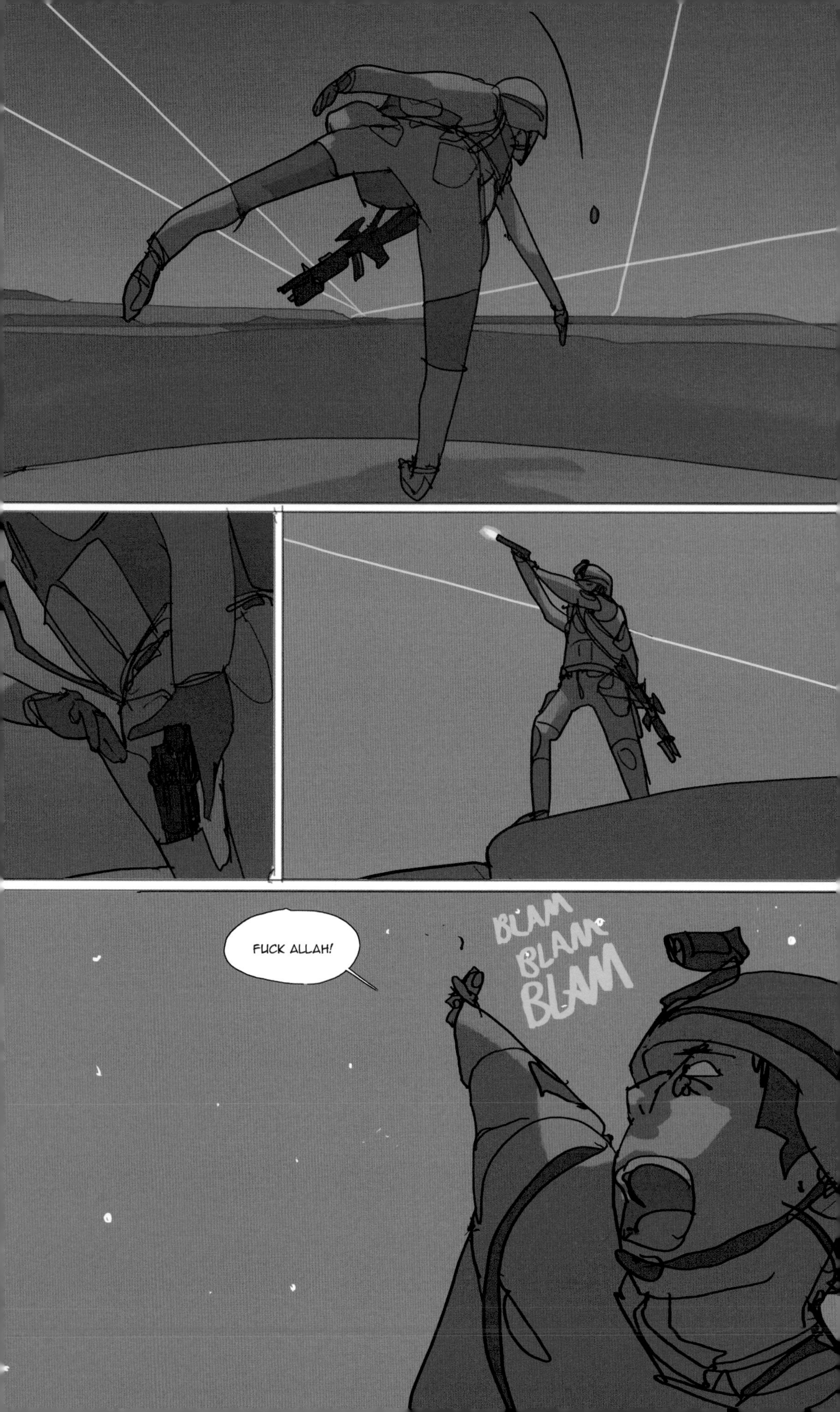
FUCK ALLAH!
BLAM
BLAM
BLAM

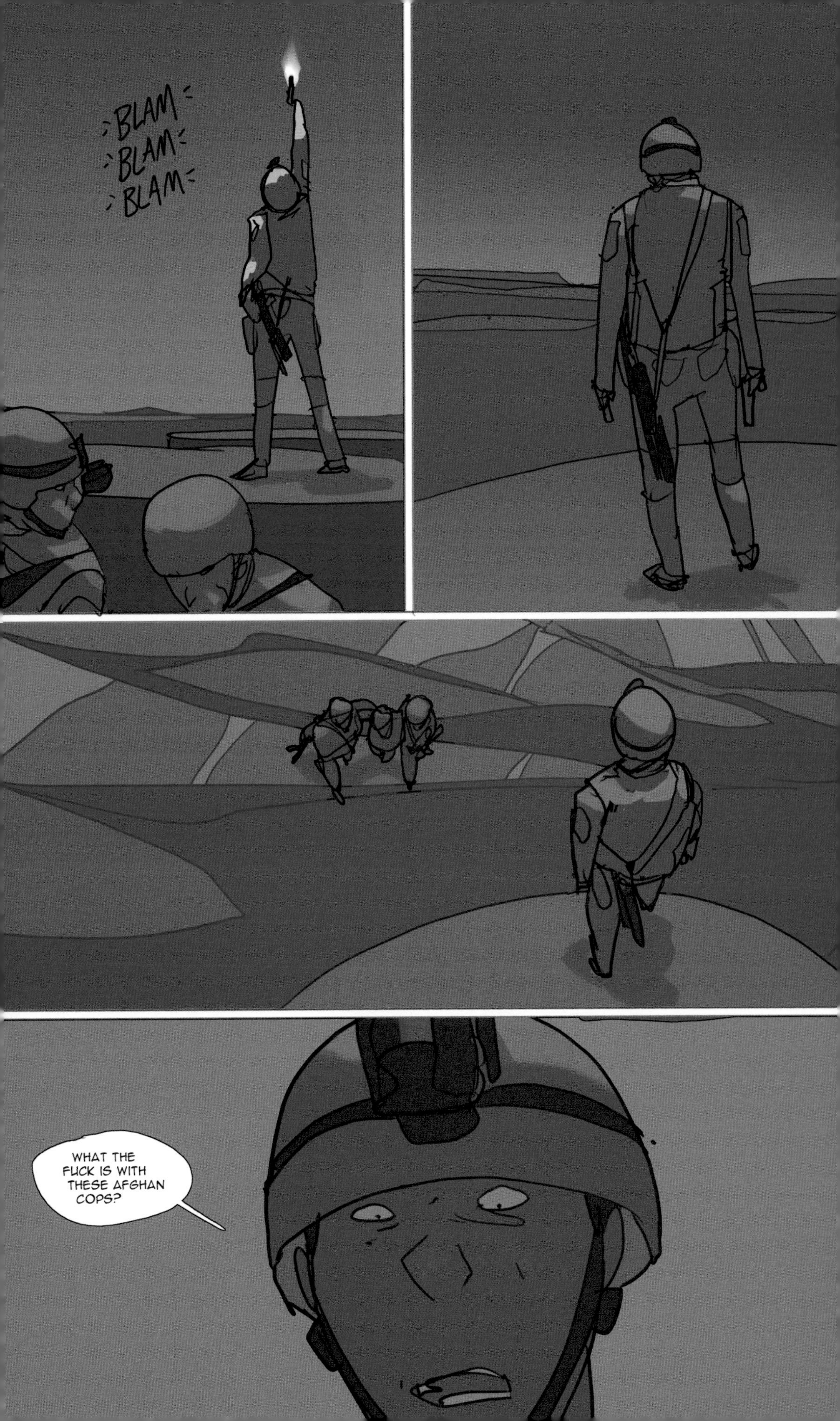
BLAM
BLAM
BLAM
WHAT THE FUCK IS WITH THESE AFGHAN COPS?

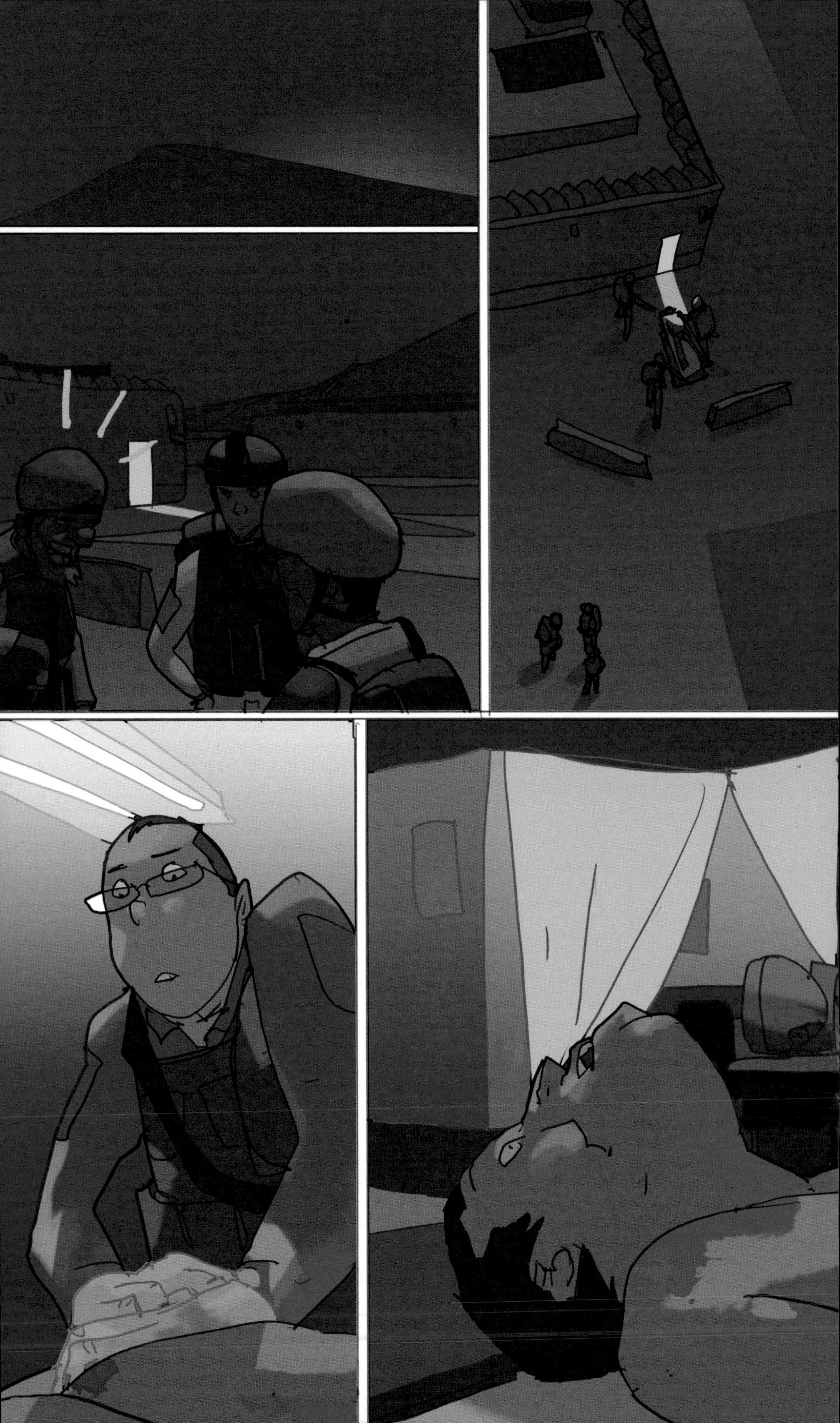

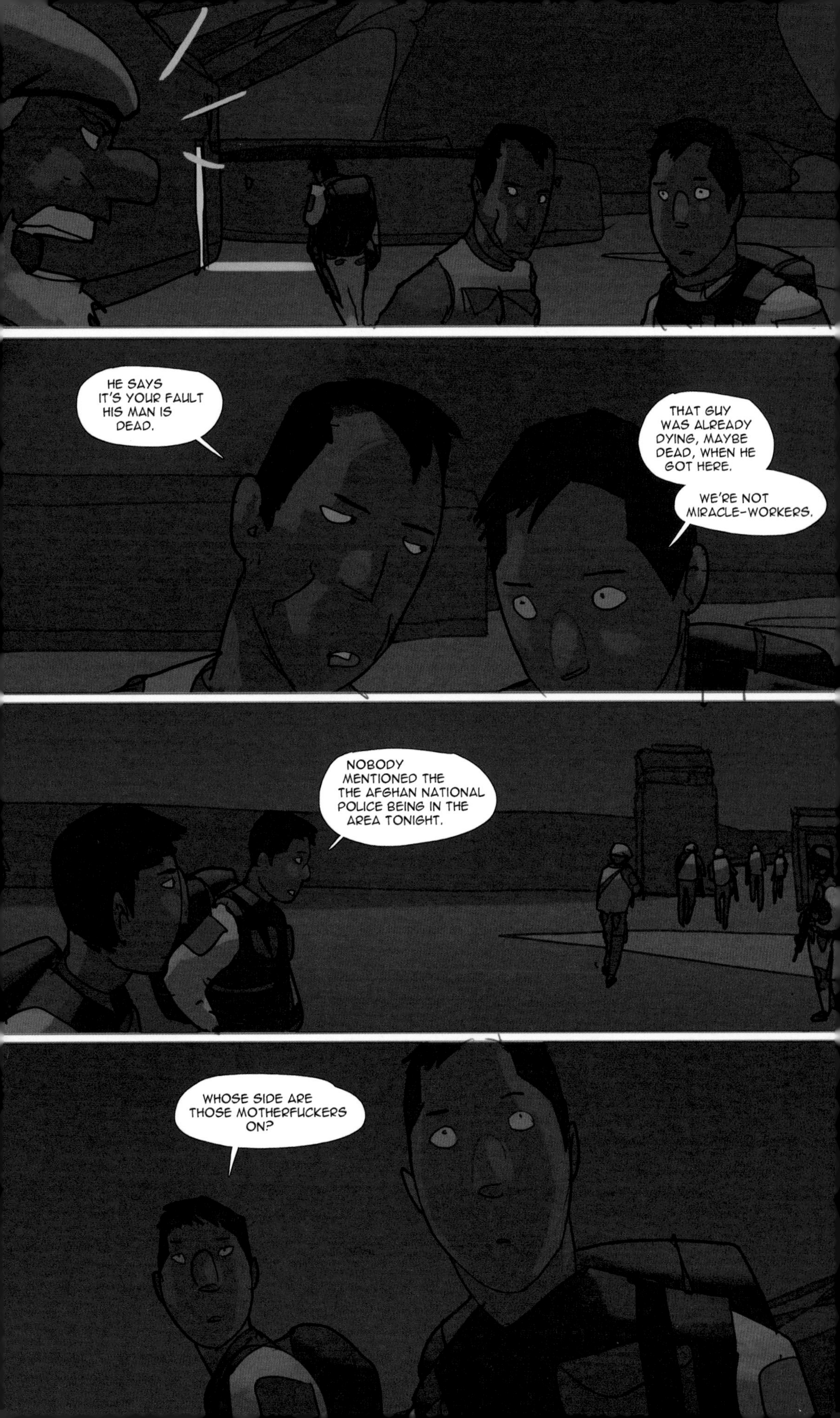
HE SAYS IT'S YOUR FAULT HIS MAN IS DEAD.
THAT GUY WAS ALREADY DYING, MAYBE DEAD, WHEN HE GOT HERE.
WE'RE NOT MIRACLE-WORKERS.
NOBODY MENTIONED THE THE AFGHAN NATIONAL POLICE BEING IN THE AREA TONIGHT.
WHOSE SIDE ARE THOSE MOTHERFUCKERS ON?

WE MEDICS TAKE TURNS LEAVING THE AID STATION TO GO OUT ON PATROLS.

YOU NEVER KNOW WHEN SOMEBODY MIGHT NEED HELP.

LATER, DULAK, WATCH YOUR STEP.

LATER, BRO.

A QUICK OVERNIGHT TRIP OUTSIDE THE WIRE. EASY.

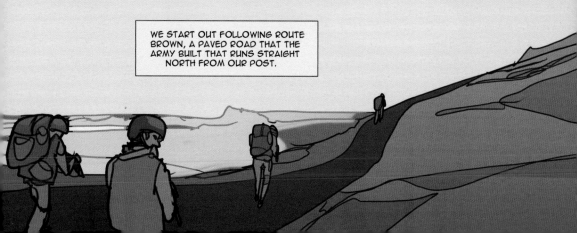

WE START OUT FOLLOWING ROUTE BROWN, A PAVED ROAD THAT THE ARMY BUILT THAT RUNS STRAIGHT NORTH FROM OUR POST.

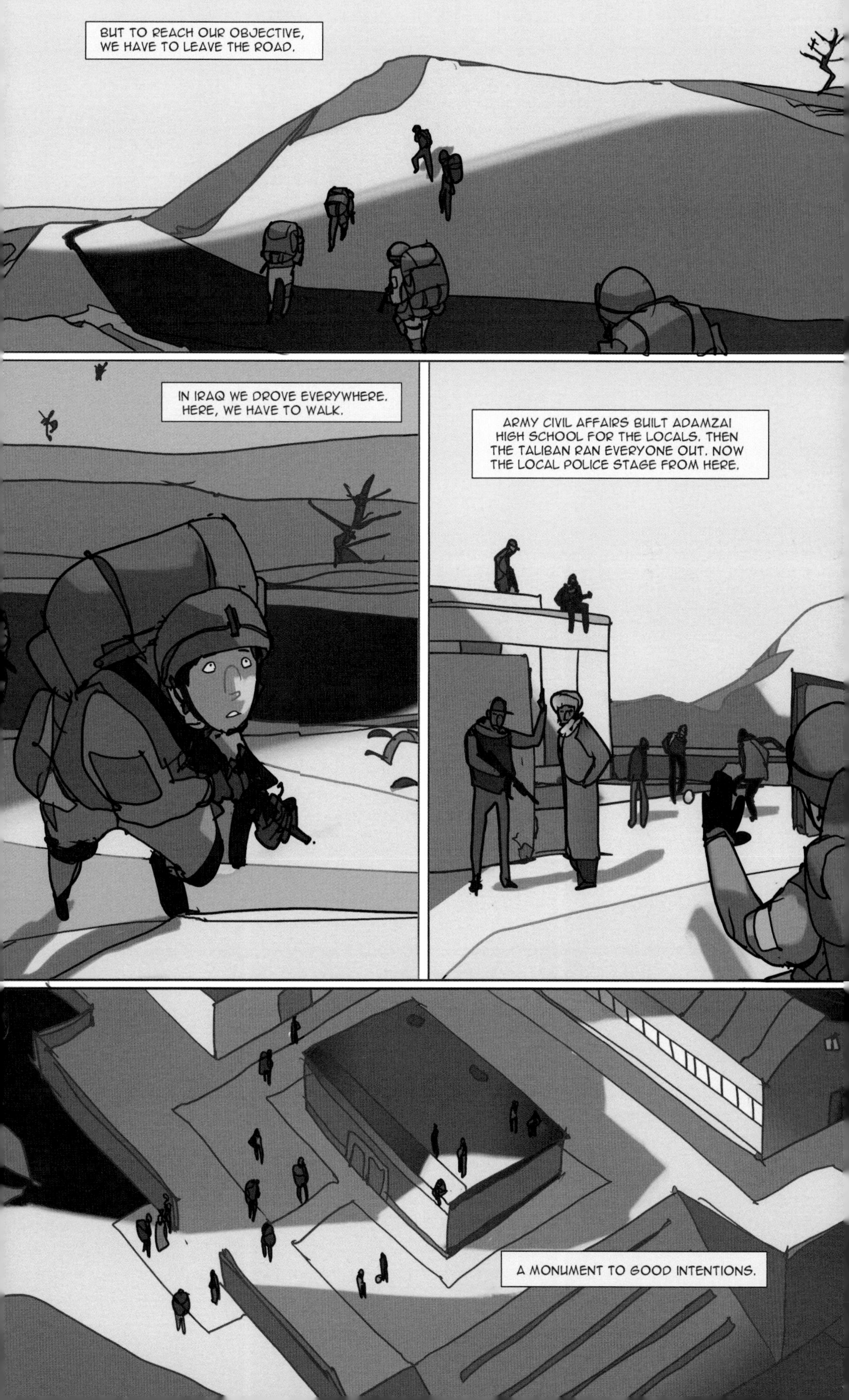
BUT TO REACH OUR OBJECTIVE, WE HAVE TO LEAVE THE ROAD.
IN IRAQ WE DROVE EVERYWHERE. HERE, WE HAVE TO WALK.
ARMY CIVIL AFFAIRS BUILT ADAMZAI HIGH SCHOOL FOR THE LOCALS. THEN THE TALIBAN RAN EVERYONE OUT. NOW THE LOCAL POLICE STAGE FROM HERE.
A MONUMENT TO GOOD INTENTIONS.

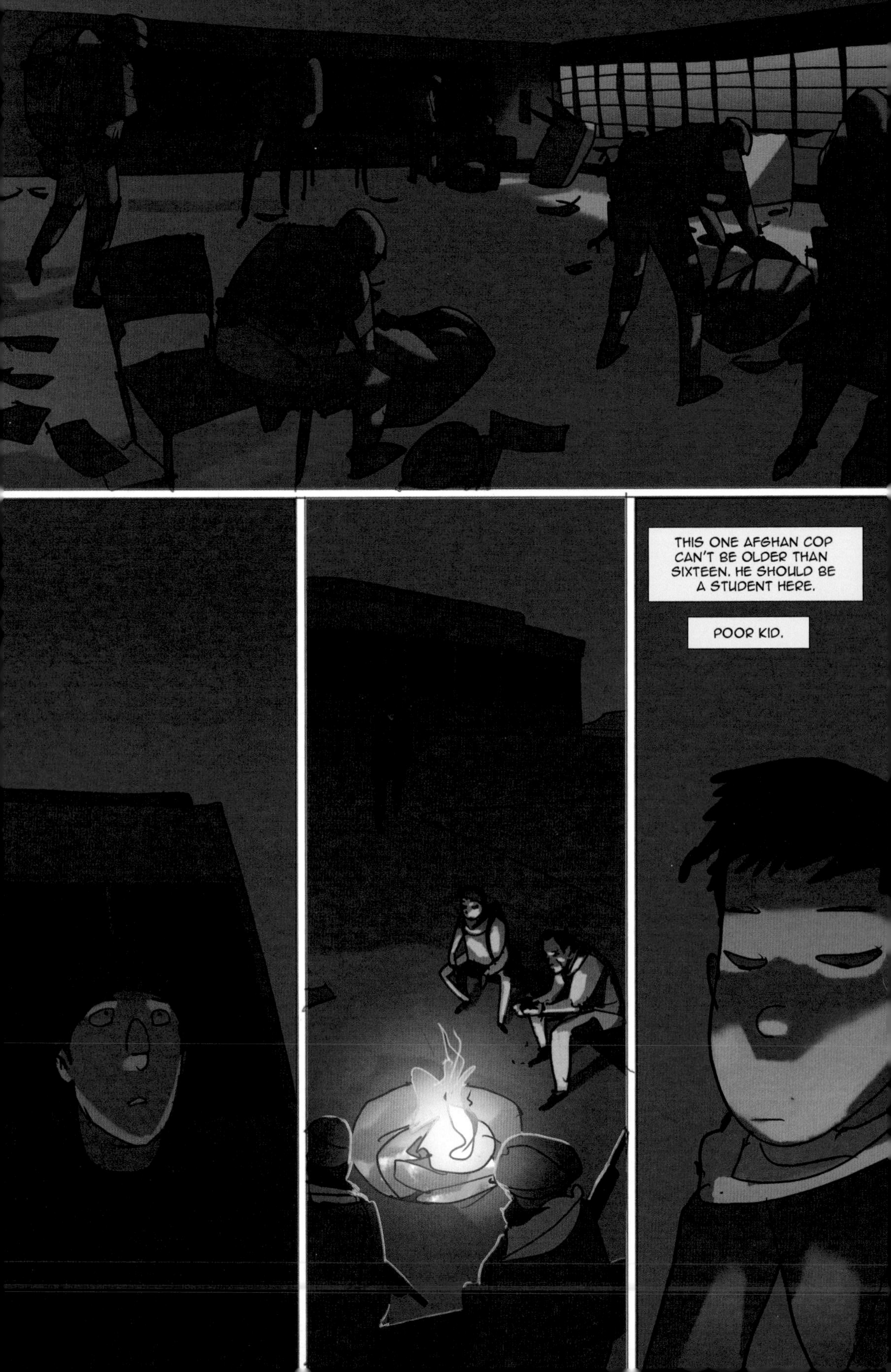
THIS ONE AFGHAN COP CAN'T BE OLDER THAN SIXTEEN. HE SHOULD BE A STUDENT HERE.
POOR KID.

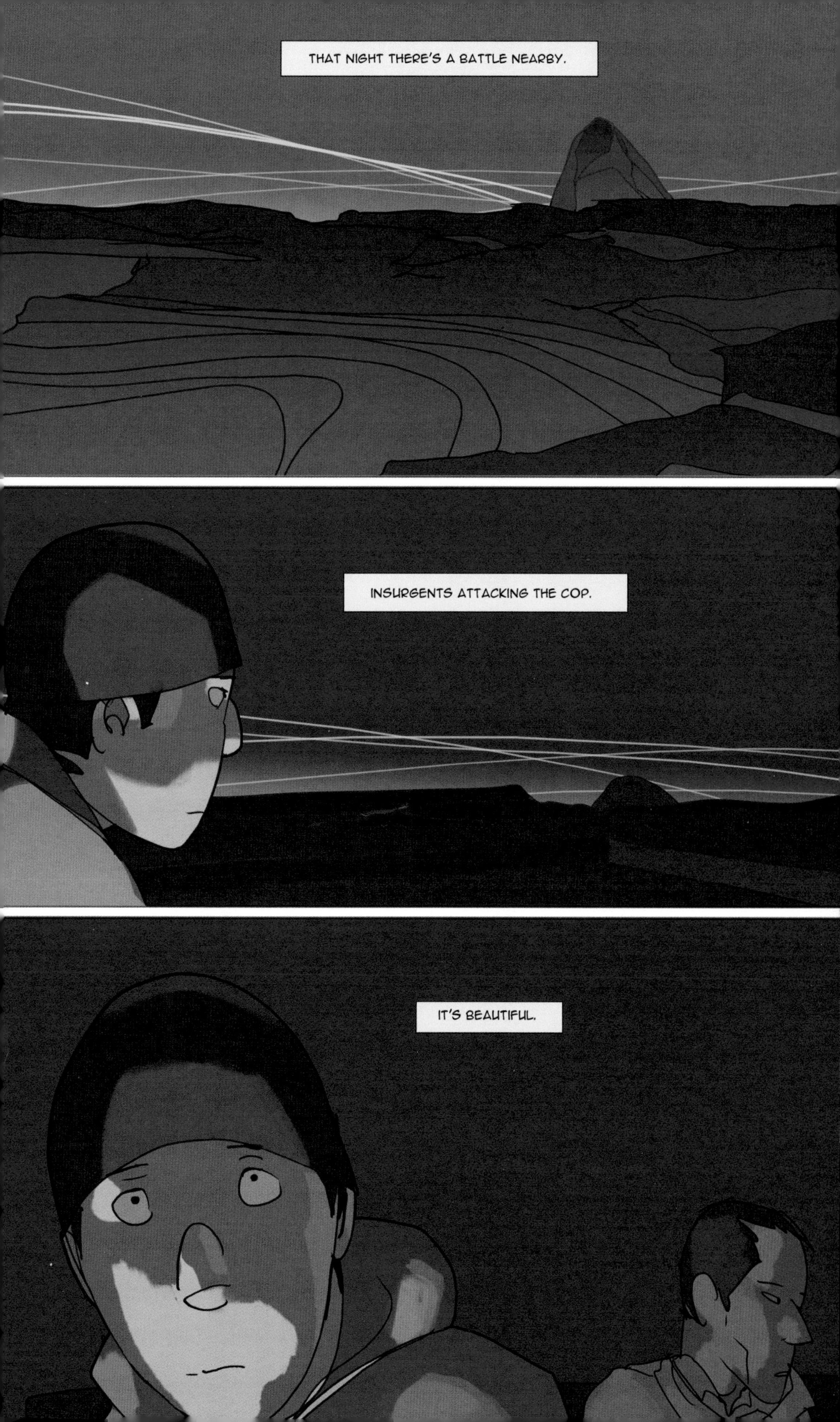
THAT NIGHT THERE'S A BATTLE NEARBY.
INSURGENTS ATTACKING THE COP.
IT'S BEAUTIFUL.

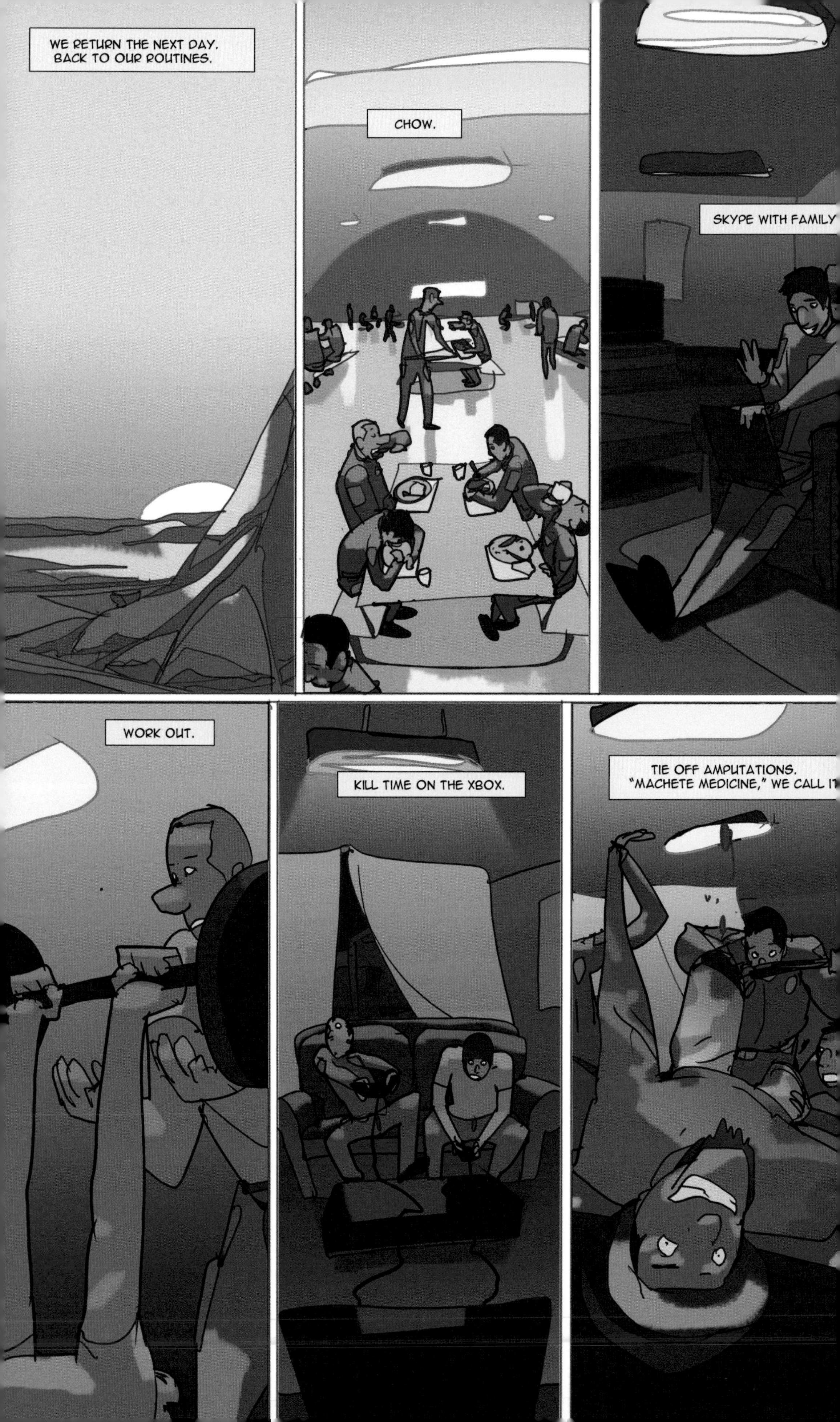
WE RETURN THE NEXT DAY.
BACK TO OUR ROUTINES.
CHOW.
SKYPE WITH FAMILY
WORK OUT.
KILL TIME ON THE XBOX.
TIE OFF AMPUTATIONS.
"MACHETE MEDICINE," WE CALL IT

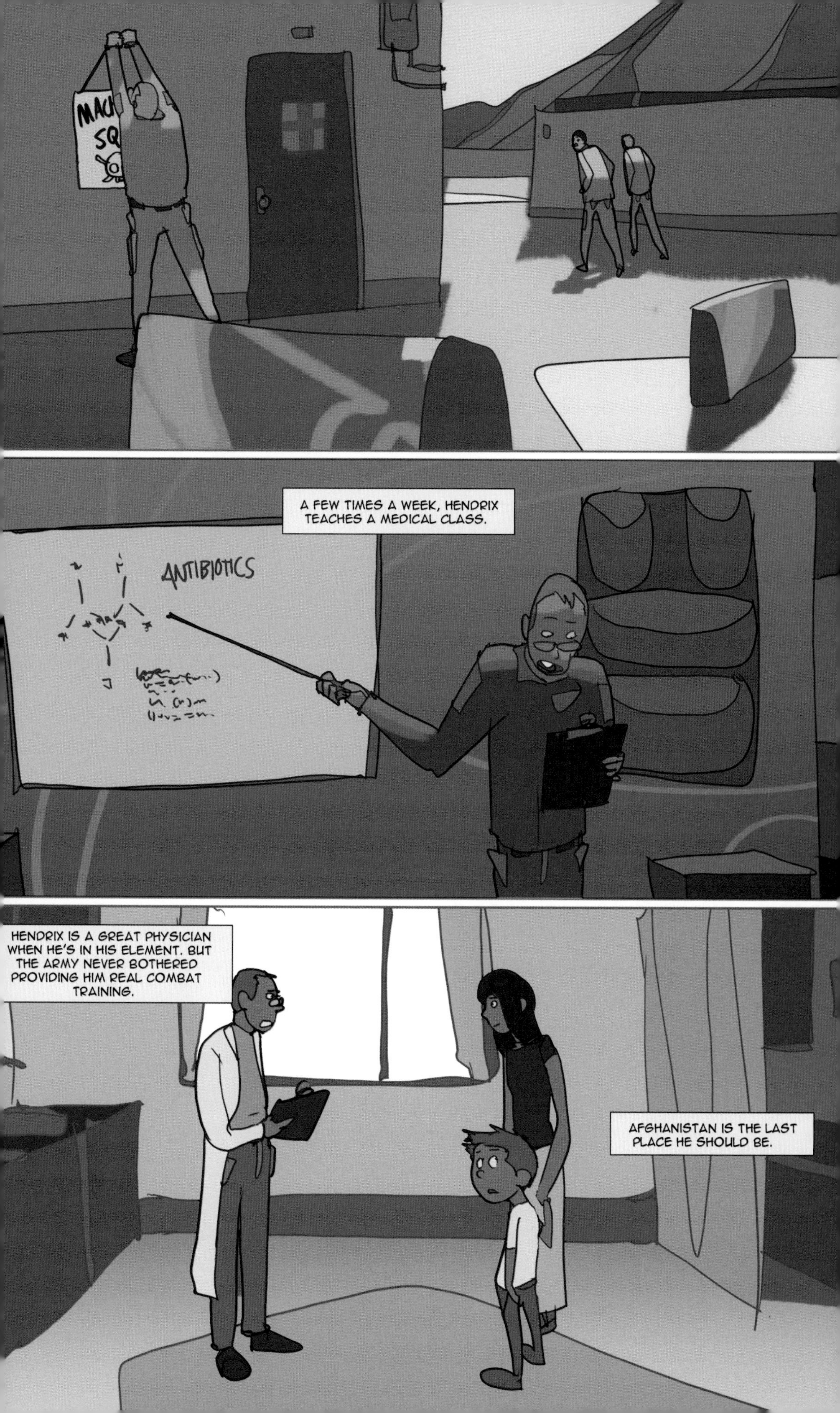
A FEW TIMES A WEEK, HENDRIX TEACHES A MEDICAL CLASS.
ANTIBIOTICS
HENDRIX IS A GREAT PHYSICIAN WHEN HE'S IN HIS ELEMENT. BUT THE ARMY NEVER BOTHERED PROVIDING HIM REAL COMBAT TRAINING.
AFGHANISTAN IS THE LAST PLACE HE SHOULD BE.

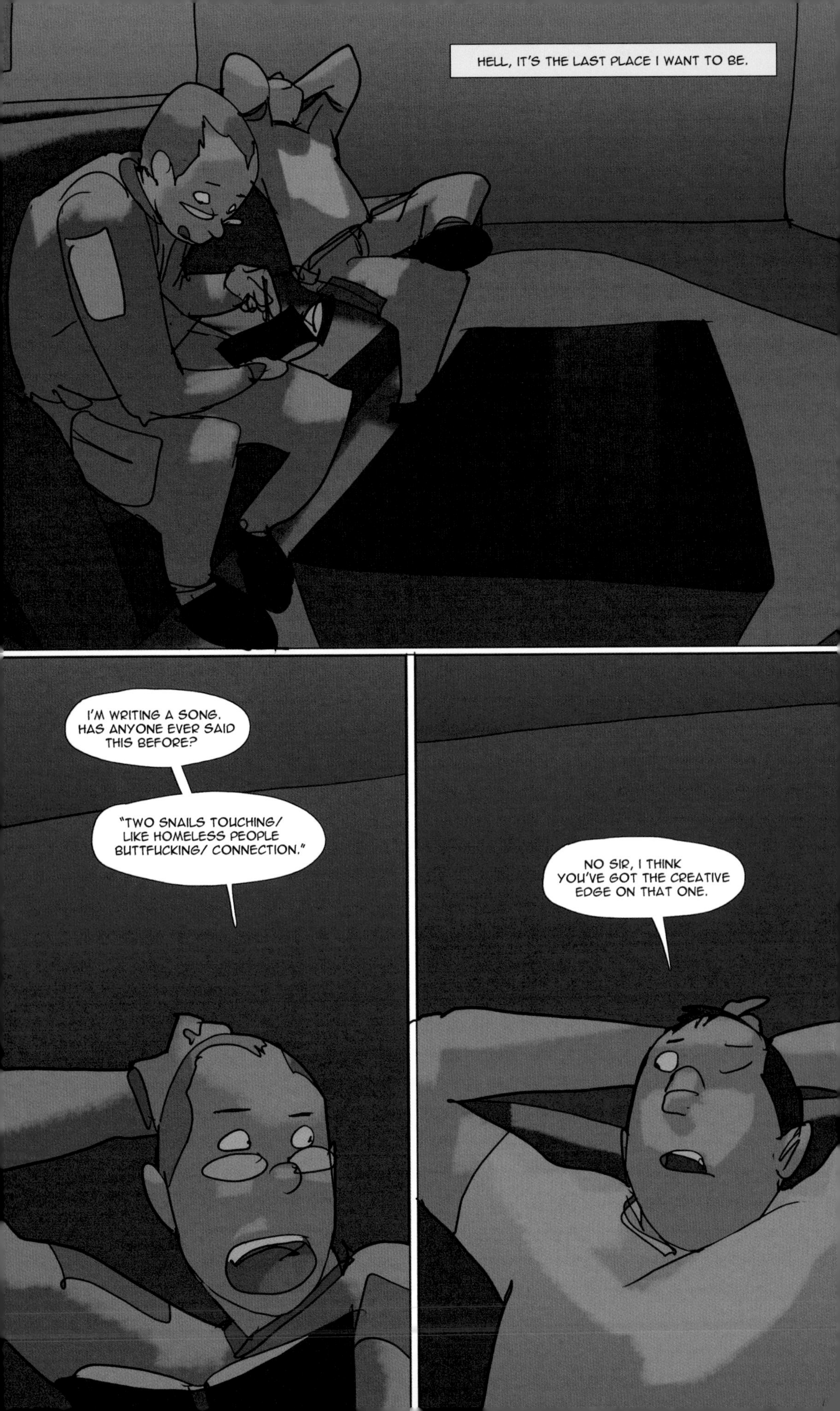
HELL, IT'S THE LAST PLACE I WANT TO BE.
I'M WRITING A SONG. HAS ANYONE EVER SAID THIS BEFORE?
"TWO SNAILS TOUCHING/ LIKE HOMELESS PEOPLE BUTTFUCKING/ CONNECTION."
NO SIR, I THINK YOU'VE GOT THE CREATIVE EDGE ON THAT ONE.

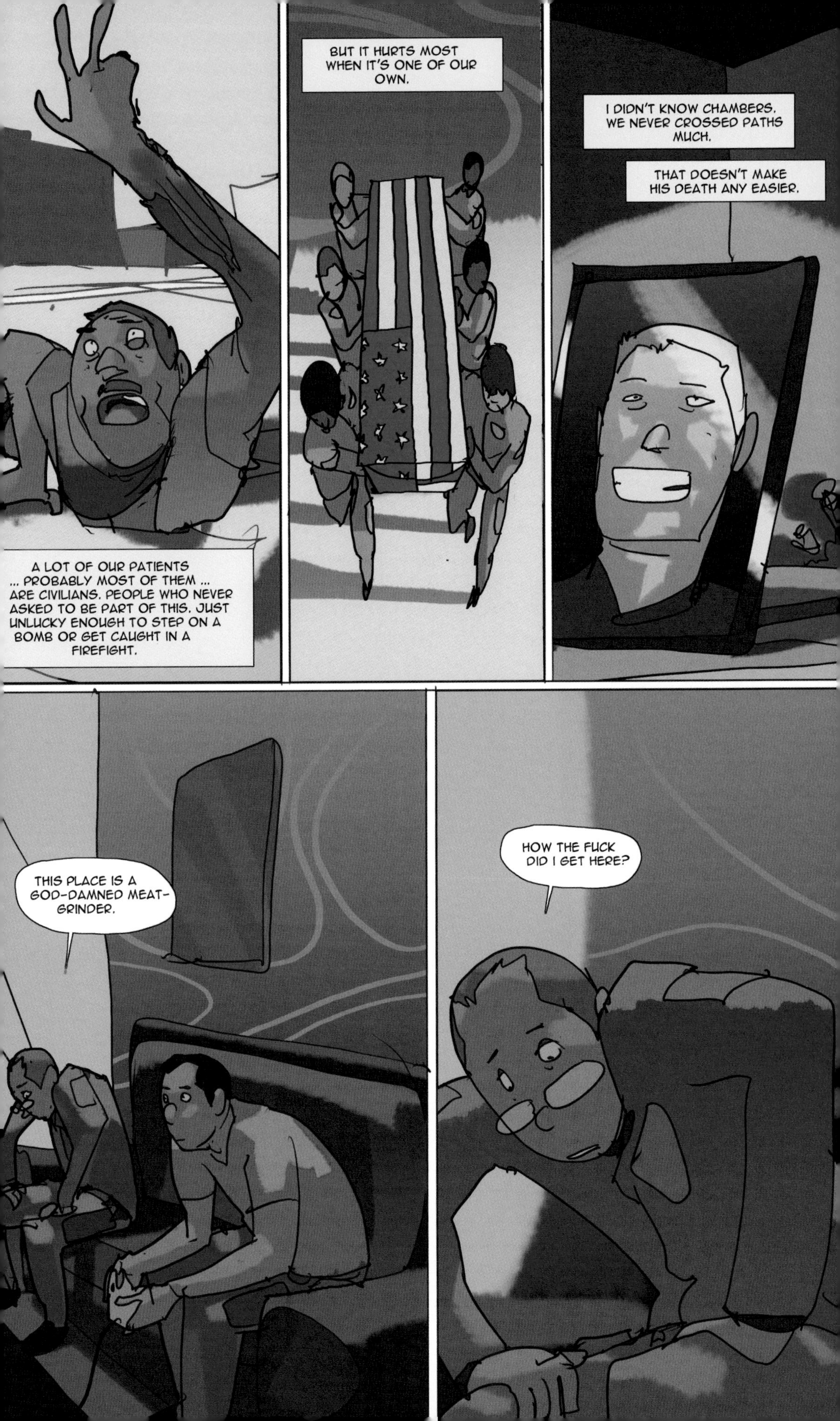
A LOT OF OUR PATIENTS ... PROBABLY MOST OF THEM ... ARE CIVILIANS. PEOPLE WHO NEVER ASKED TO BE PART OF THIS. JUST UNLUCKY ENOUGH TO STEP ON A BOMB OR GET CAUGHT IN A FIREFIGHT.
BUT IT HURTS MOST WHEN IT'S ONE OF OUR OWN.
I DIDN'T KNOW CHAMBERS. WE NEVER CROSSED PATHS MUCH.
THAT DOESN'T MAKE HIS DEATH ANY EASIER.
THIS PLACE IS A GOD-DAMNED MEAT-GRINDER.
HOW THE FUCK DID I GET HERE?

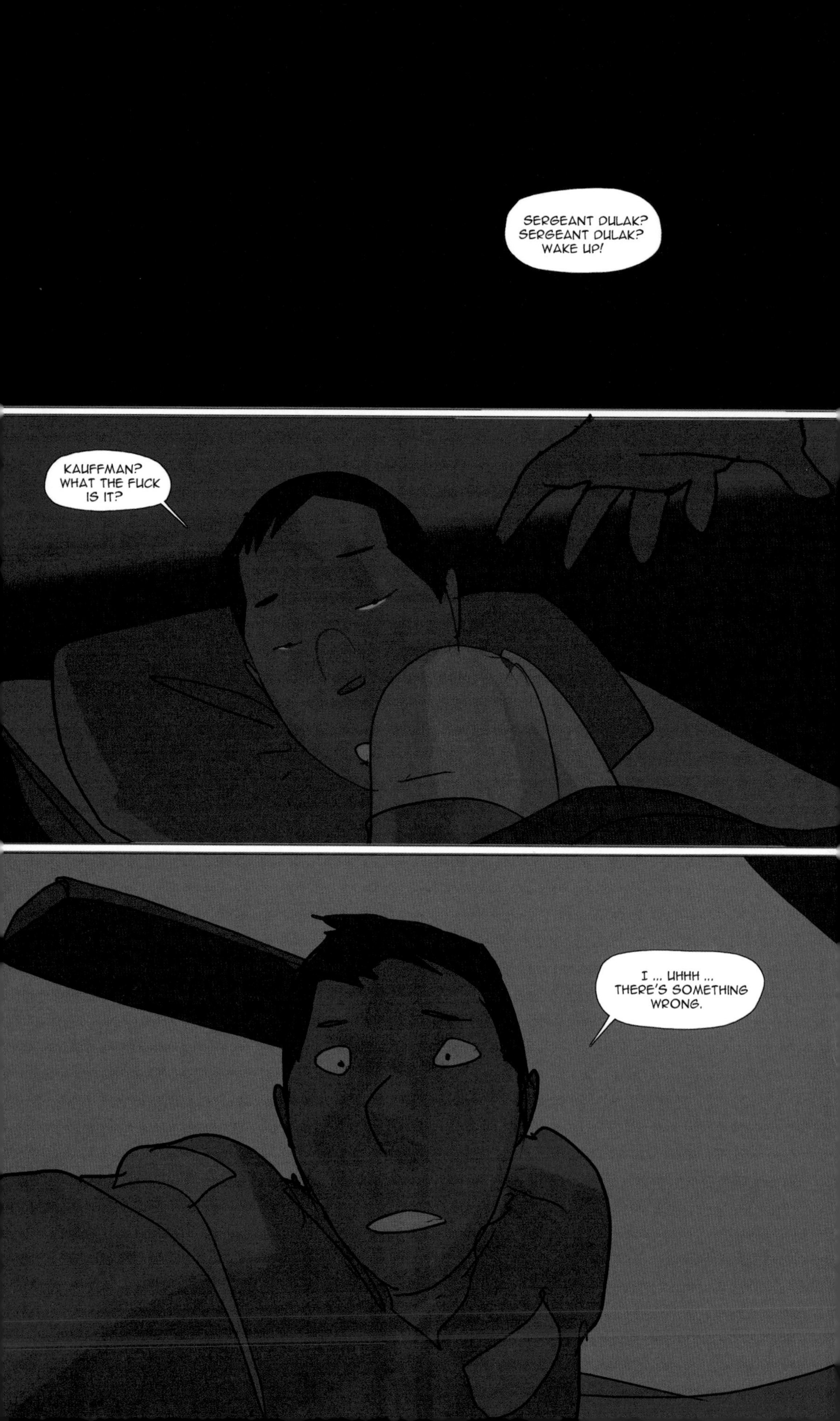
SERGEANT DULAK? SERGEANT DULAK? WAKE UP!
KAUFFMAN? WHAT THE FUCK IS IT?
I ... UHHH ... THERE'S SOMETHING WRONG.

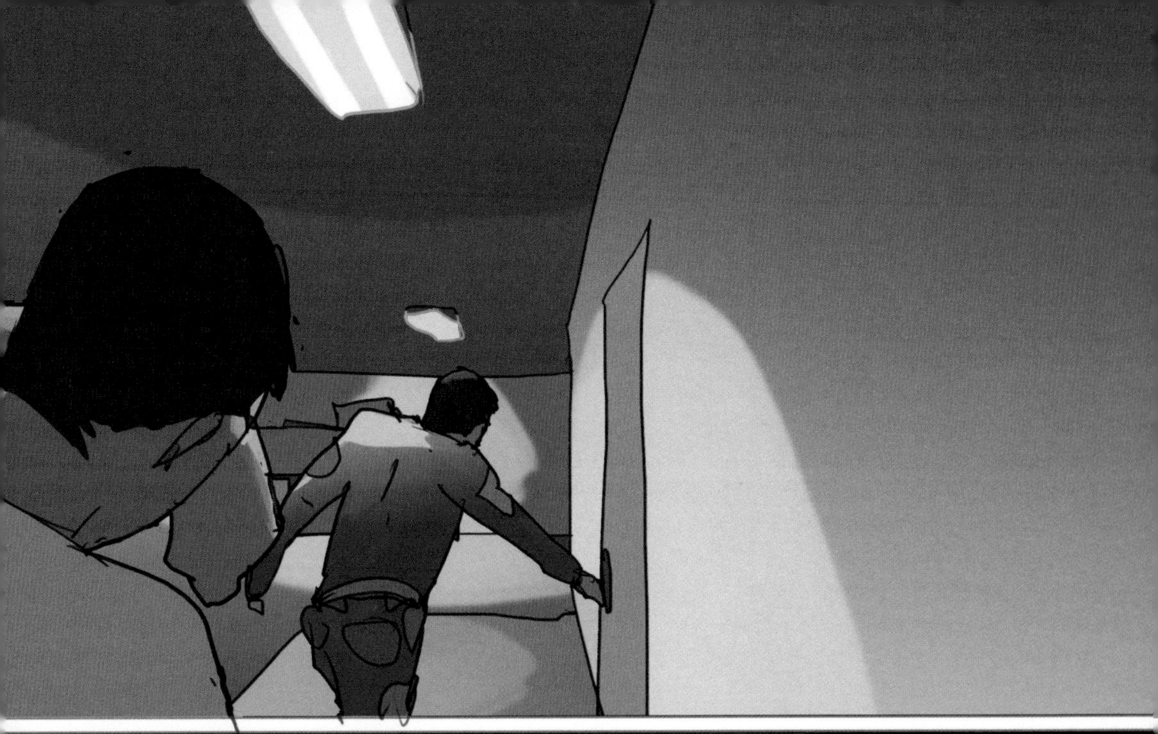

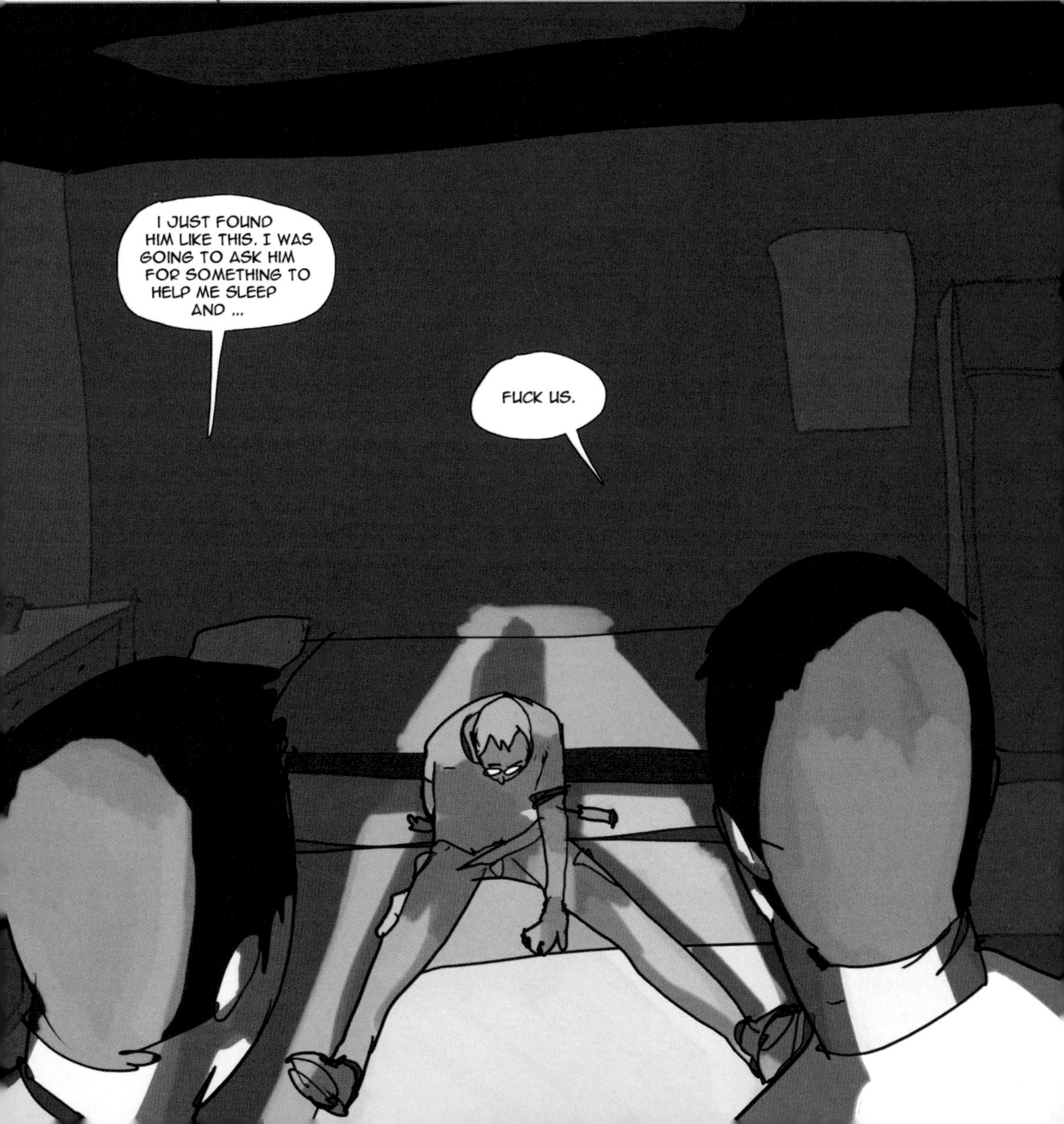
I JUST FOUND HIM LIKE THIS. I WAS GOING TO ASK HIM FOR SOMETHING TO HELP ME SLEEP AND ...
FUCK US.

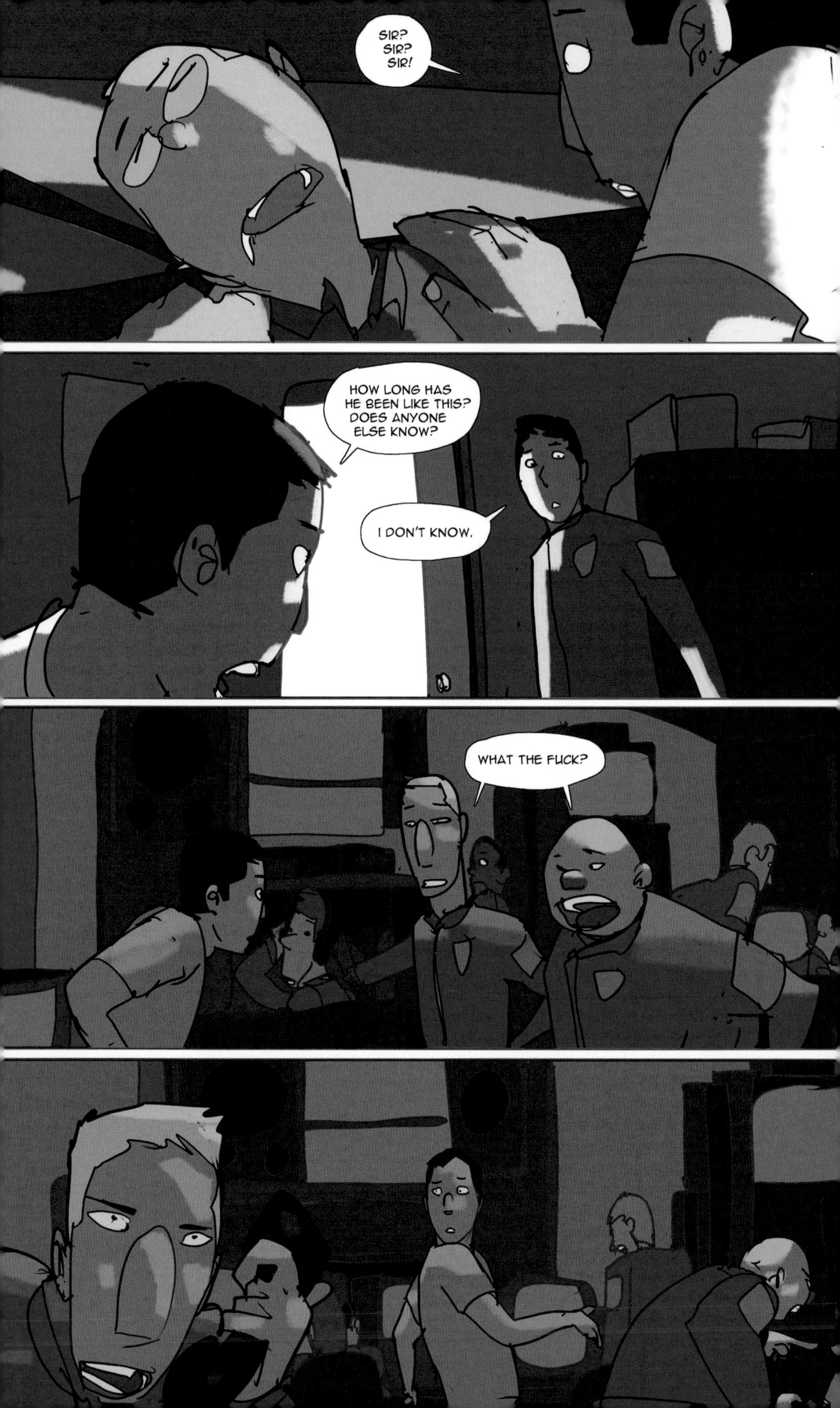
SIR?
SIR?
SIR!
HOW LONG HAS HE BEEN LIKE THIS? DOES ANYONE ELSE KNOW?
I DON'T KNOW.
WHAT THE FUCK?

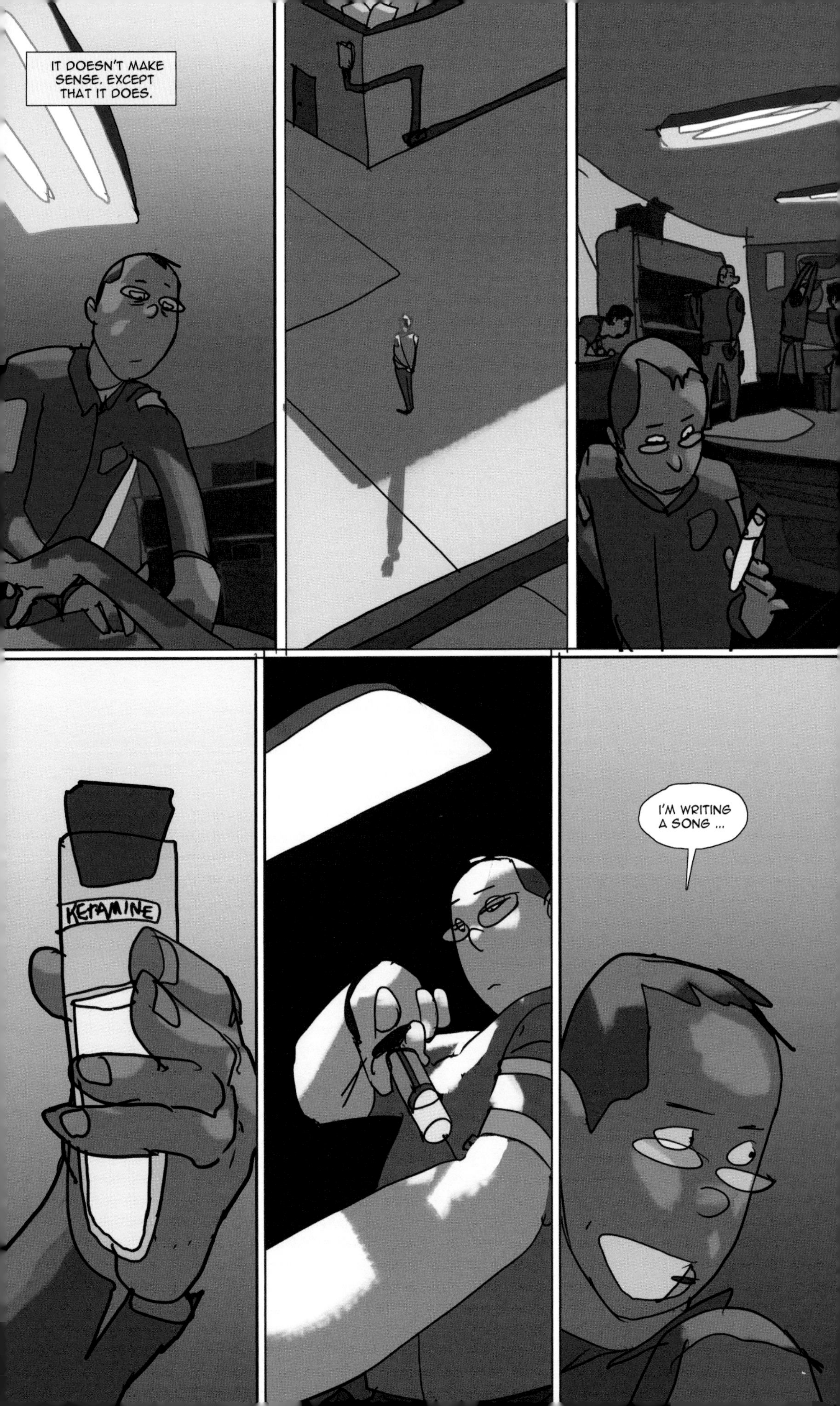
IT DOESN'T MAKE SENSE. EXCEPT THAT IT DOES.
KETAMINE
I'M WRITING A SONG ...

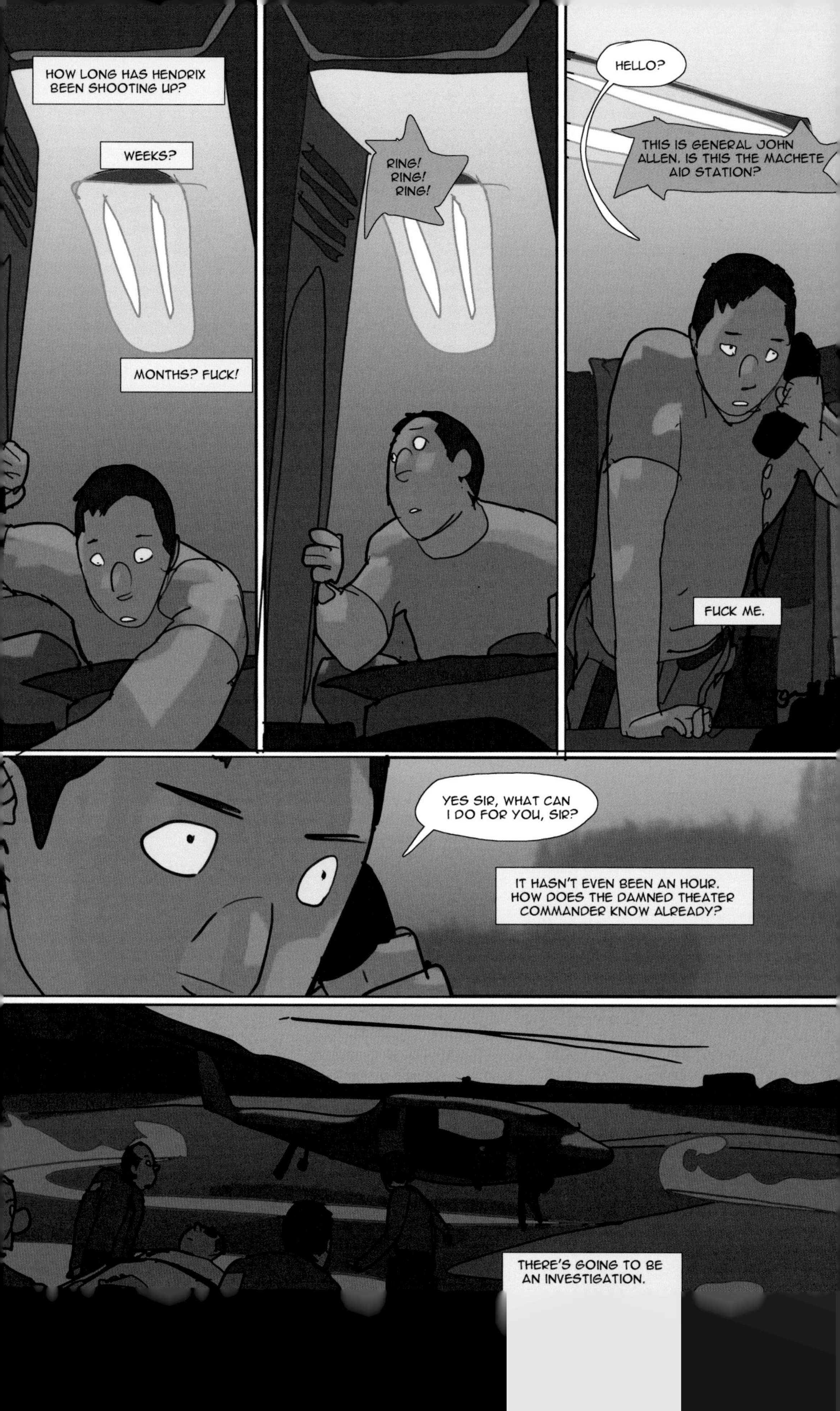
HOW LONG HAS HENDRIX BEEN SHOOTING UP?
WEEKS?
MONTHS? FUCK!
RING! RING! RING!
HELLO?
THIS IS GENERAL JOHN ALLEN. IS THIS THE MACHETE AID STATION?
FUCK ME.
YES SIR, WHAT CAN I DO FOR YOU, SIR?
IT HASN'T EVEN BEEN AN HOUR. HOW DOES THE DAMNED THEATER COMMANDER KNOW ALREADY?
THERE'S GOING TO BE AN INVESTIGATION.

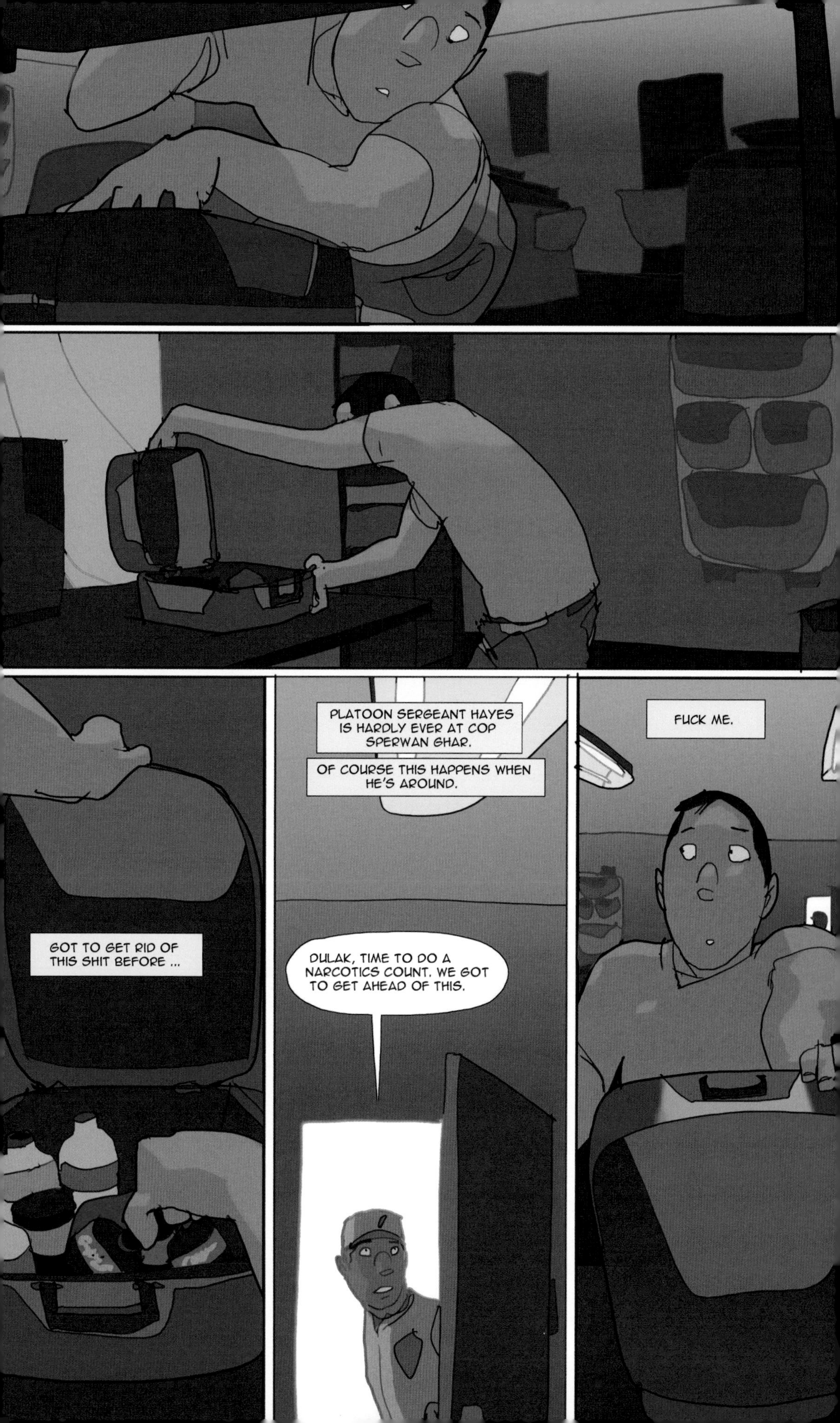
GOT TO GET RID OF THIS SHIT BEFORE ...
PLATOON SERGEANT HAYES IS HARDLY EVER AT COP SPERWAN GHAR.
OF COURSE THIS HAPPENS WHEN HE'S AROUND.
DULAK, TIME TO DO A NARCOTICS COUNT. WE GOT TO GET AHEAD OF THIS.
FUCK ME.

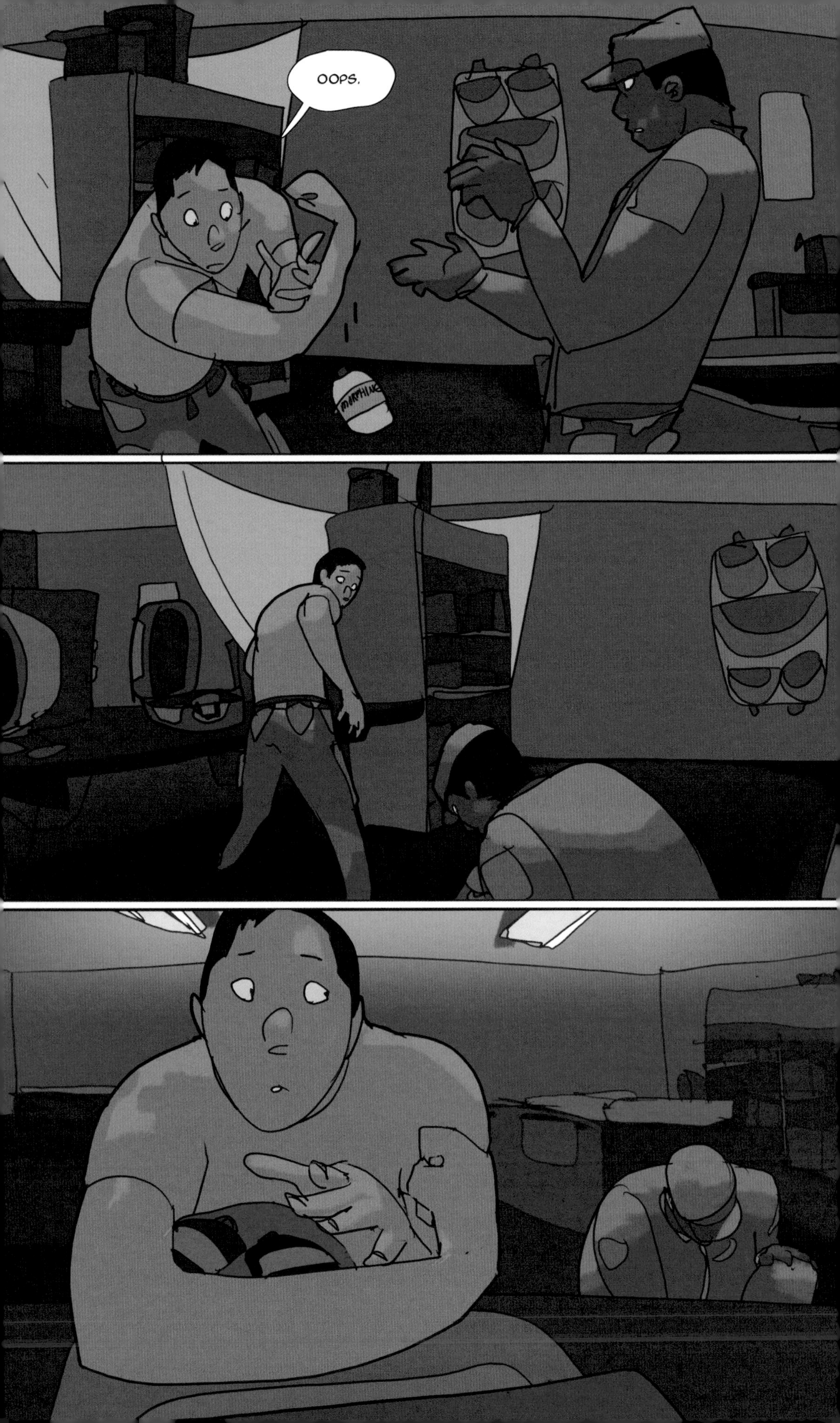
OOPS.
MORPHINE

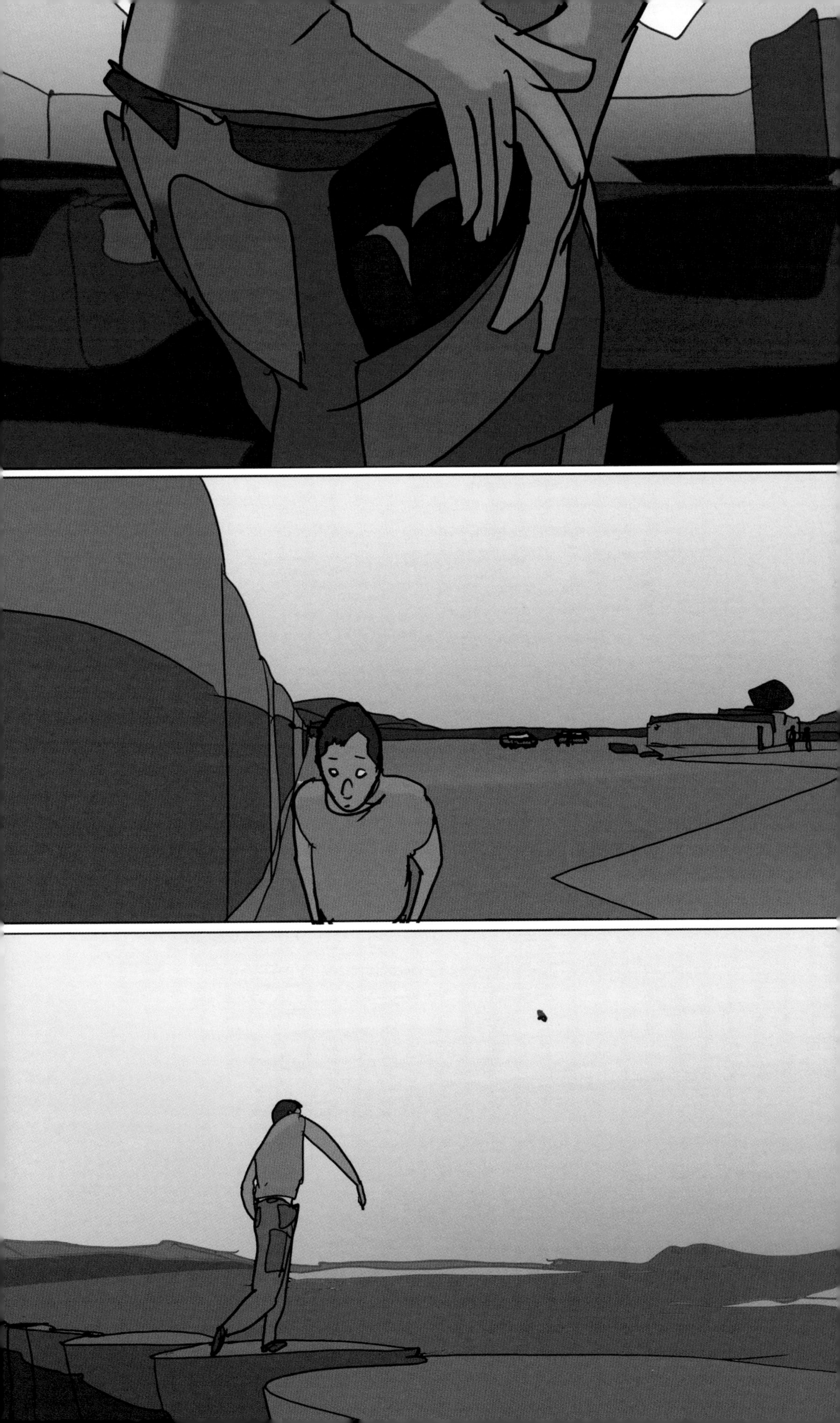

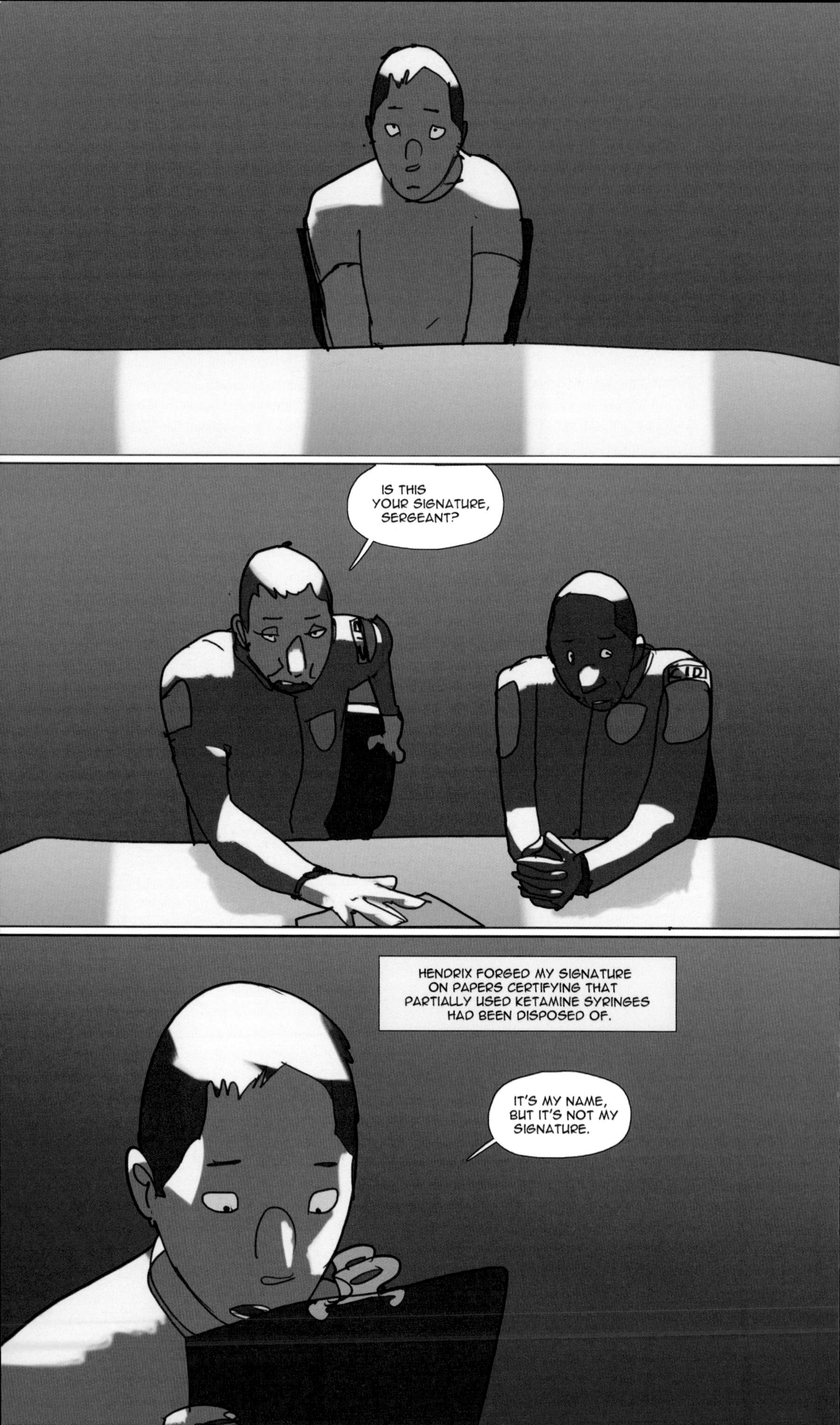
IS THIS YOUR SIGNATURE, SERGEANT?
CID
CID
HENDRIX FORGED MY SIGNATURE ON PAPERS CERTIFYING THAT PARTIALLY USED KETAMINE SYRINGES HAD BEEN DISPOSED OF.
IT'S MY NAME, BUT IT'S NOT MY SIGNATURE.

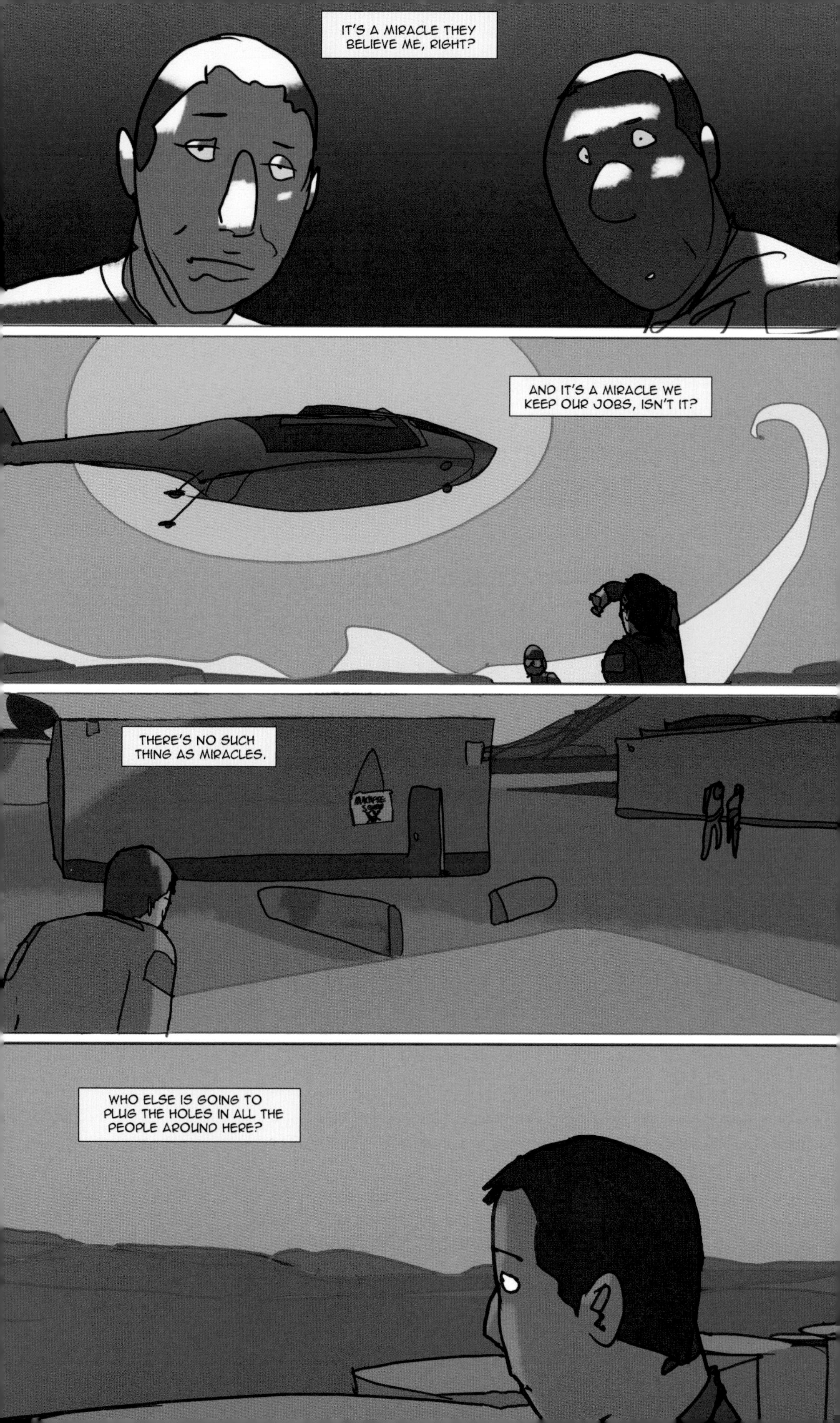
IT'S A MIRACLE THEY BELIEVE ME, RIGHT?
AND IT'S A MIRACLE WE KEEP OUR JOBS, ISN'T IT?
THERE'S NO SUCH THING AS MIRACLES.
WHO ELSE IS GOING TO PLUG THE HOLES IN ALL THE PEOPLE AROUND HERE?

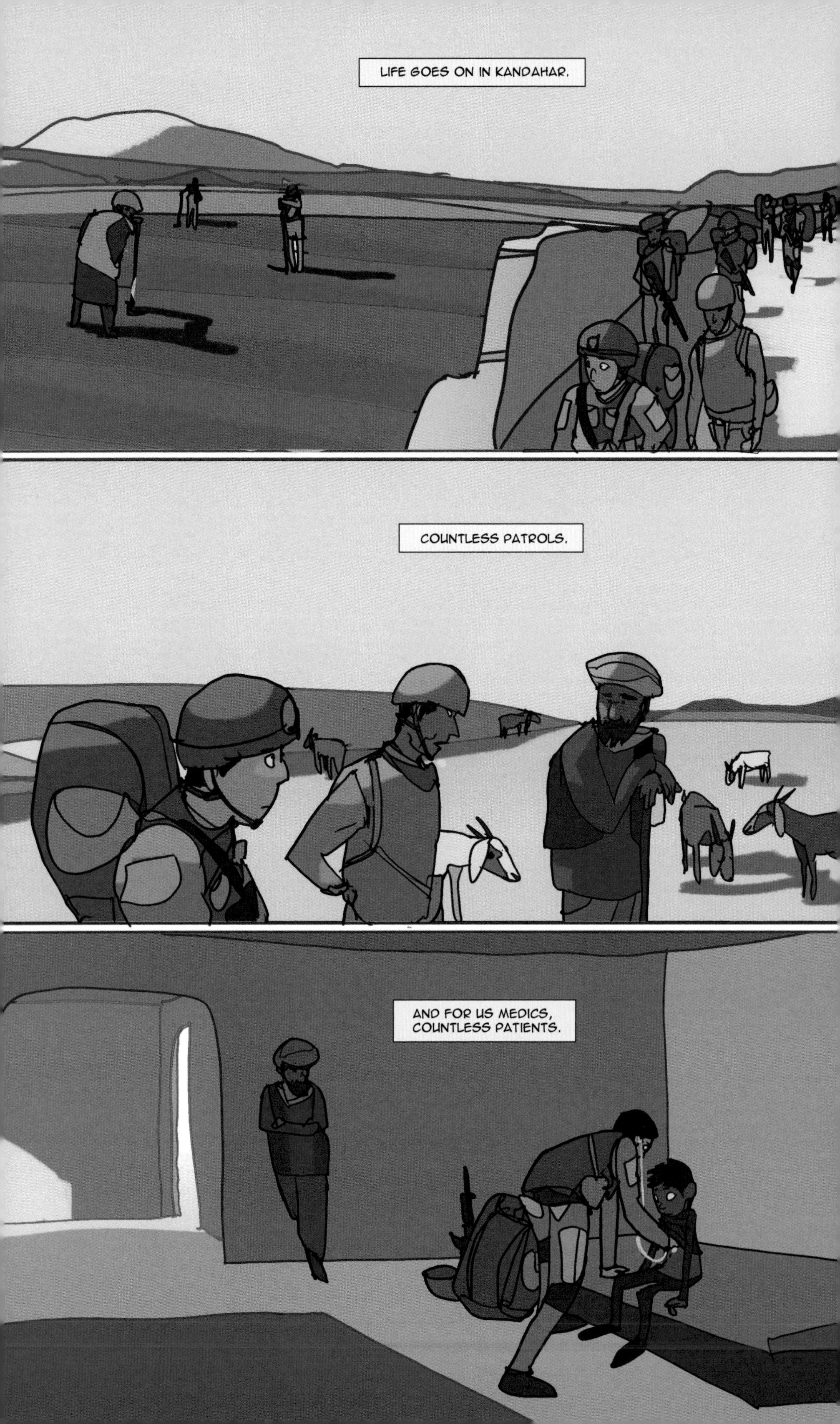
LIFE GOES ON IN KANDAHAR.
COUNTLESS PATROLS.
AND FOR US MEDICS, COUNTLESS PATIENTS.

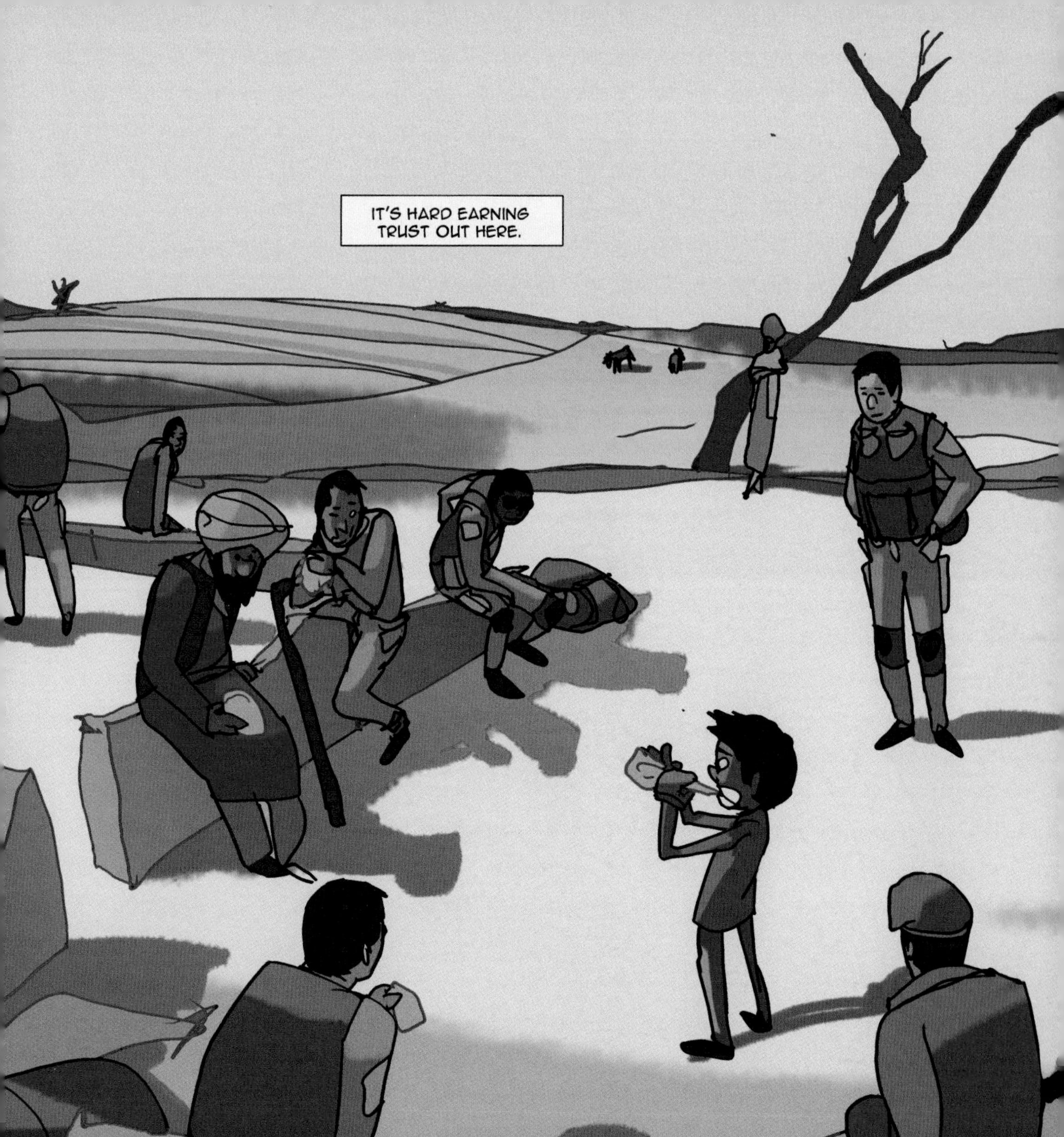
IT'S HARD EARNING TRUST OUT HERE.

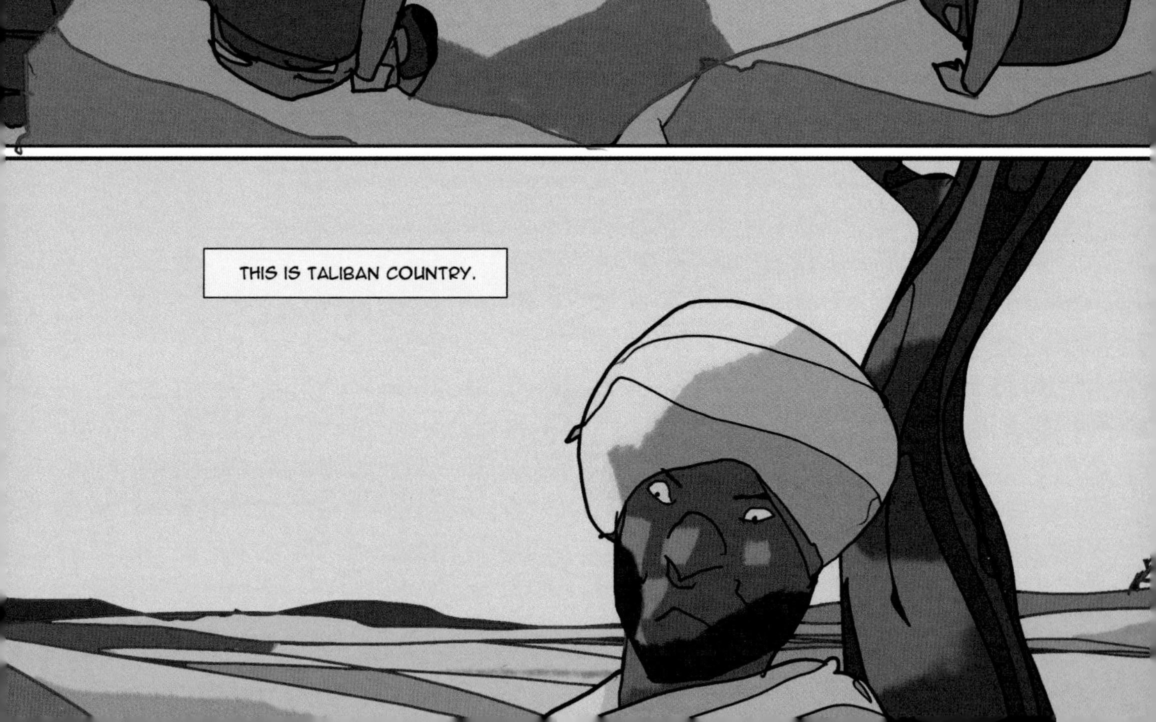
THIS IS TALIBAN COUNTRY.

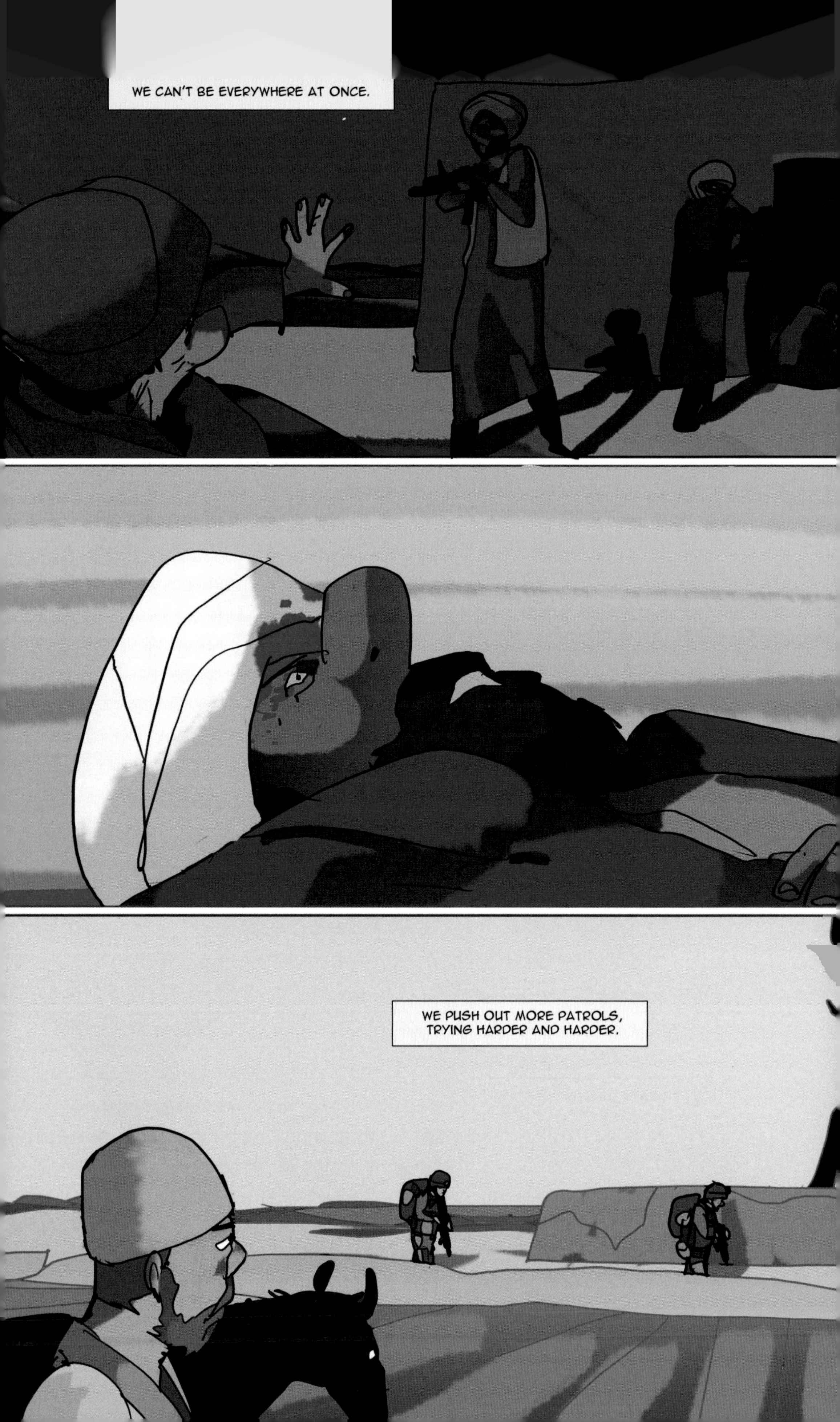
WE CAN'T BE EVERYWHERE AT ONCE.
WE PUSH OUT MORE PATROLS, TRYING HARDER AND HARDER.

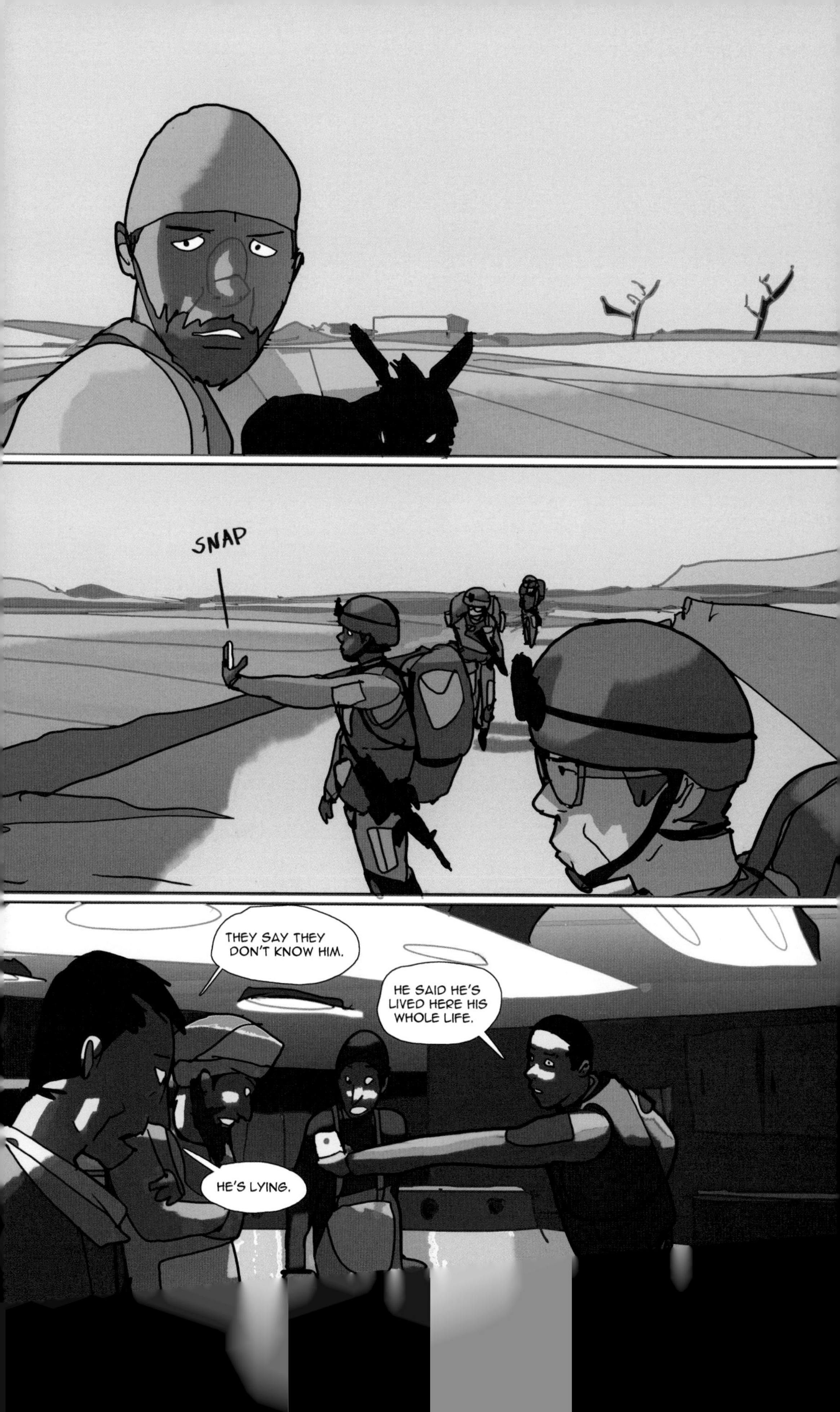
SNAP
THEY SAY THEY DON'T KNOW HIM.
HE SAID HE'S LIVED HERE HIS WHOLE LIFE.
HE'S LYING.

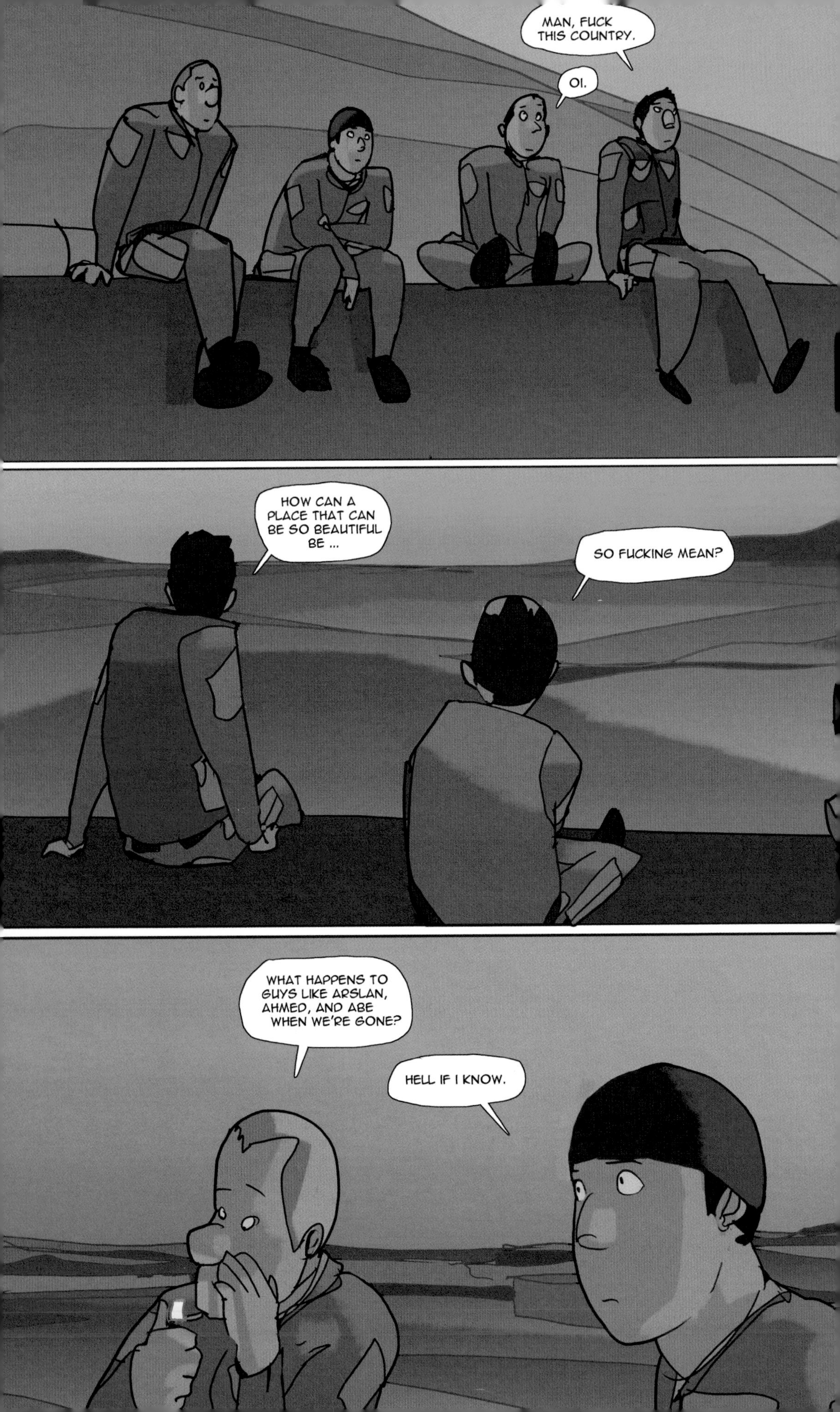
MAN, FUCK THIS COUNTRY.
OI.
HOW CAN A PLACE THAT CAN BE SO BEAUTIFUL BE ...
SO FUCKING MEAN?
WHAT HAPPENS TO GUYS LIKE ARSLAN, AHMED, AND ABE WHEN WE'RE GONE?
HELL IF I KNOW.

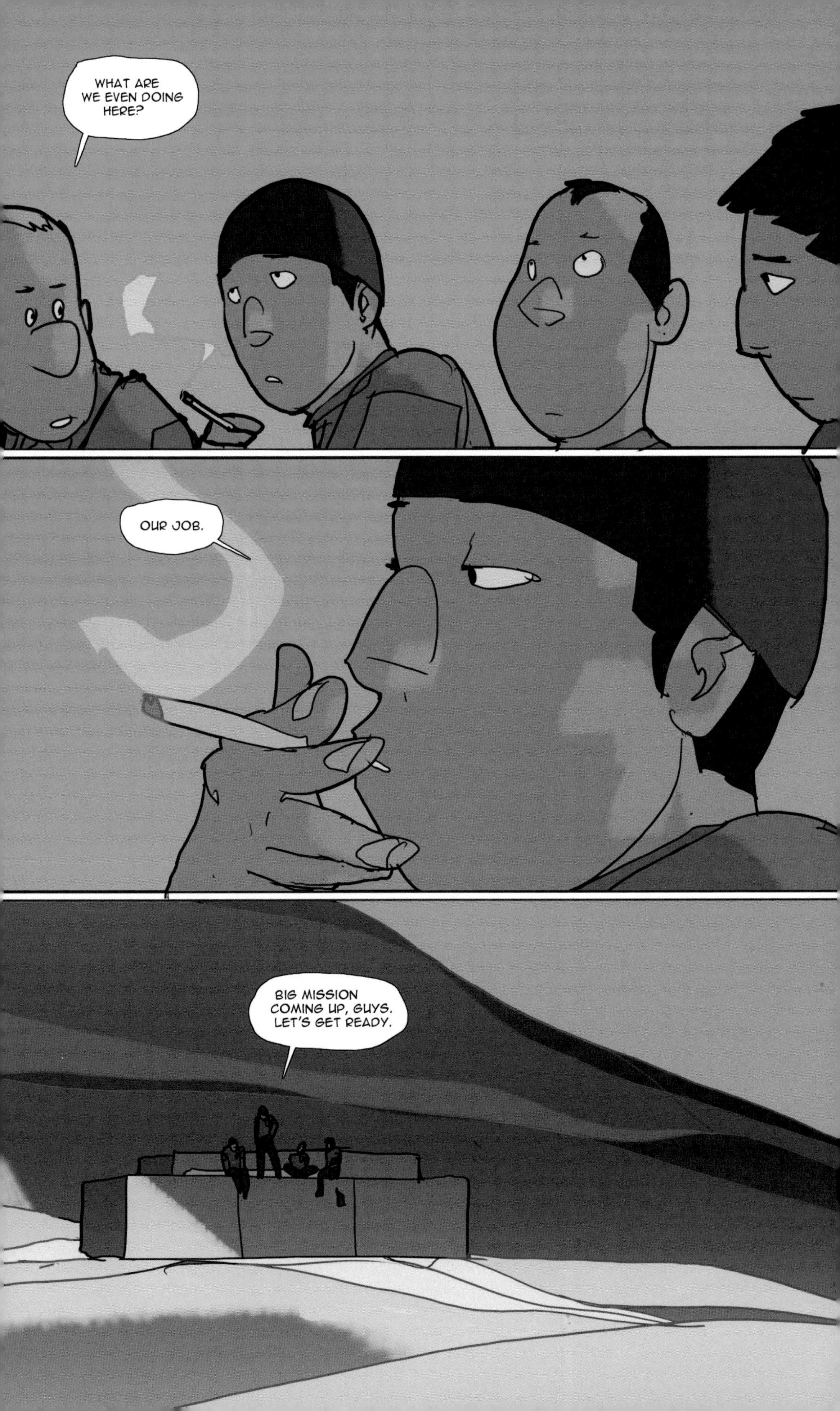
WHAT ARE WE EVEN DOING HERE?
OUR JOB.
BIG MISSION COMING UP, GUYS. LET'S GET READY.

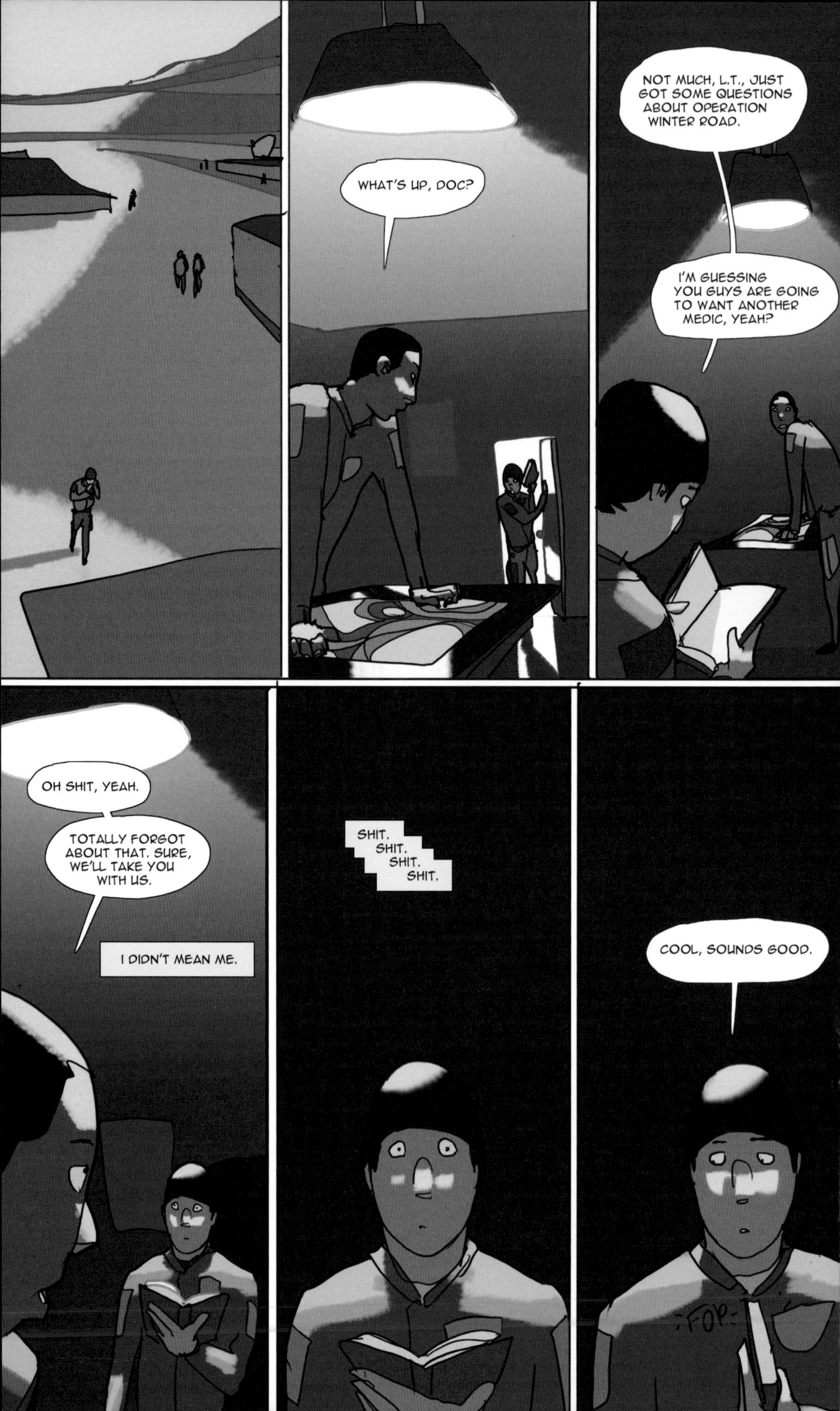
WHAT'S UP, DOC?
NOT MUCH, L.T., JUST GOT SOME QUESTIONS ABOUT OPERATION WINTER ROAD.
I'M GUESSING YOU GUYS ARE GOING TO WANT ANOTHER MEDIC, YEAH?
OH SHIT, YEAH.
TOTALLY FORGOT ABOUT THAT. SURE, WE'LL TAKE YOU WITH US.
I DIDN'T MEAN ME.
SHIT.
SHIT.
SHIT.
SHIT.
COOL, SOUNDS GOOD.
FOP

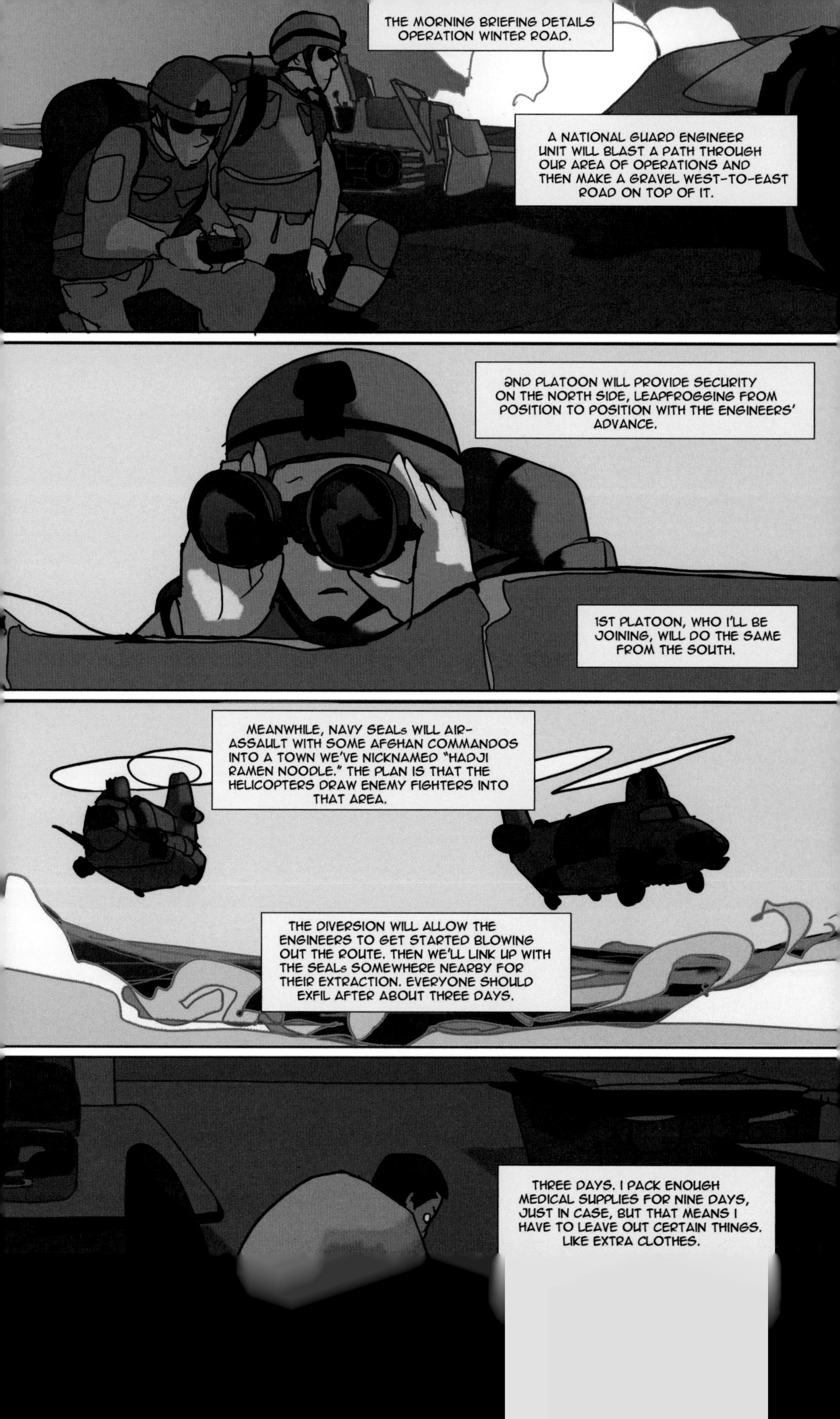
THE MORNING BRIEFING DETAILS OPERATION WINTER ROAD.
A NATIONAL GUARD ENGINEER UNIT WILL BLAST A PATH THROUGH OUR AREA OF OPERATIONS AND THEN MAKE A GRAVEL WEST-TO-EAST ROAD ON TOP OF IT.
2ND PLATOON WILL PROVIDE SECURITY ON THE NORTH SIDE, LEAPFROGGING FROM POSITION TO POSITION WITH THE ENGINEERS' ADVANCE.
1ST PLATOON, WHO I'LL BE JOINING, WILL DO THE SAME FROM THE SOUTH.
MEANWHILE, NAVY SEALs WILL AIR-ASSAULT WITH SOME AFGHAN COMMANDOS INTO A TOWN WE'VE NICKNAMED "HADJI RAMEN NOODLE." THE PLAN IS THAT THE HELICOPTERS DRAW ENEMY FIGHTERS INTO THAT AREA.
THE DIVERSION WILL ALLOW THE ENGINEERS TO GET STARTED BLOWING OUT THE ROUTE. THEN WE'LL LINK UP WITH THE SEALs SOMEWHERE NEARBY FOR THEIR EXTRACTION. EVERYONE SHOULD EXFIL AFTER ABOUT THREE DAYS.
THREE DAYS. I PACK ENOUGH MEDICAL SUPPLIES FOR NINE DAYS, JUST IN CASE, BUT THAT MEANS I HAVE TO LEAVE OUT CERTAIN THINGS. LIKE EXTRA CLOTHES.

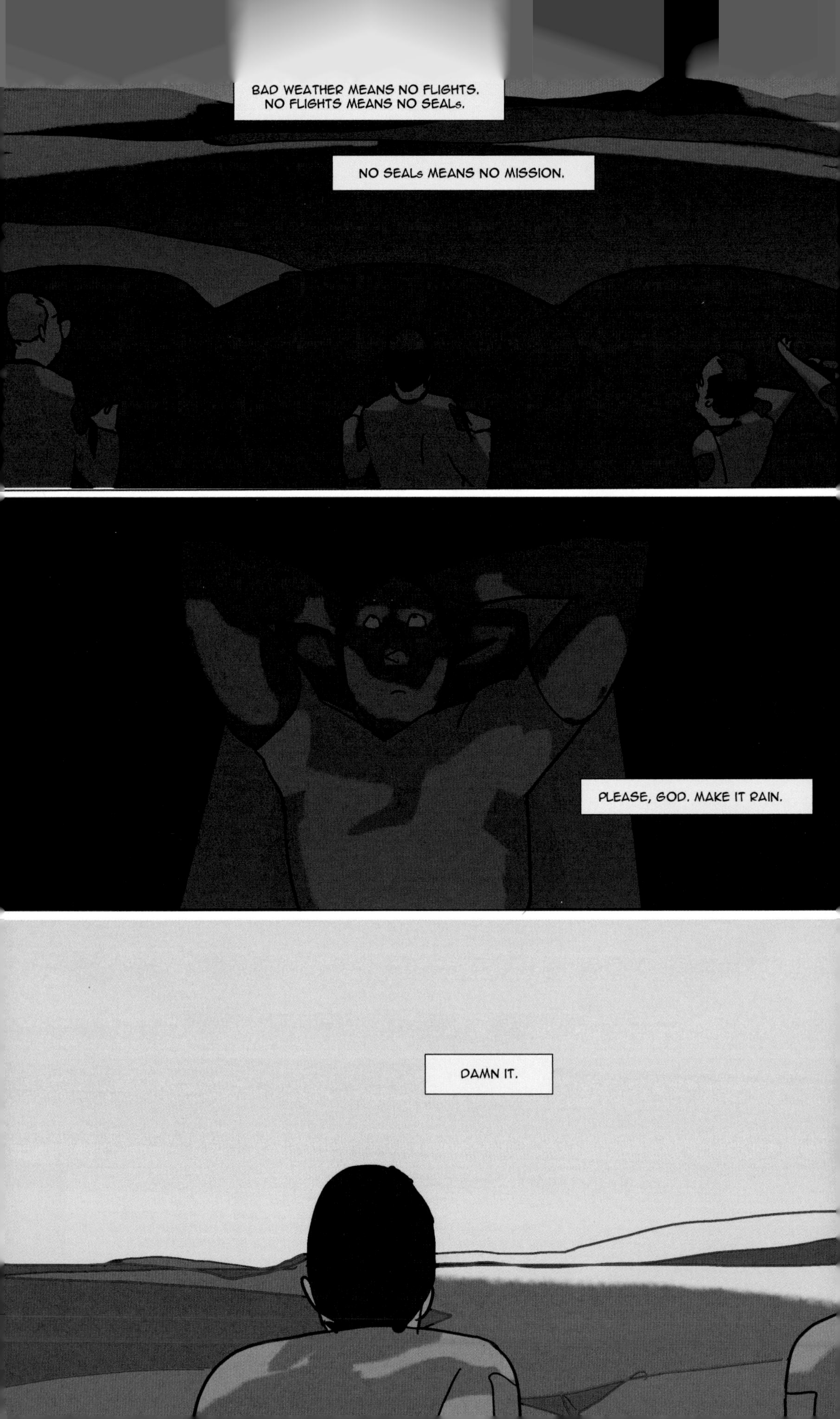
BAD WEATHER MEANS NO FLIGHTS.
NO FLIGHTS MEANS NO SEALs.
NO SEALs MEANS NO MISSION.
PLEASE, GOD. MAKE IT RAIN.
DAMN IT.

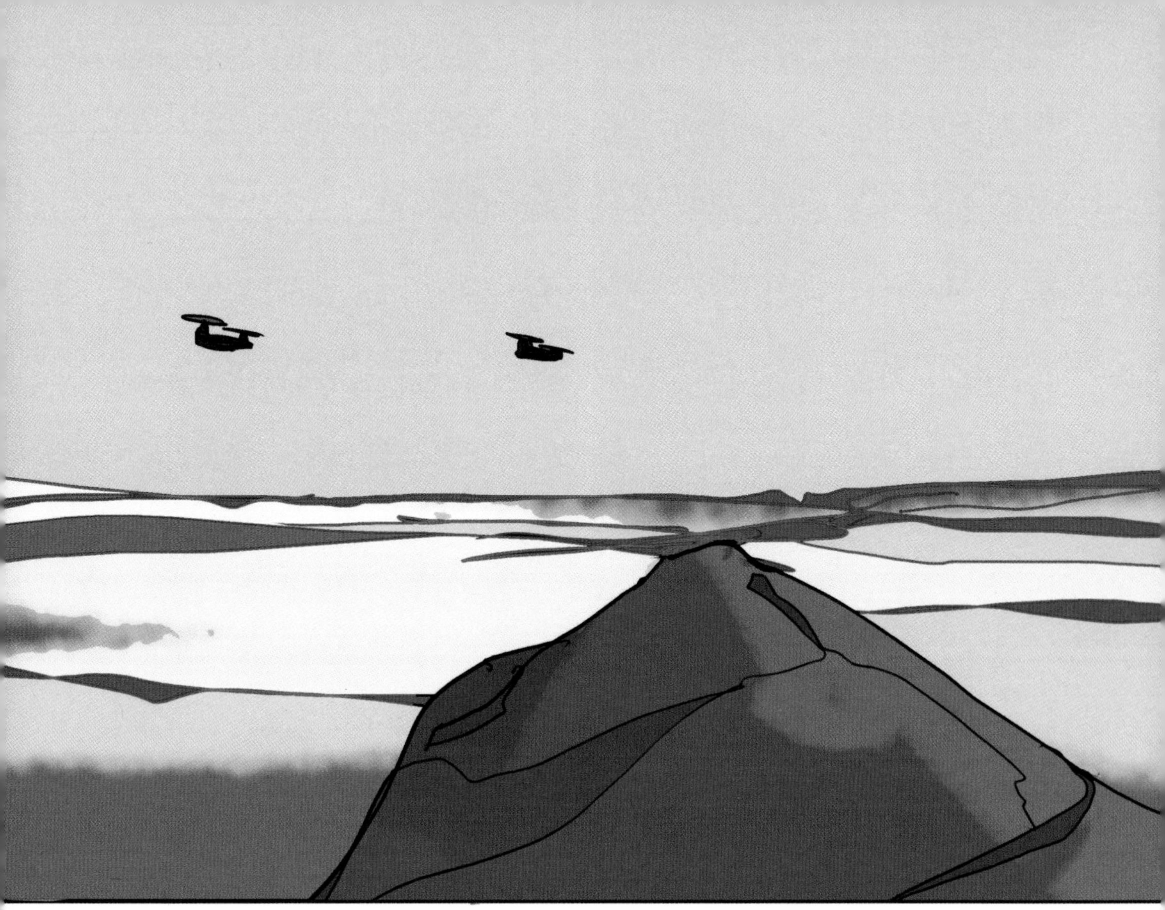

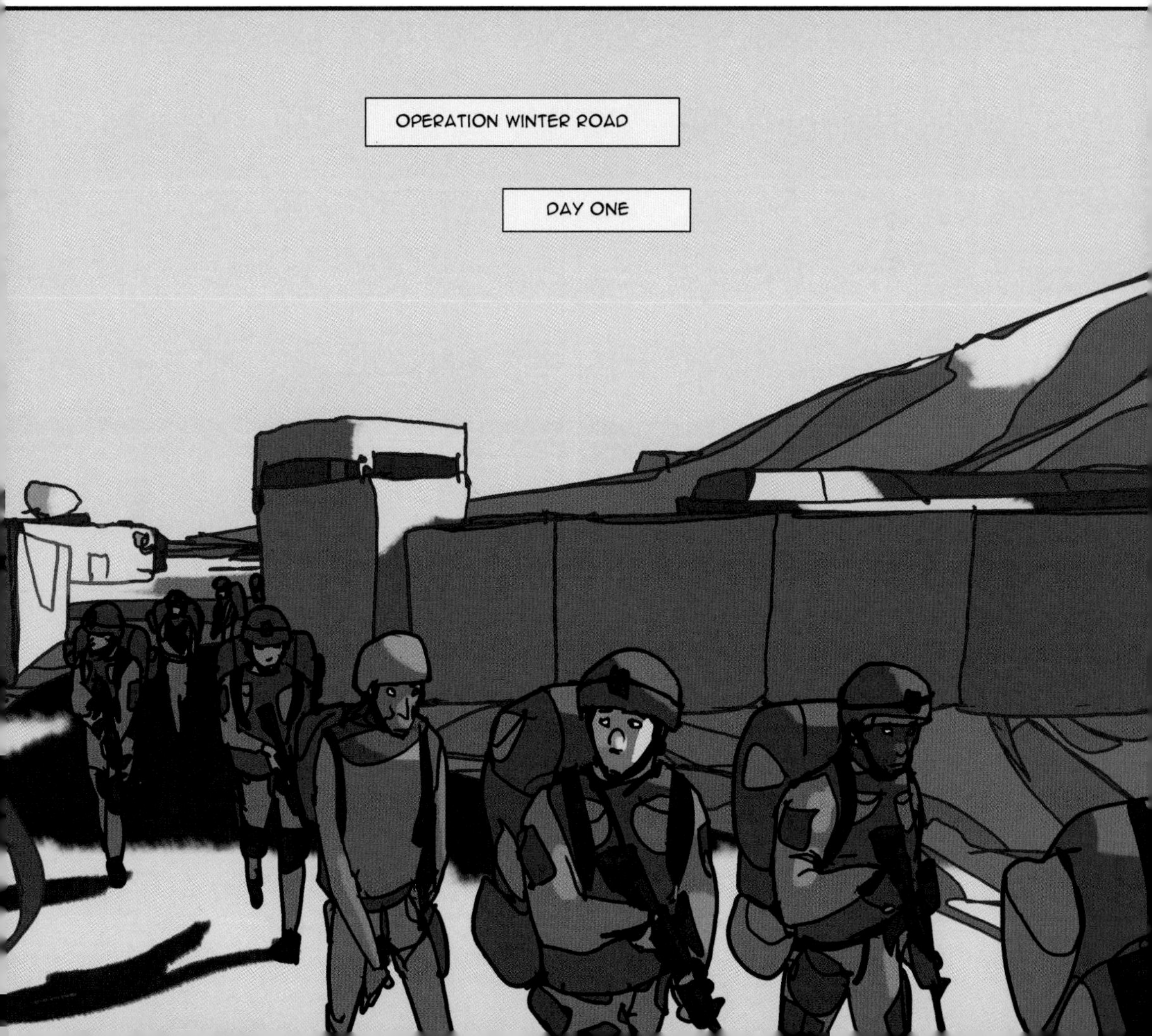
OPERATION WINTER ROAD
DAY ONE

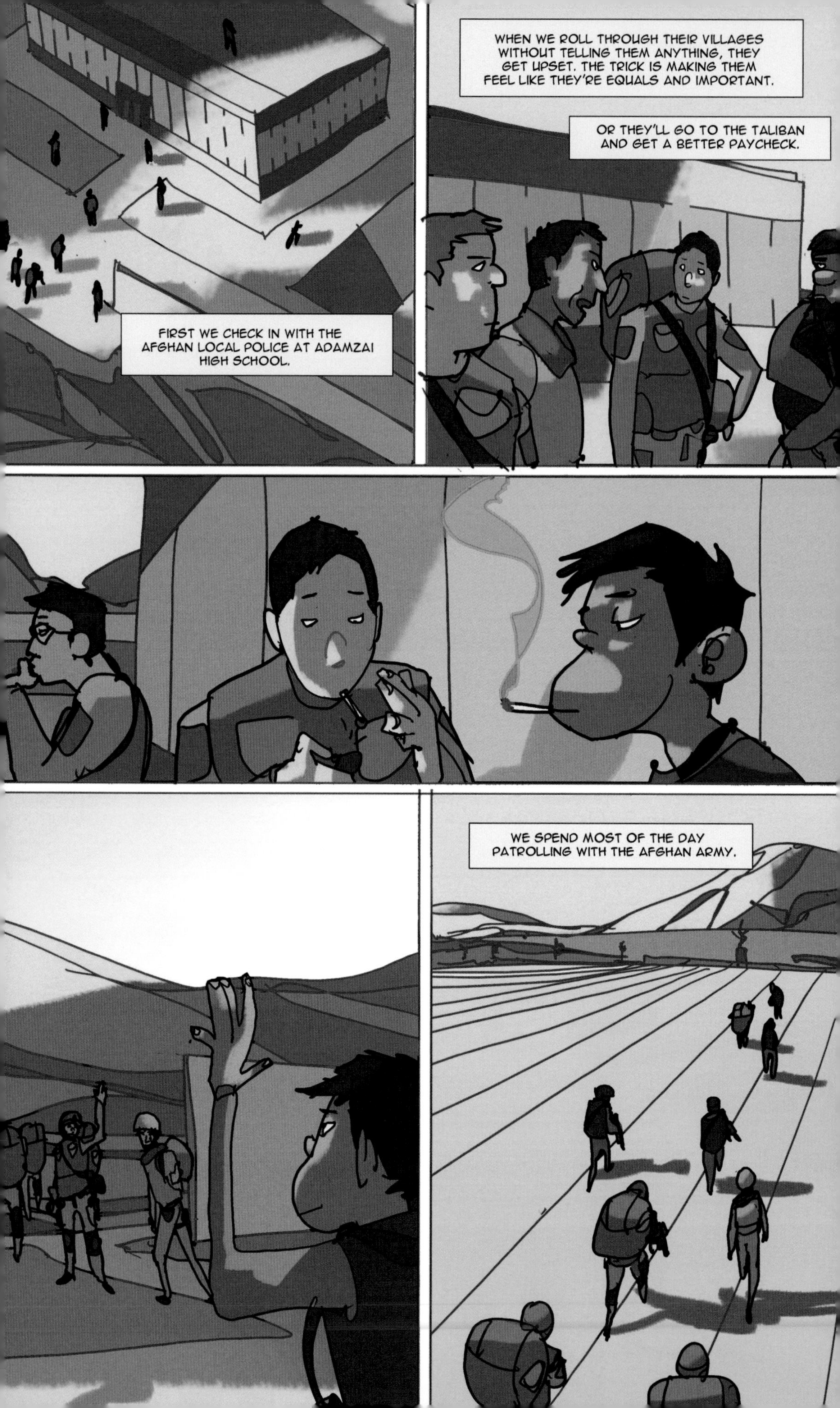
FIRST WE CHECK IN WITH THE AFGHAN LOCAL POLICE AT ADAMZAI HIGH SCHOOL.
WHEN WE ROLL THROUGH THEIR VILLAGES WITHOUT TELLING THEM ANYTHING, THEY GET UPSET. THE TRICK IS MAKING THEM FEEL LIKE THEY'RE EQUALS AND IMPORTANT.
OR THEY'LL GO TO THE TALIBAN AND GET A BETTER PAYCHECK.
WE SPEND MOST OF THE DAY PATROLLING WITH THE AFGHAN ARMY.

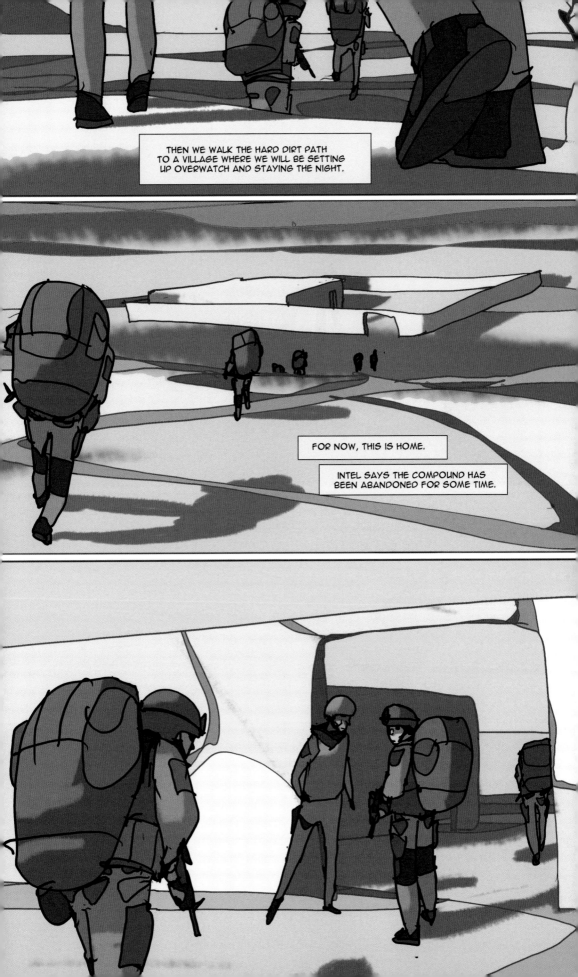

THEN WE WALK THE HARD DIRT PATH TO A VILLAGE WHERE WE WILL BE SETTING UP OVERWATCH AND STAYING THE NIGHT.

FOR NOW, THIS IS HOME.

INTEL SAYS THE COMPOUND HAS BEEN ABANDONED FOR SOME TIME.

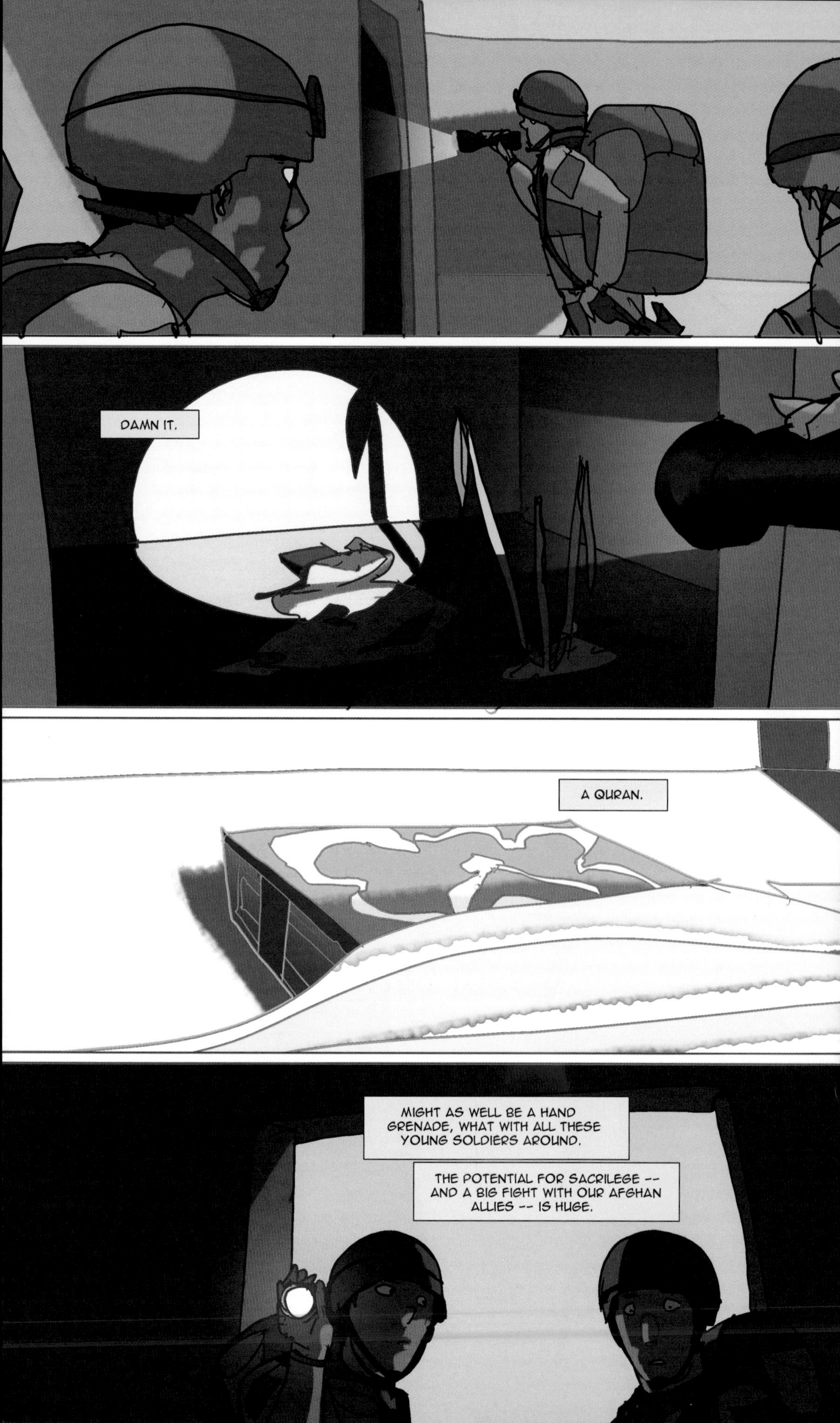
DAMN IT.
A QURAN.
MIGHT AS WELL BE A HAND GRENADE, WHAT WITH ALL THESE YOUNG SOLDIERS AROUND.
THE POTENTIAL FOR SACRILEGE -- AND A BIG FIGHT WITH OUR AFGHAN ALLIES -- IS HUGE.

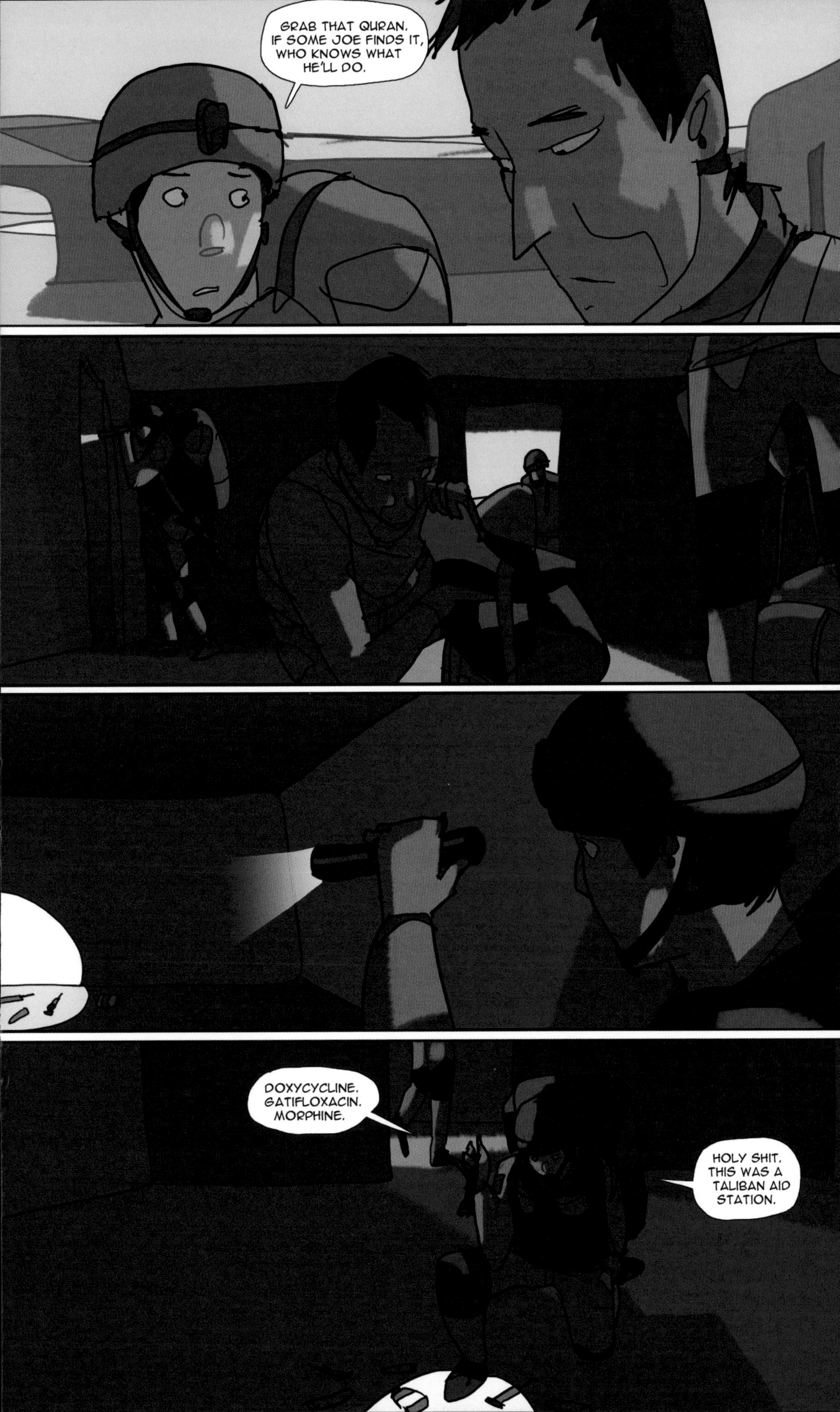
GRAB THAT QURAN. IF SOME JOE FINDS IT, WHO KNOWS WHAT HE'LL DO.
DOXYCYCLINE. GATIFLOXACIN. MORPHINE.
HOLY SHIT. THIS WAS A TALIBAN AID STATION.

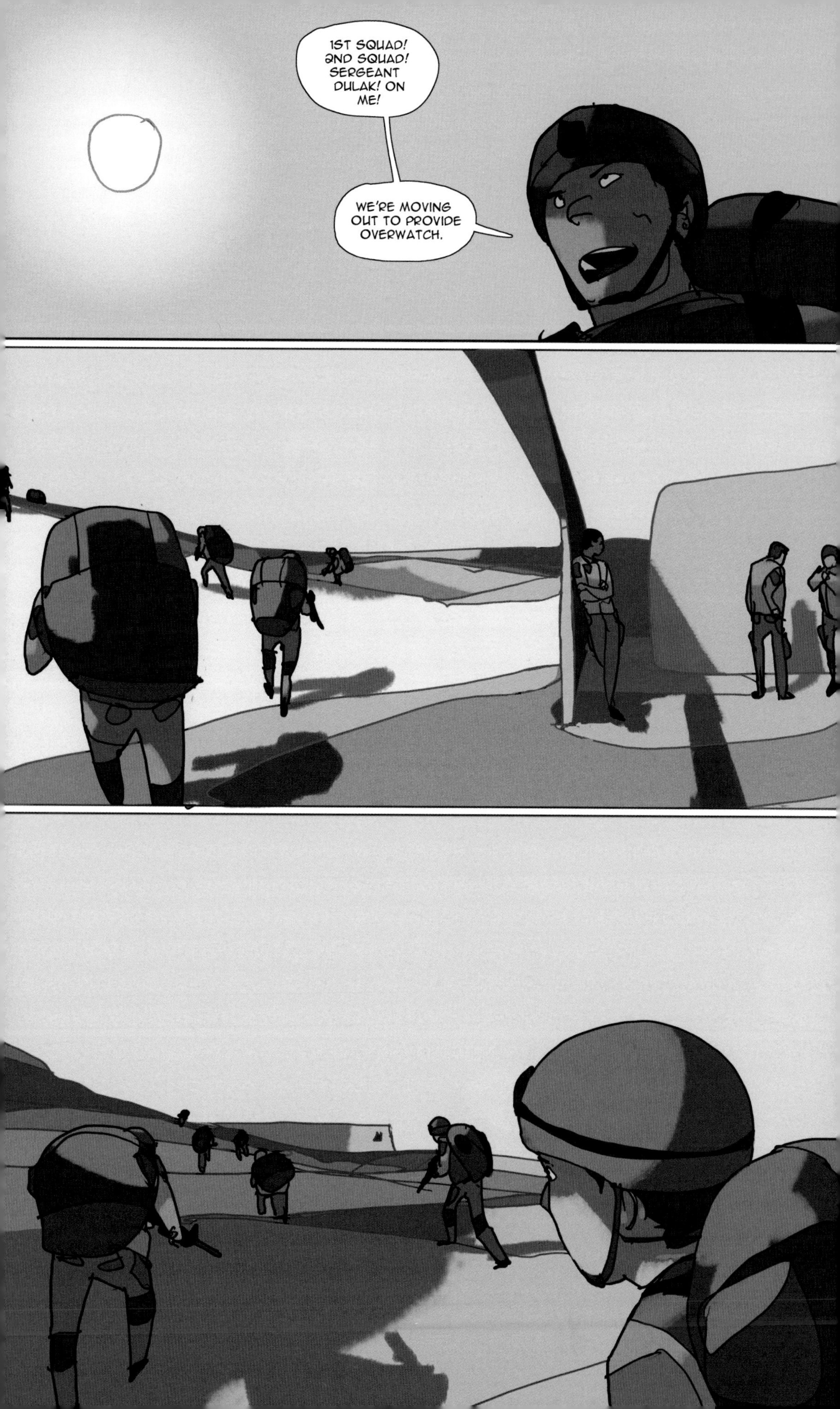
1ST SQUAD! 2ND SQUAD! SERGEANT DULAK! ON ME!
WE'RE MOVING OUT TO PROVIDE OVERWATCH.

YOU GUYS TAKE UP A WATCH POSITION ON THE ROOF.

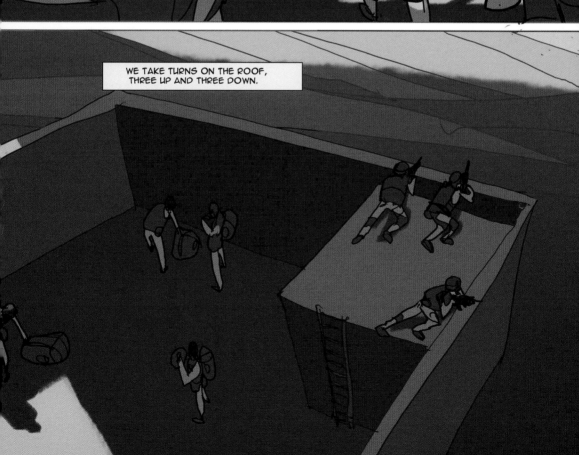

WE TAKE TURNS ON THE ROOF, THREE UP AND THREE DOWN.

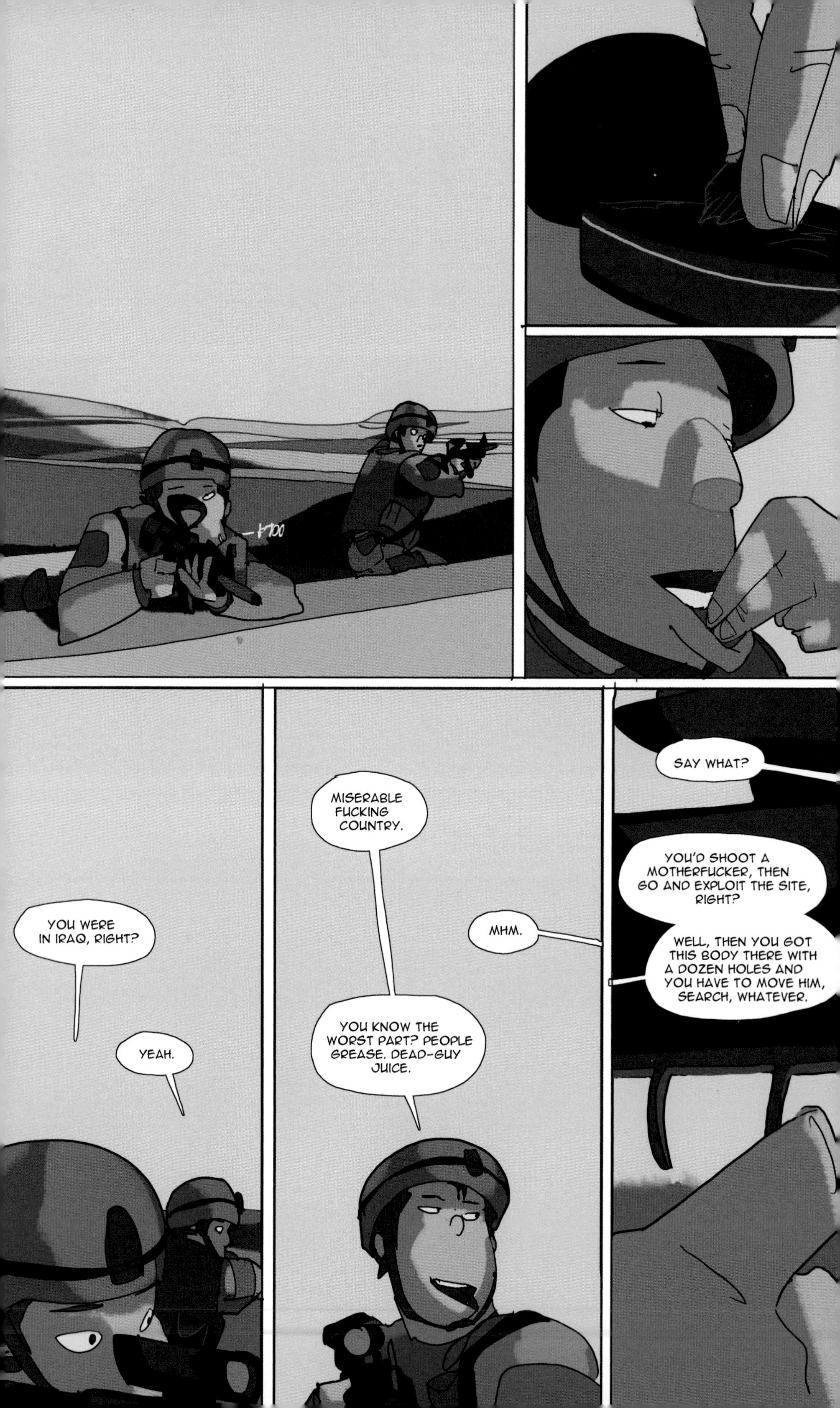

SAY WHAT?
YOU'D SHOOT A MOTHERFUCKER, THEN GO AND EXPLOIT THE SITE, RIGHT?
WELL, THEN YOU GOT THIS BODY THERE WITH A DOZEN HOLES AND YOU HAVE TO MOVE HIM, SEARCH, WHATEVER.
MHM.
MISERABLE FUCKING COUNTRY.
YOU KNOW THE WORST PART? PEOPLE GREASE. DEAD-GUY JUICE.
YOU WERE IN IRAQ, RIGHT?
YEAH.

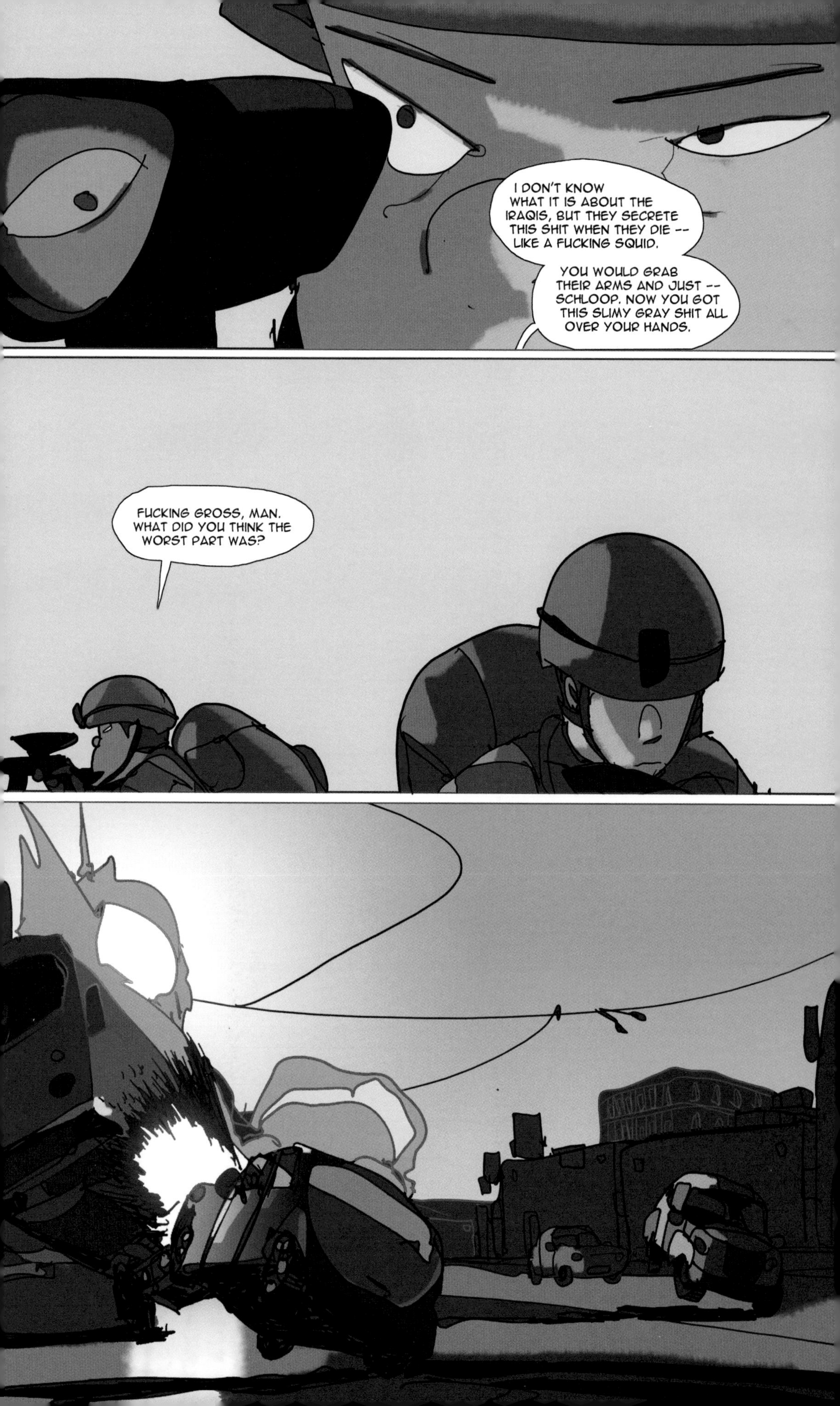
I DON'T KNOW WHAT IT IS ABOUT THE IRAQIS, BUT THEY SECRETE THIS SHIT WHEN THEY DIE -- LIKE A FUCKING SQUID.
YOU WOULD GRAB THEIR ARMS AND JUST -- SCHLOOP. NOW YOU GOT THIS SLIMY GRAY SHIT ALL OVER YOUR HANDS.
FUCKING GROSS, MAN. WHAT DID YOU THINK THE WORST PART WAS?

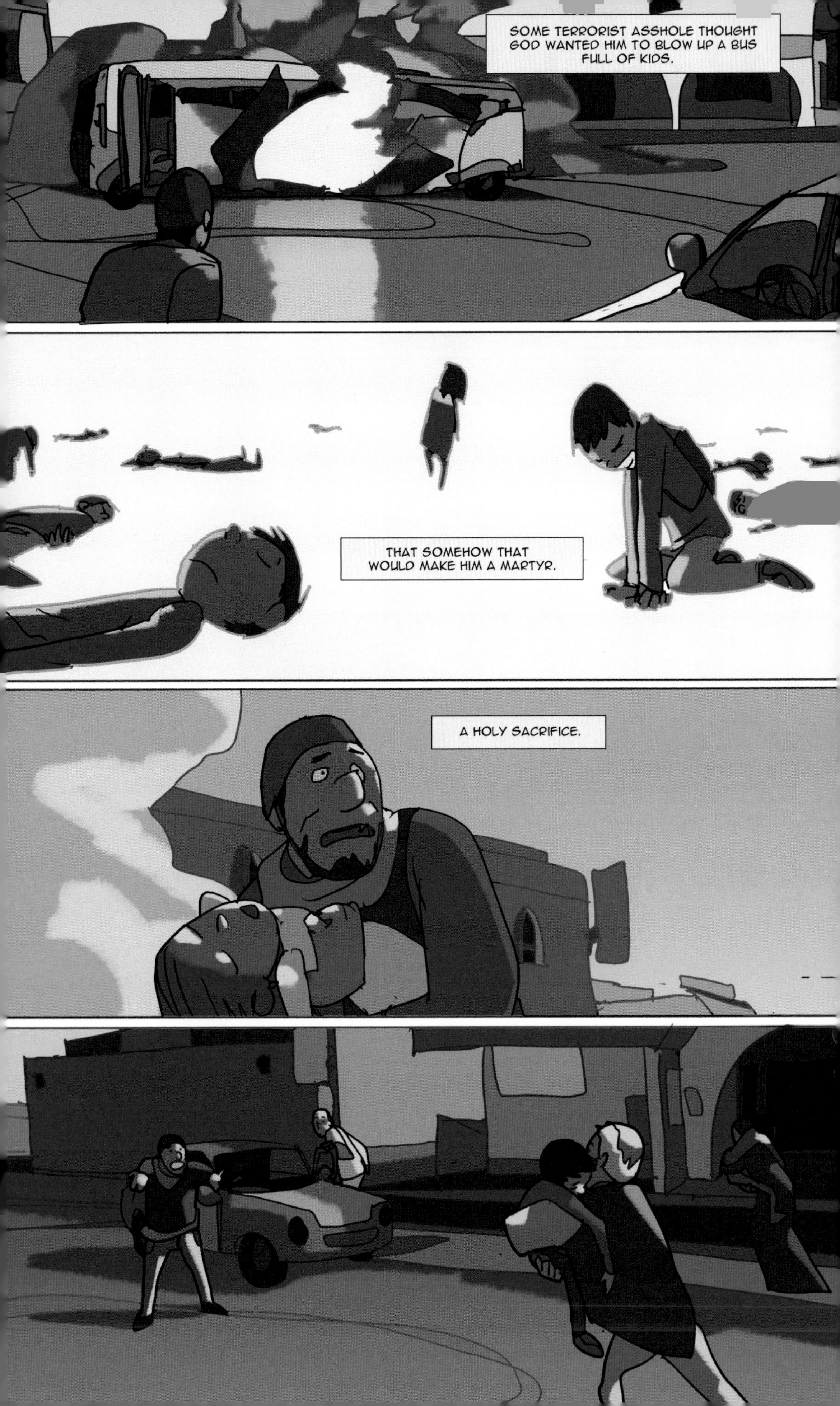
SOME TERRORIST ASSHOLE THOUGHT GOD WANTED HIM TO BLOW UP A BUS FULL OF KIDS.
THAT SOMEHOW THAT WOULD MAKE HIM A MARTYR.
A HOLY SACRIFICE.

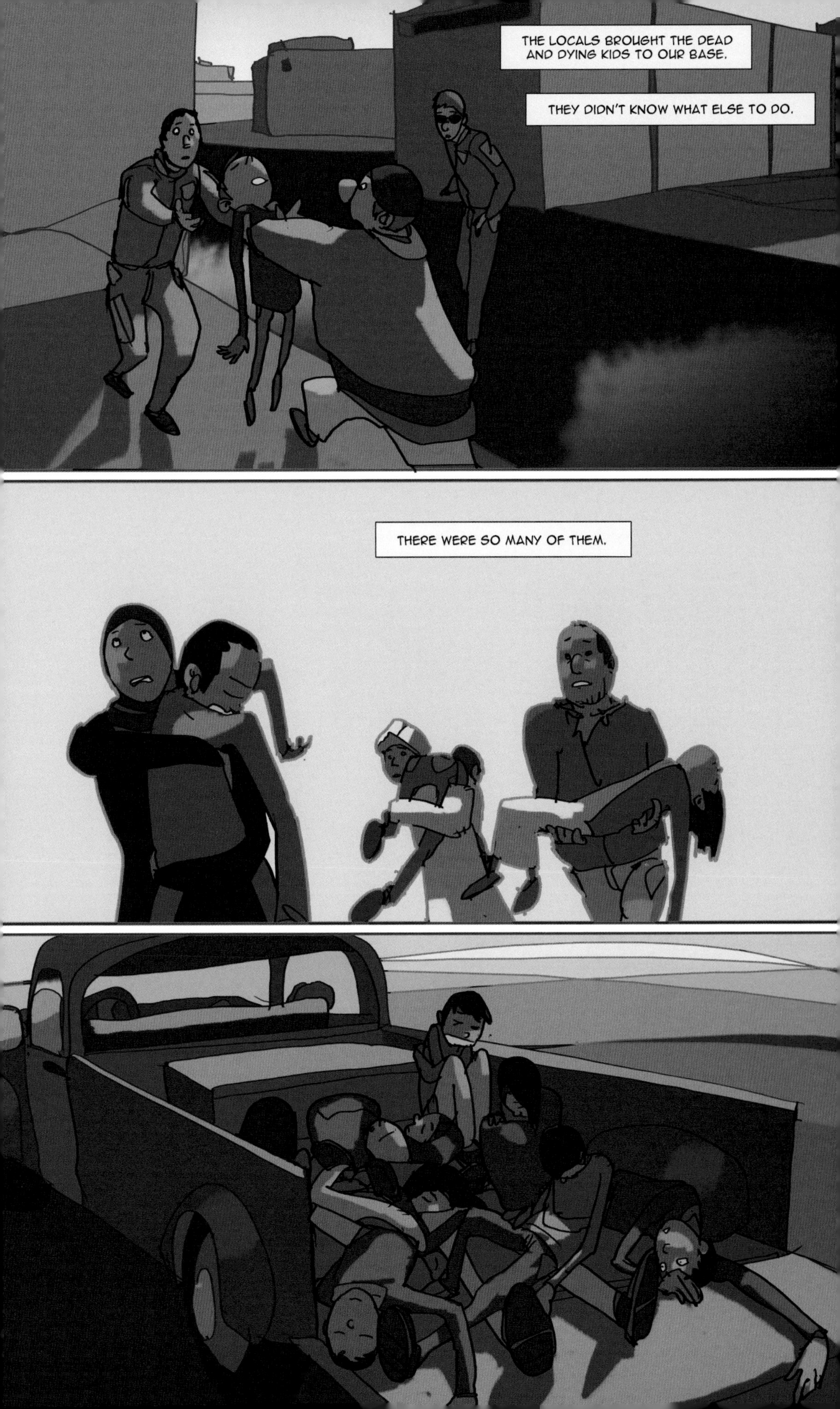
THE LOCALS BROUGHT THE DEAD AND DYING KIDS TO OUR BASE.
THEY DIDN'T KNOW WHAT ELSE TO DO.
THERE WERE SO MANY OF THEM.

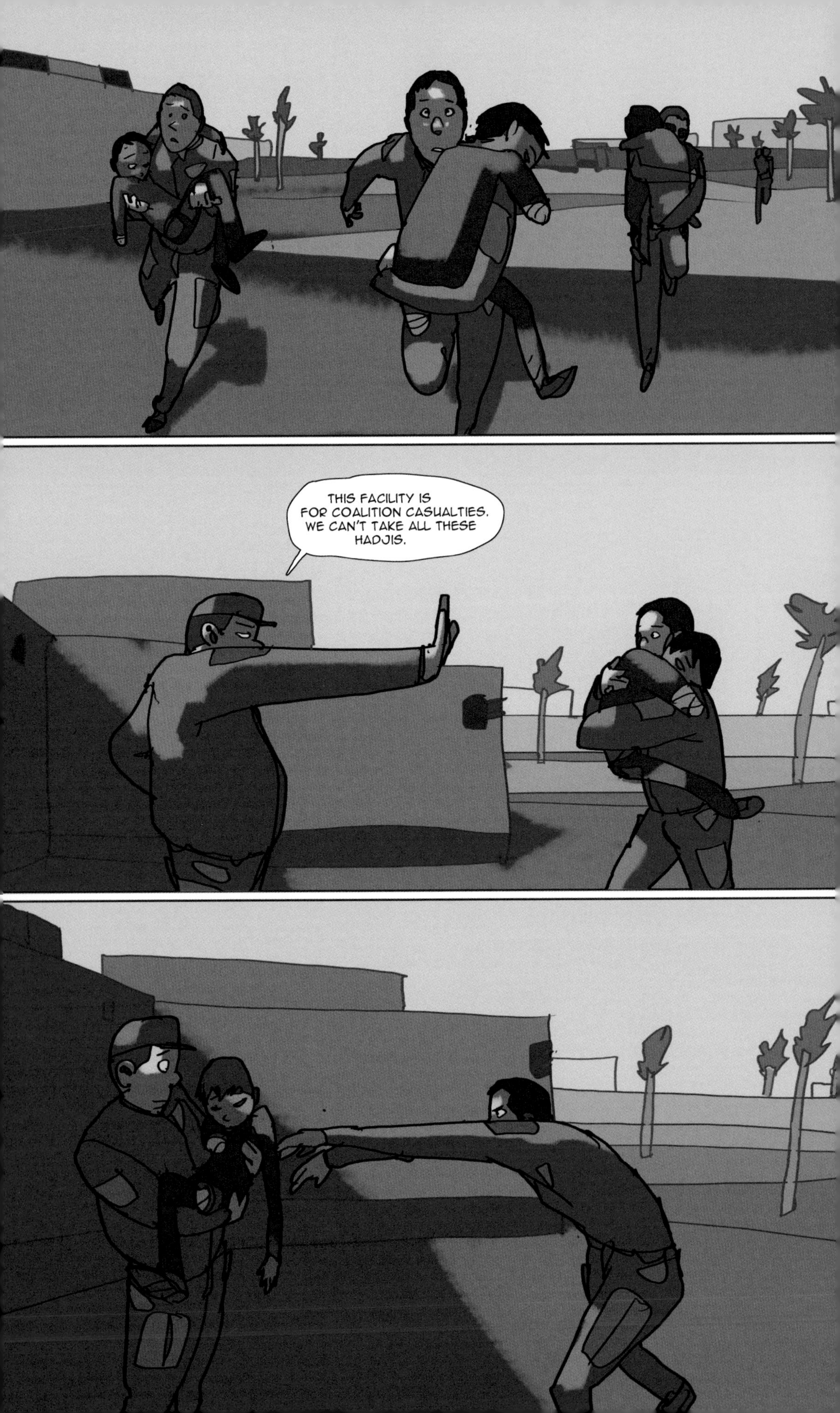
THIS FACILITY IS FOR COALITION CASUALTIES. WE CAN'T TAKE ALL THESE HADJIS.

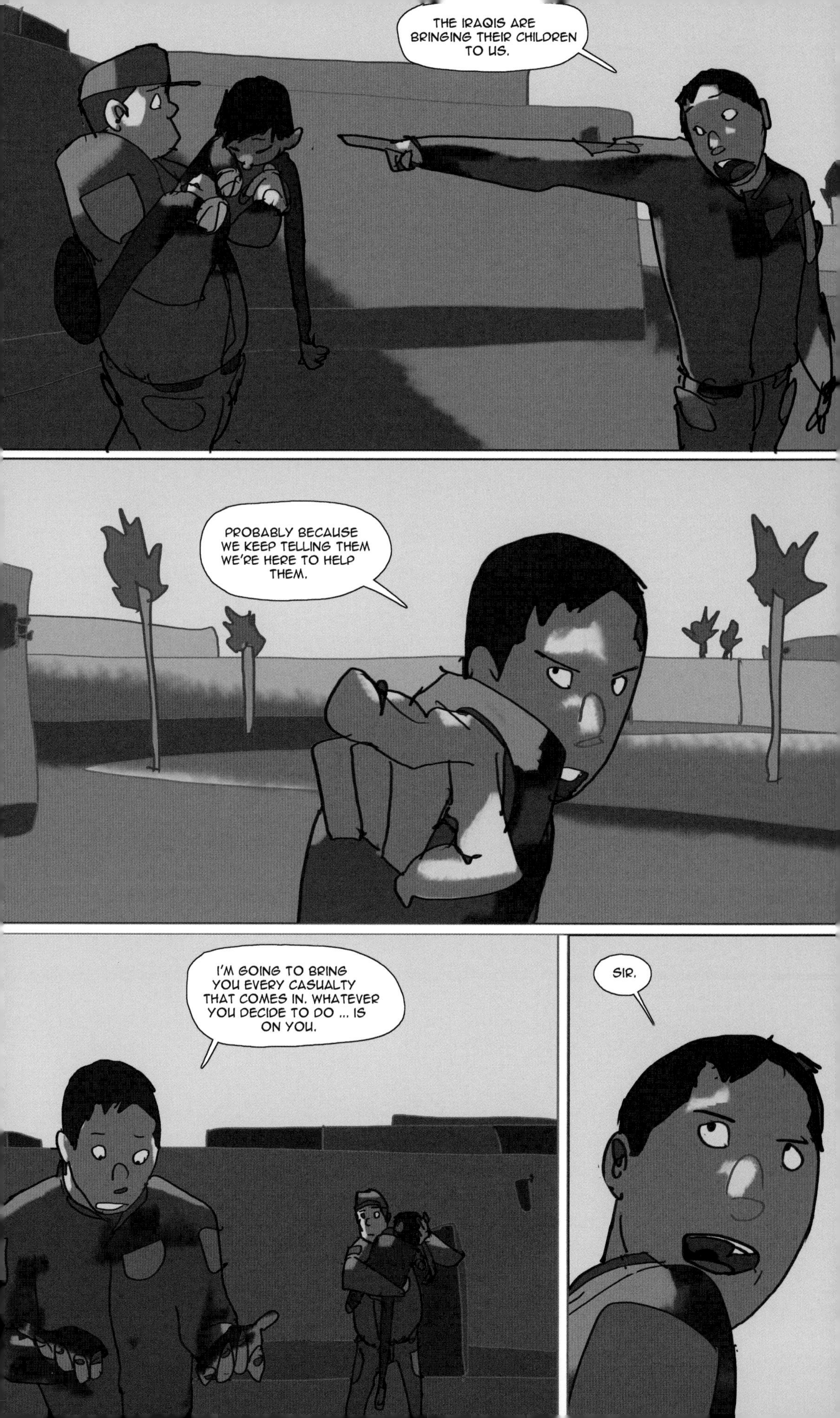
THE IRAQIS ARE BRINGING THEIR CHILDREN TO US.
PROBABLY BECAUSE WE KEEP TELLING THEM WE'RE HERE TO HELP THEM.
I'M GOING TO BRING YOU EVERY CASUALTY THAT COMES IN. WHATEVER YOU DECIDE TO DO ... IS ON YOU.
SIR.

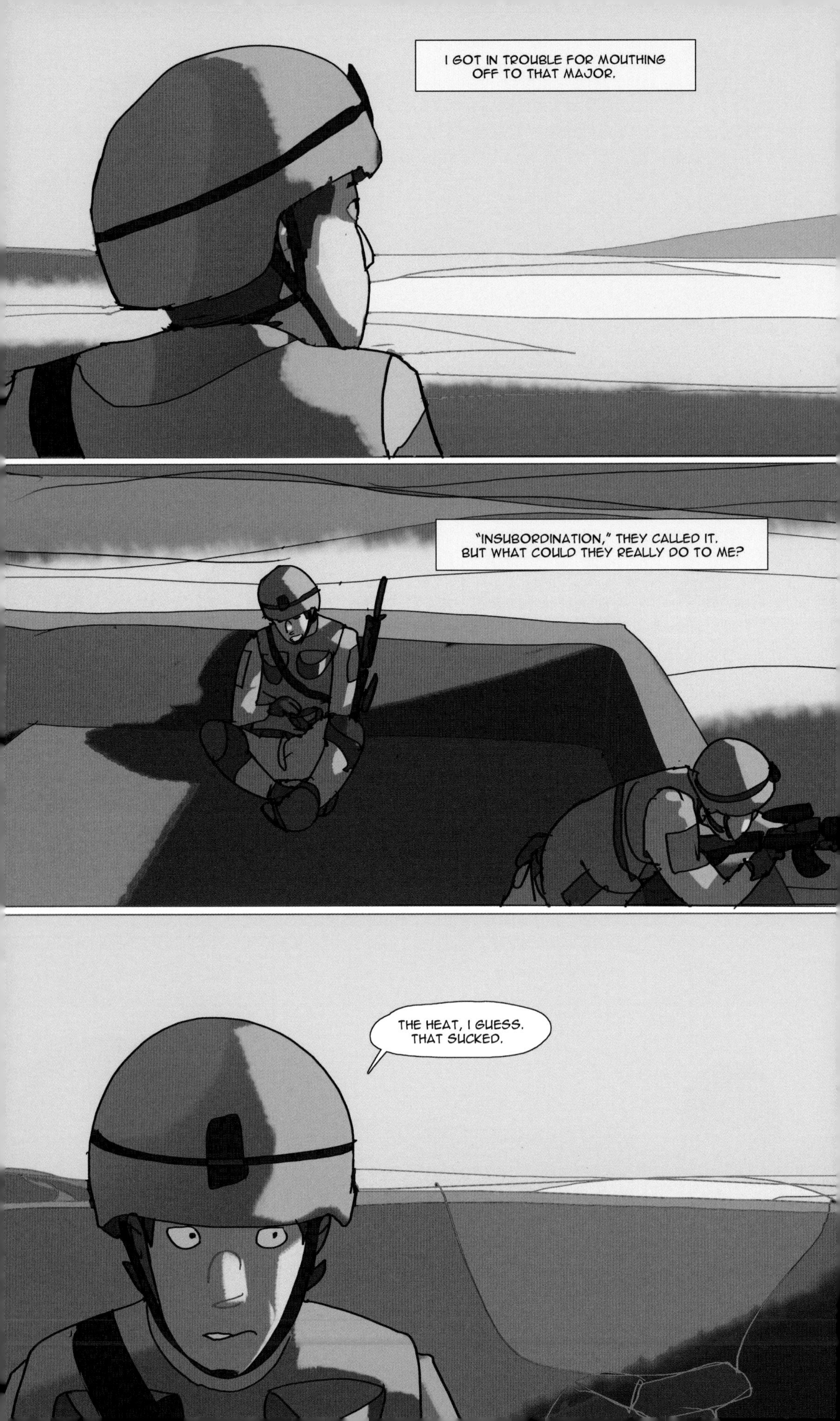
I GOT IN TROUBLE FOR MOUTHING OFF TO THAT MAJOR.
"INSUBORDINATION," THEY CALLED IT. BUT WHAT COULD THEY REALLY DO TO ME?
THE HEAT, I GUESS. THAT SUCKED.

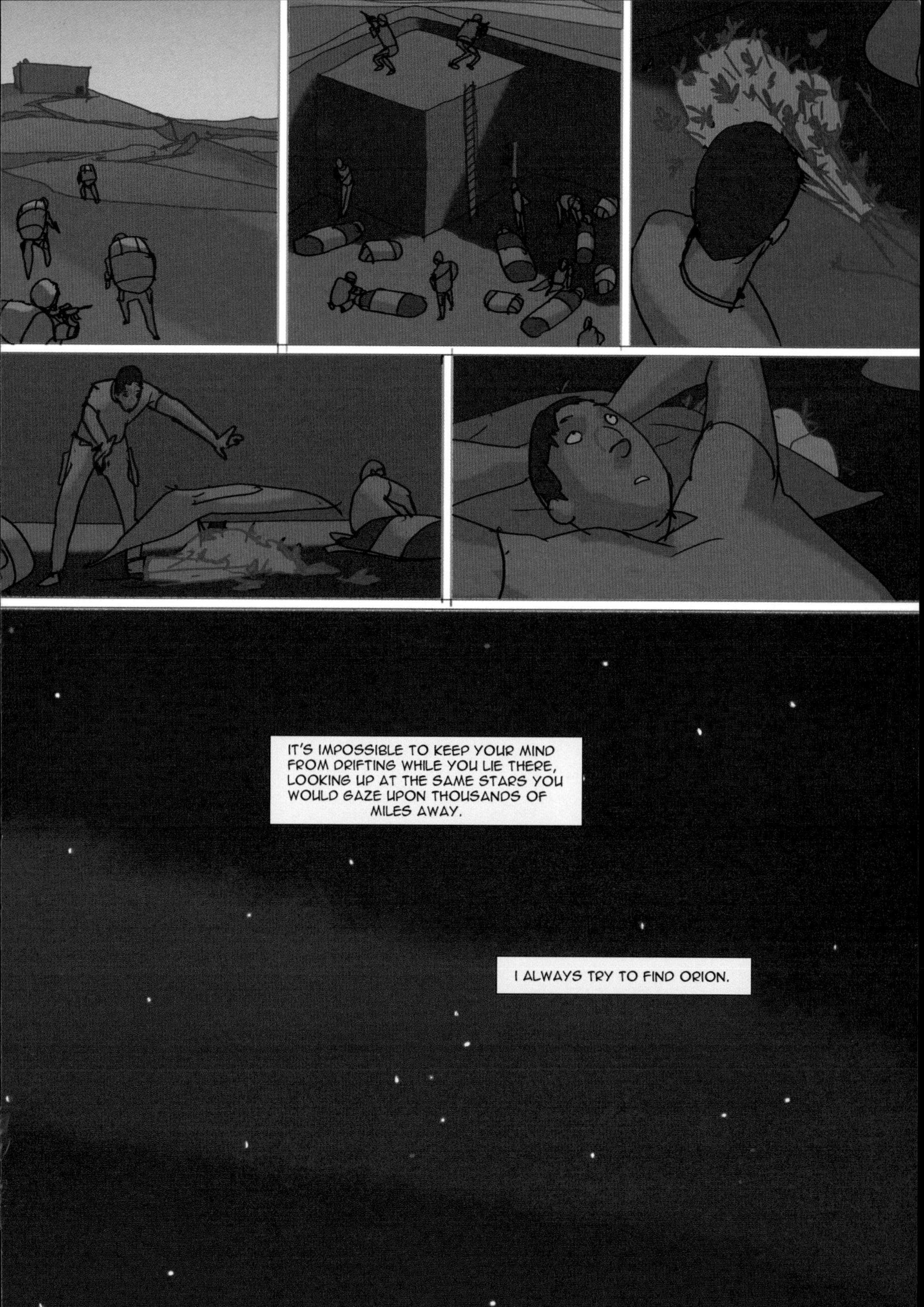
IT'S IMPOSSIBLE TO KEEP YOUR MIND FROM DRIFTING WHILE YOU LIE THERE, LOOKING UP AT THE SAME STARS YOU WOULD GAZE UPON THOUSANDS OF MILES AWAY.
I ALWAYS TRY TO FIND ORION.

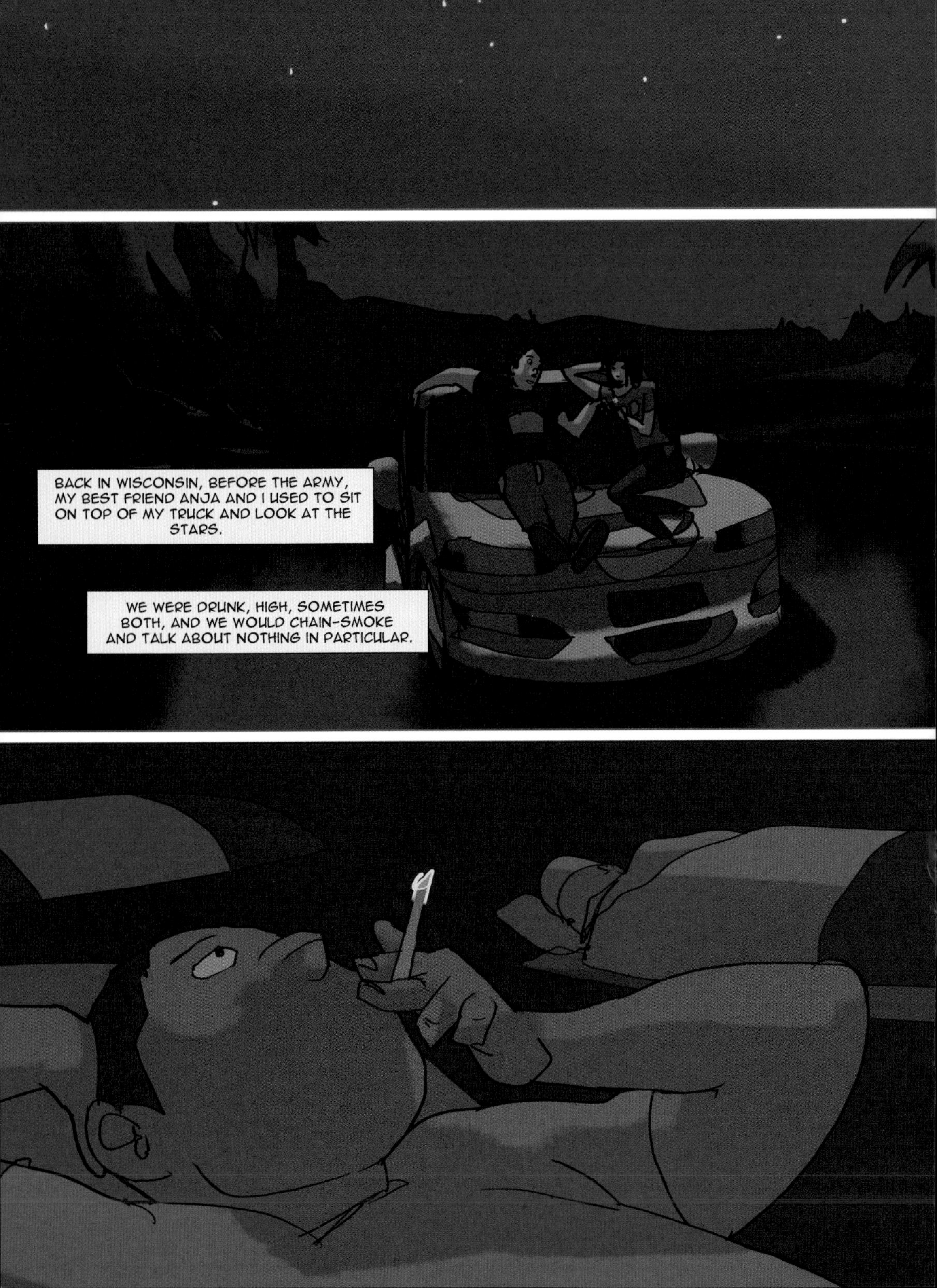
BACK IN WISCONSIN, BEFORE THE ARMY, MY BEST FRIEND ANJA AND I USED TO SIT ON TOP OF MY TRUCK AND LOOK AT THE STARS.
WE WERE DRUNK, HIGH, SOMETIMES BOTH, AND WE WOULD CHAIN-SMOKE AND TALK ABOUT NOTHING IN PARTICULAR.

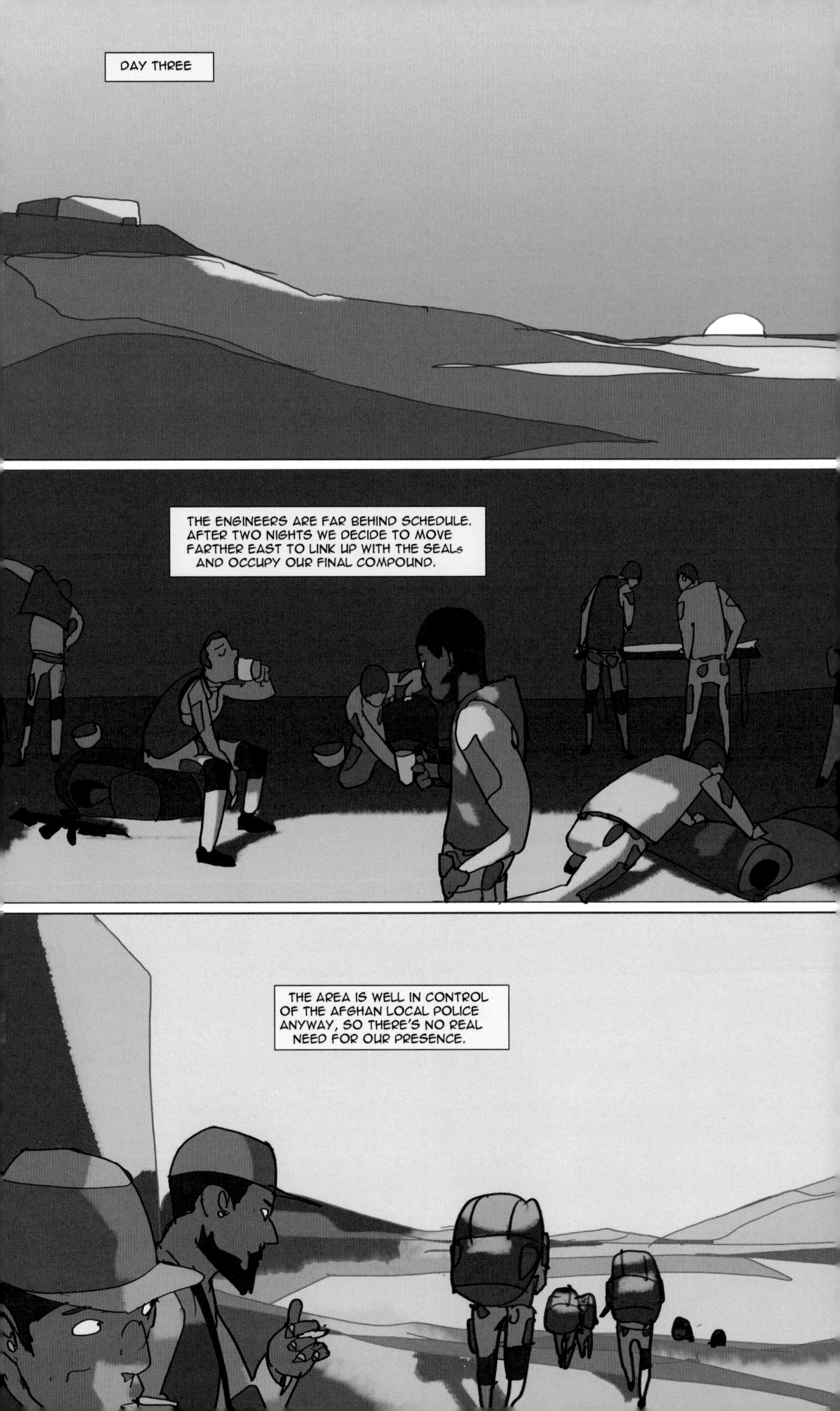
DAY THREE
THE ENGINEERS ARE FAR BEHIND SCHEDULE. AFTER TWO NIGHTS WE DECIDE TO MOVE FARTHER EAST TO LINK UP WITH THE SEALs AND OCCUPY OUR FINAL COMPOUND.
THE AREA IS WELL IN CONTROL OF THE AFGHAN LOCAL POLICE ANYWAY, SO THERE'S NO REAL NEED FOR OUR PRESENCE.

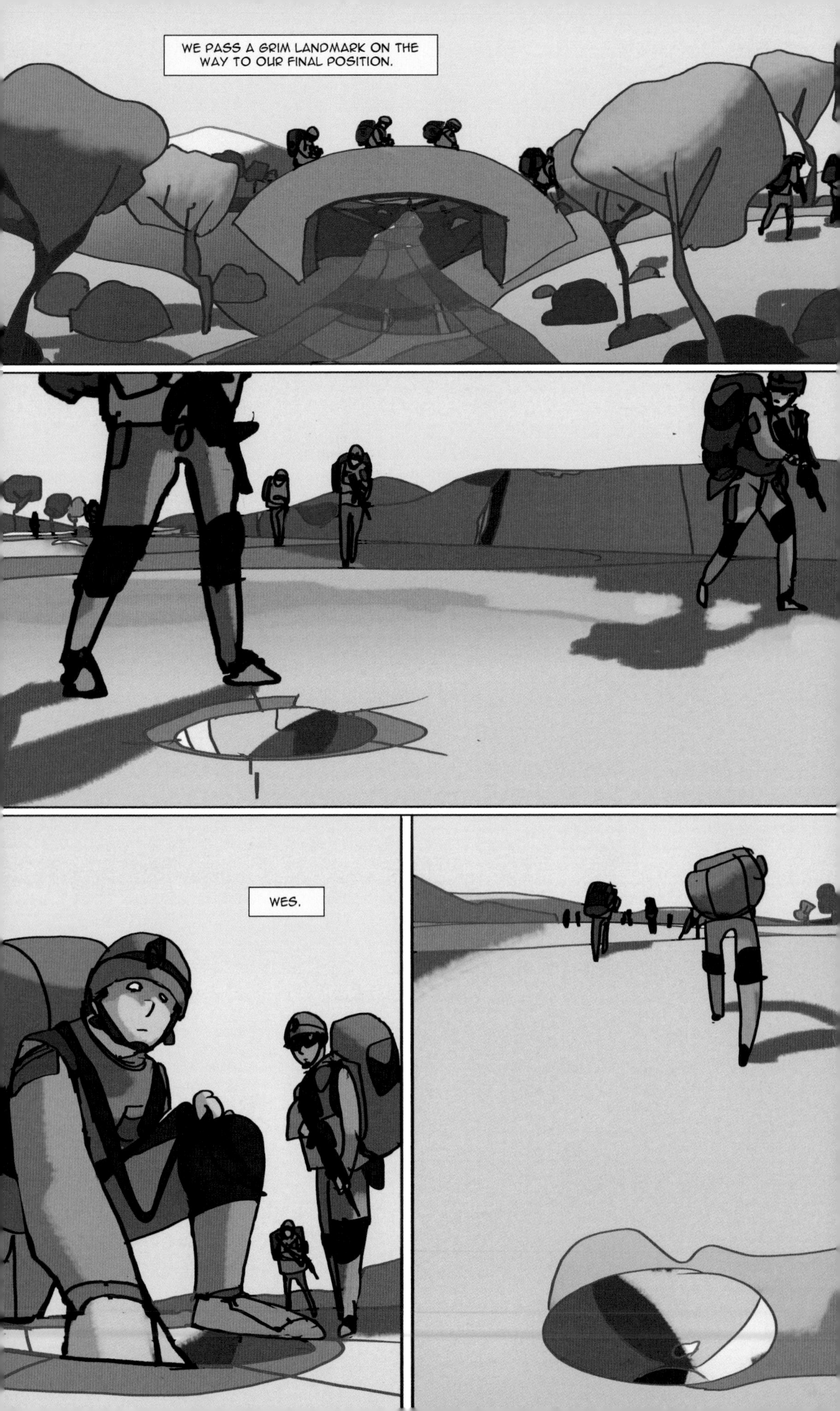
WE PASS A GRIM LANDMARK ON THE WAY TO OUR FINAL POSITION.
WES.

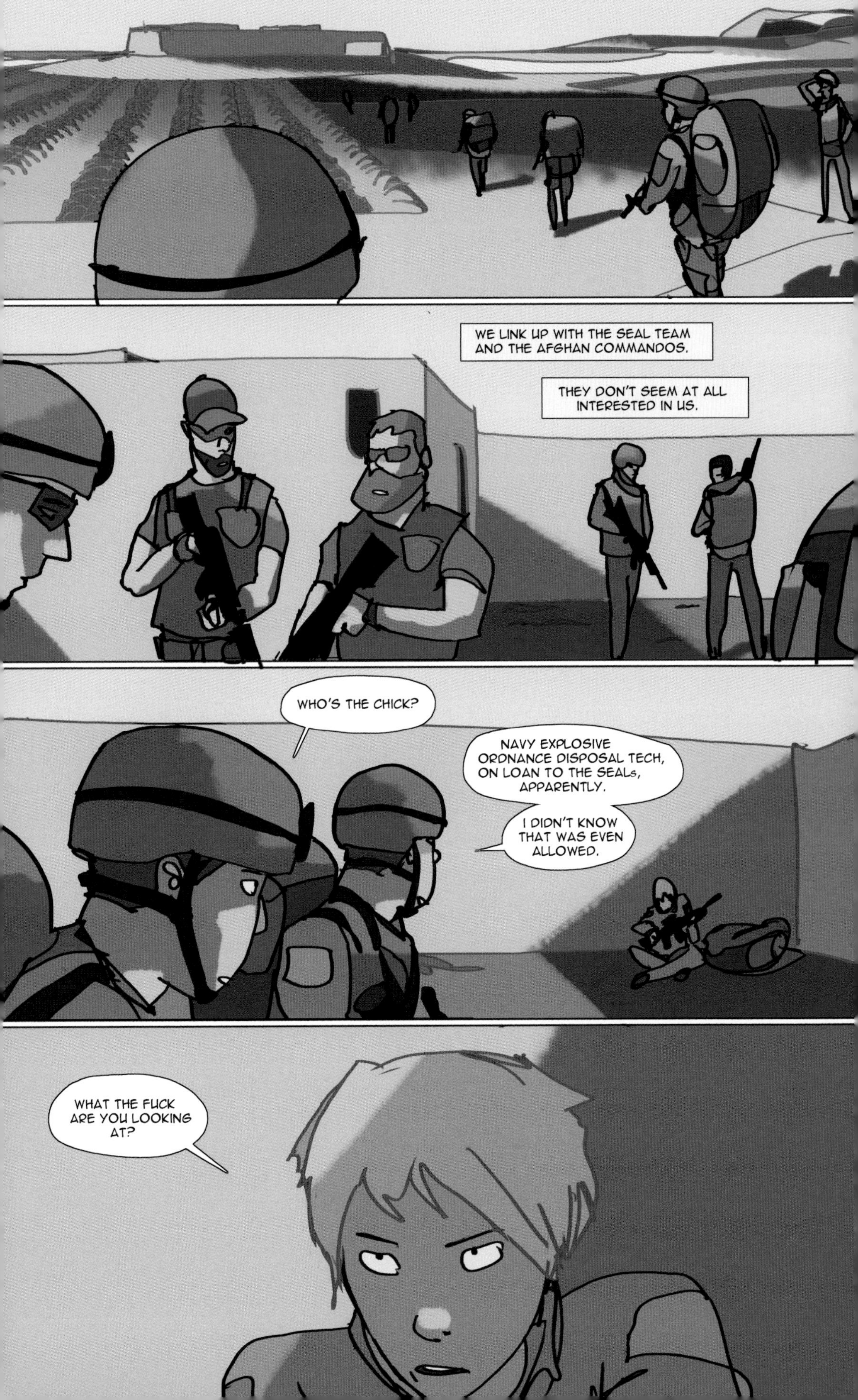
WE LINK UP WITH THE SEAL TEAM AND THE AFGHAN COMMANDOS.
THEY DON'T SEEM AT ALL INTERESTED IN US.
WHO'S THE CHICK?
NAVY EXPLOSIVE ORDNANCE DISPOSAL TECH, ON LOAN TO THE SEALs, APPARENTLY.
I DIDN'T KNOW THAT WAS EVEN ALLOWED.
WHAT THE FUCK ARE YOU LOOKING AT?

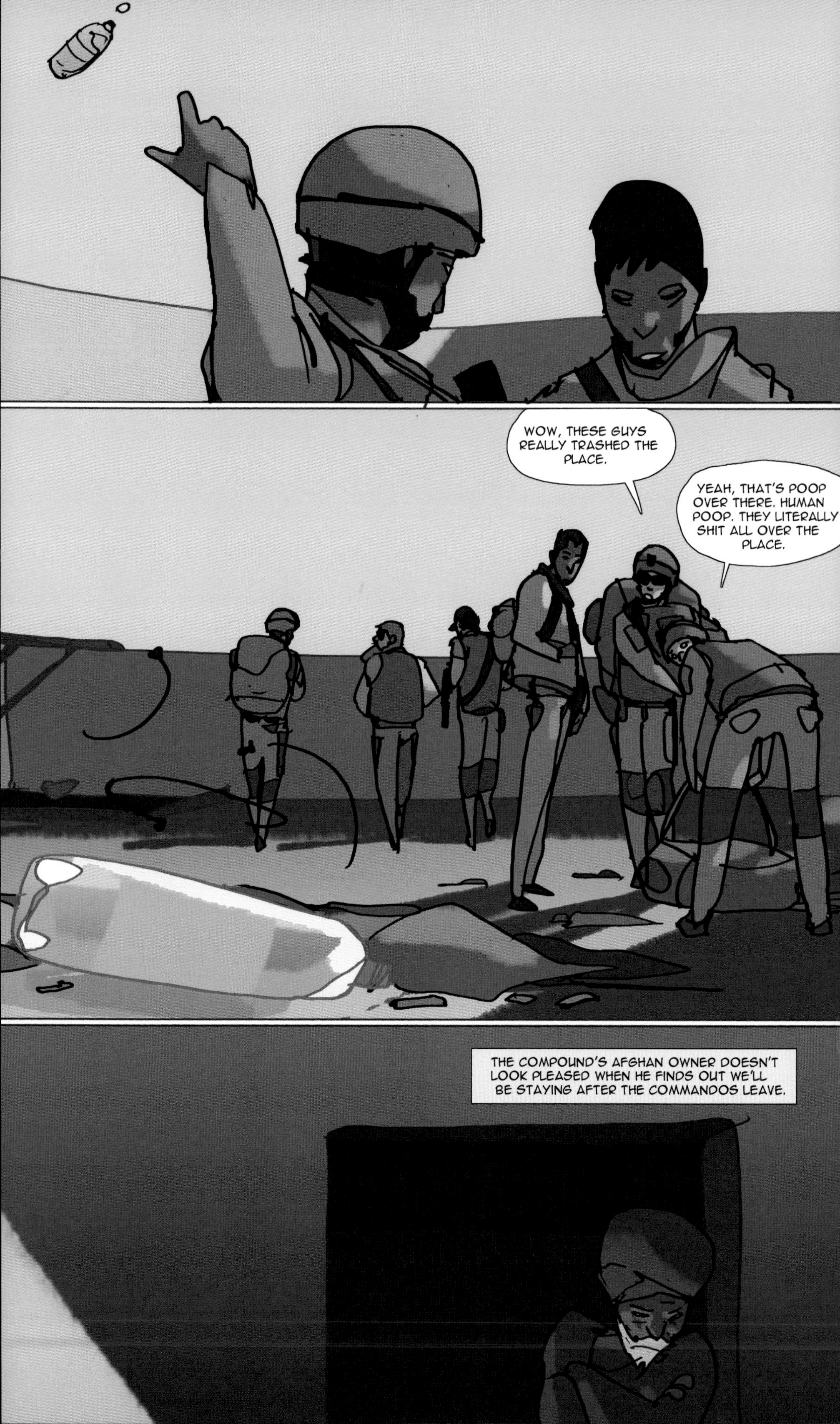
WOW, THESE GUYS REALLY TRASHED THE PLACE.
YEAH, THAT'S POOP OVER THERE. HUMAN POOP. THEY LITERALLY SHIT ALL OVER THE PLACE.
THE COMPOUND'S AFGHAN OWNER DOESN'T LOOK PLEASED WHEN HE FINDS OUT WE'LL BE STAYING AFTER THE COMMANDOS LEAVE.

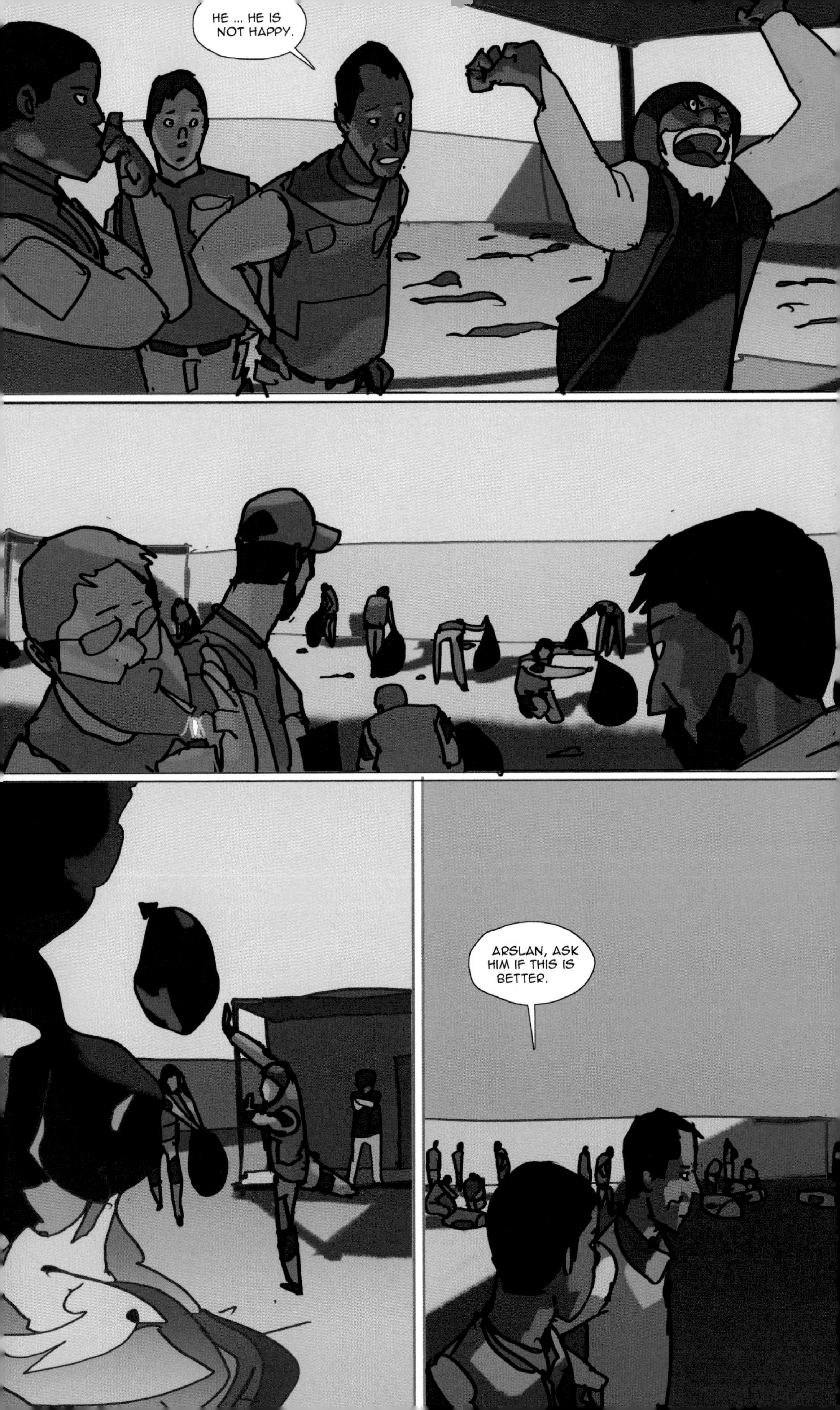
HE ... HE IS NOT HAPPY.
ARSLAN, ASK HIM IF THIS IS BETTER.

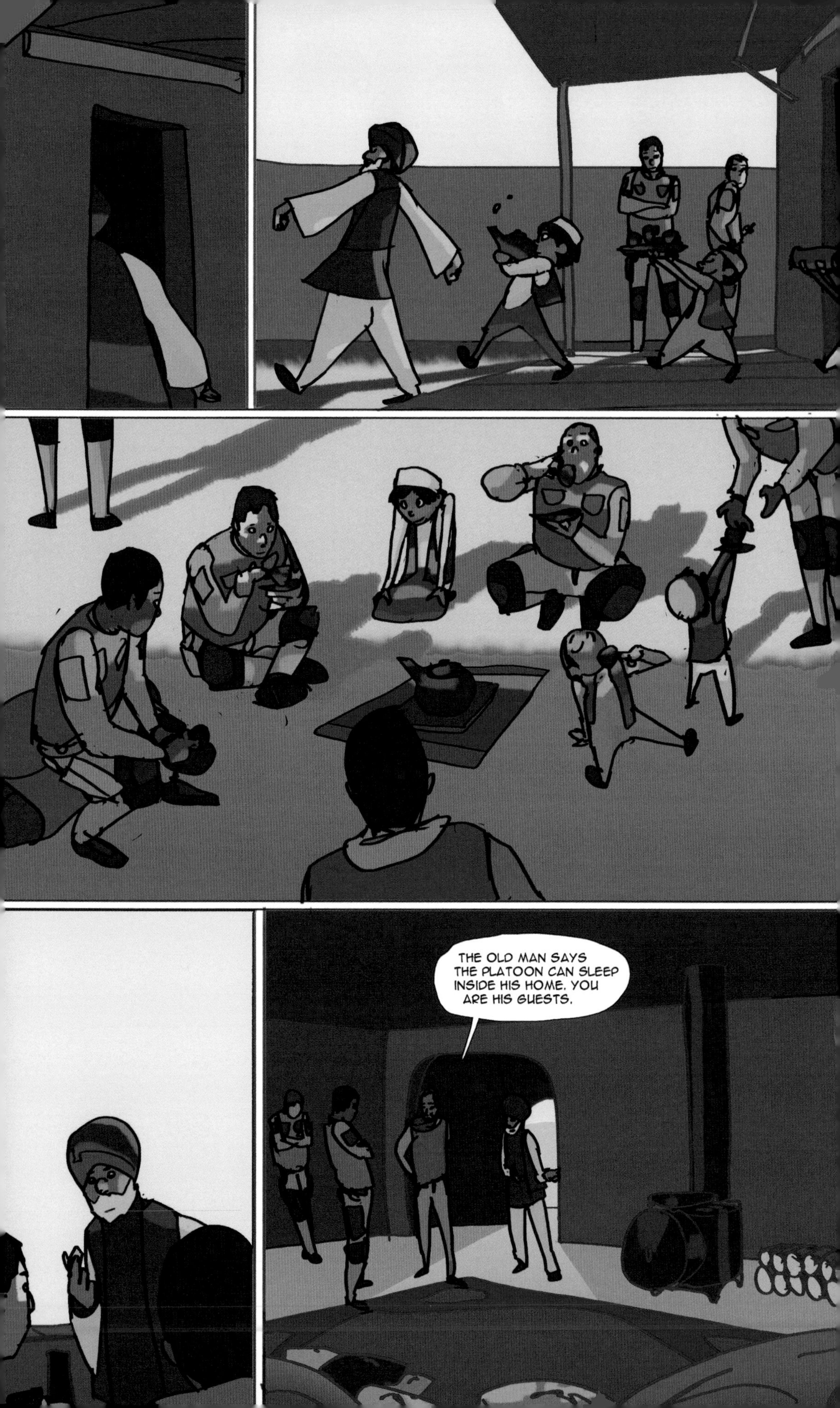
THE OLD MAN SAYS THE PLATOON CAN SLEEP INSIDE HIS HOME. YOU ARE HIS GUESTS.

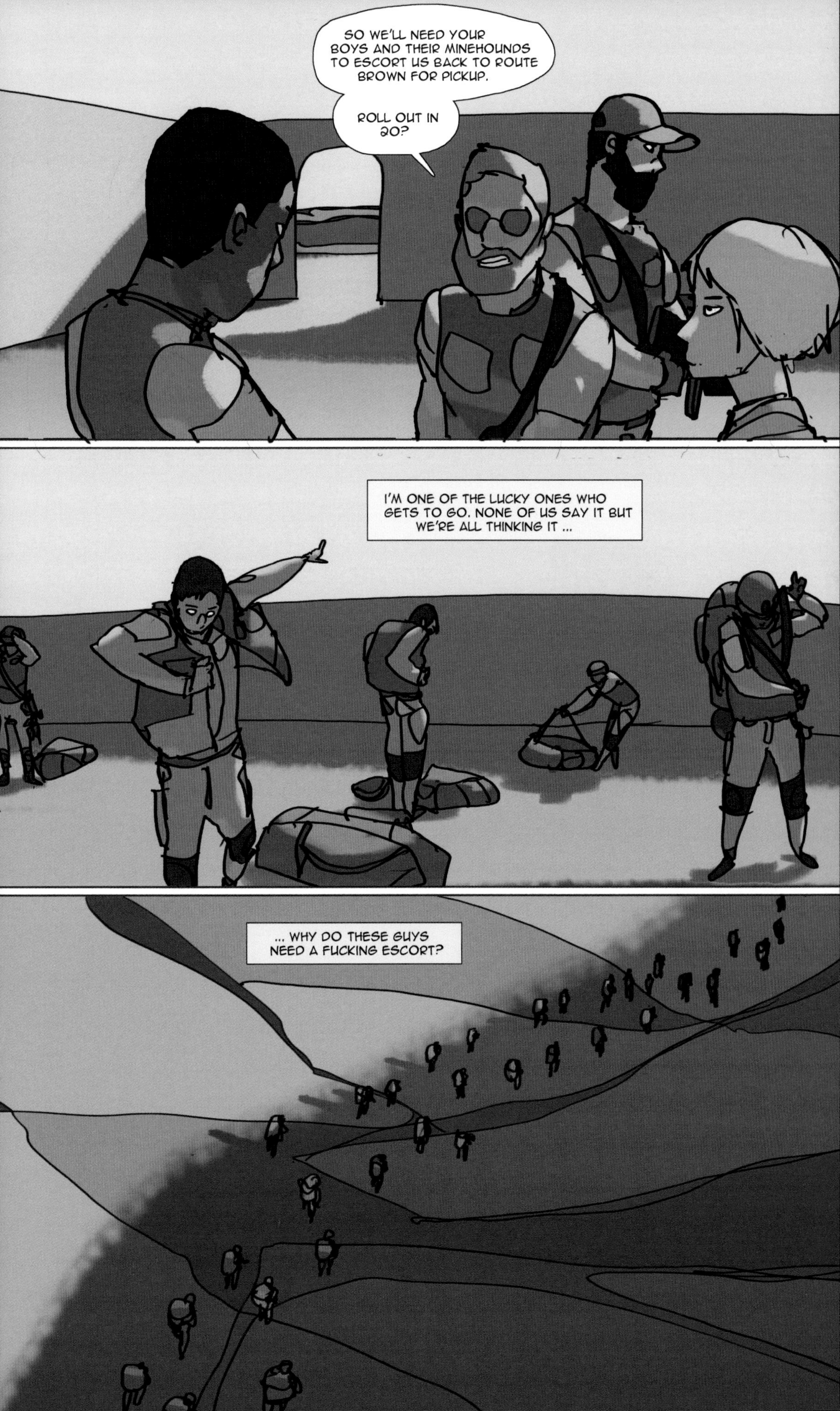
SO WE'LL NEED YOUR BOYS AND THEIR MINEHOUNDS TO ESCORT US BACK TO ROUTE BROWN FOR PICKUP.
ROLL OUT IN 20?
I'M ONE OF THE LUCKY ONES WHO GETS TO GO. NONE OF US SAY IT BUT WE'RE ALL THINKING IT ...
... WHY DO THESE GUYS NEED A FUCKING ESCORT?

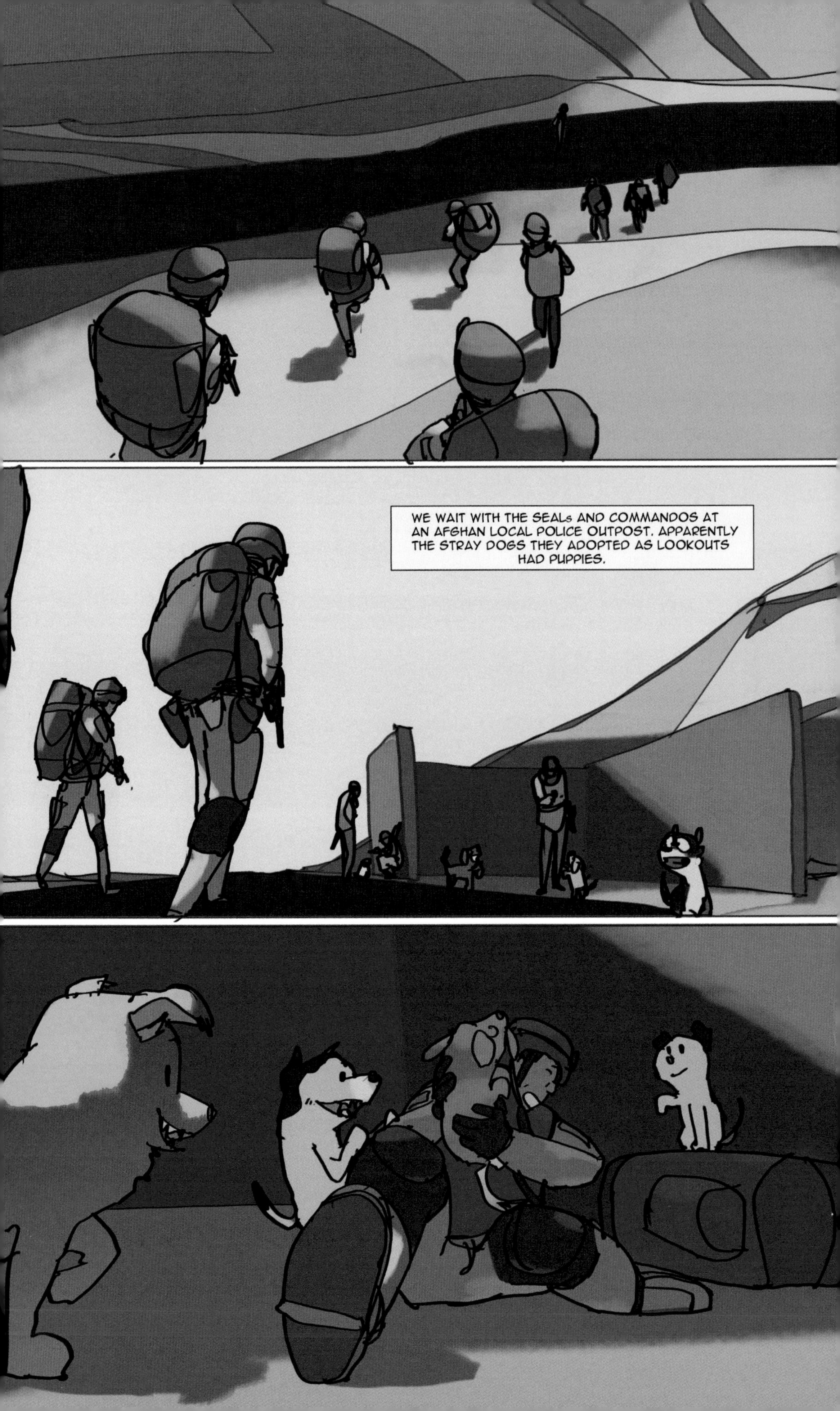
WE WAIT WITH THE SEALs AND COMMANDOS AT AN AFGHAN LOCAL POLICE OUTPOST. APPARENTLY THE STRAY DOGS THEY ADOPTED AS LOOKOUTS HAD PUPPIES.

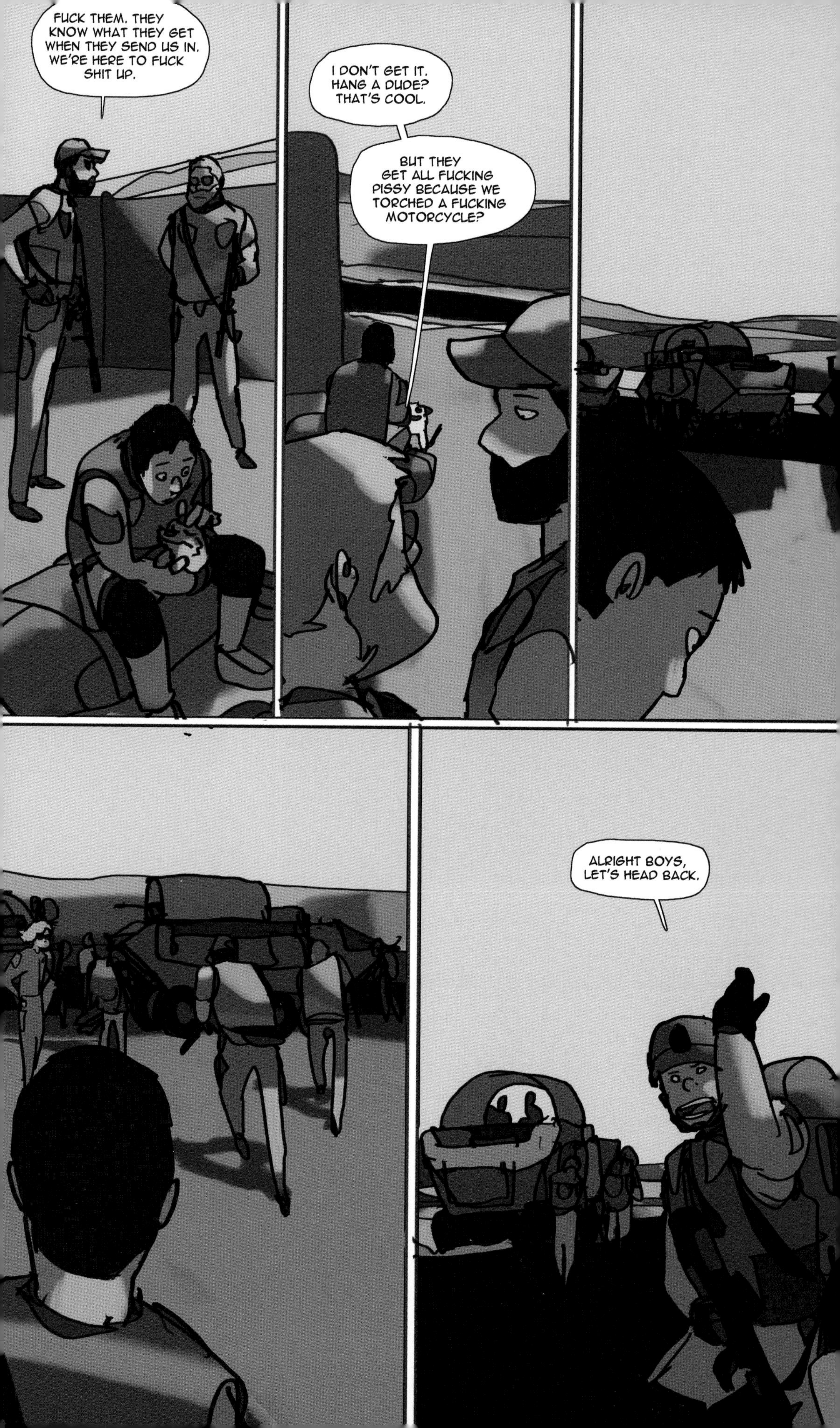
FUCK THEM. THEY KNOW WHAT THEY GET WHEN THEY SEND US IN. WE'RE HERE TO FUCK SHIT UP.
I DON'T GET IT. HANG A DUDE? THAT'S COOL.
BUT THEY GET ALL FUCKING PISSY BECAUSE WE TORCHED A FUCKING MOTORCYCLE?
ALRIGHT BOYS, LET'S HEAD BACK.

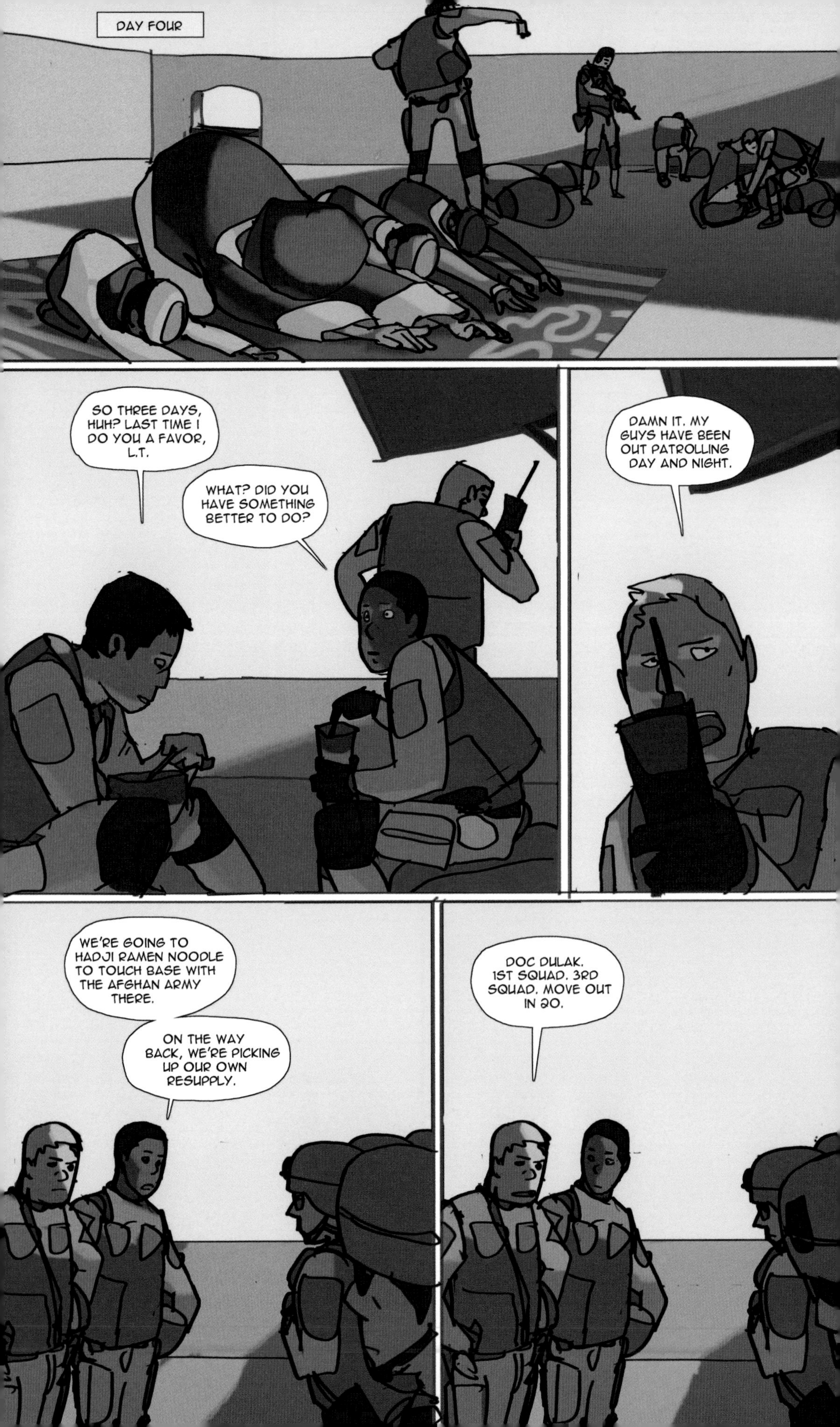
DAY FOUR
SO THREE DAYS, HUH? LAST TIME I DO YOU A FAVOR, L.T.
WHAT? DID YOU HAVE SOMETHING BETTER TO DO?
DAMN IT. MY GUYS HAVE BEEN OUT PATROLLING DAY AND NIGHT.
WE'RE GOING TO HADJI RAMEN NOODLE TO TOUCH BASE WITH THE AFGHAN ARMY THERE.
ON THE WAY BACK, WE'RE PICKING UP OUR OWN RESUPPLY.
DOC DULAK. 1ST SQUAD. 3RD SQUAD. MOVE OUT IN 20.

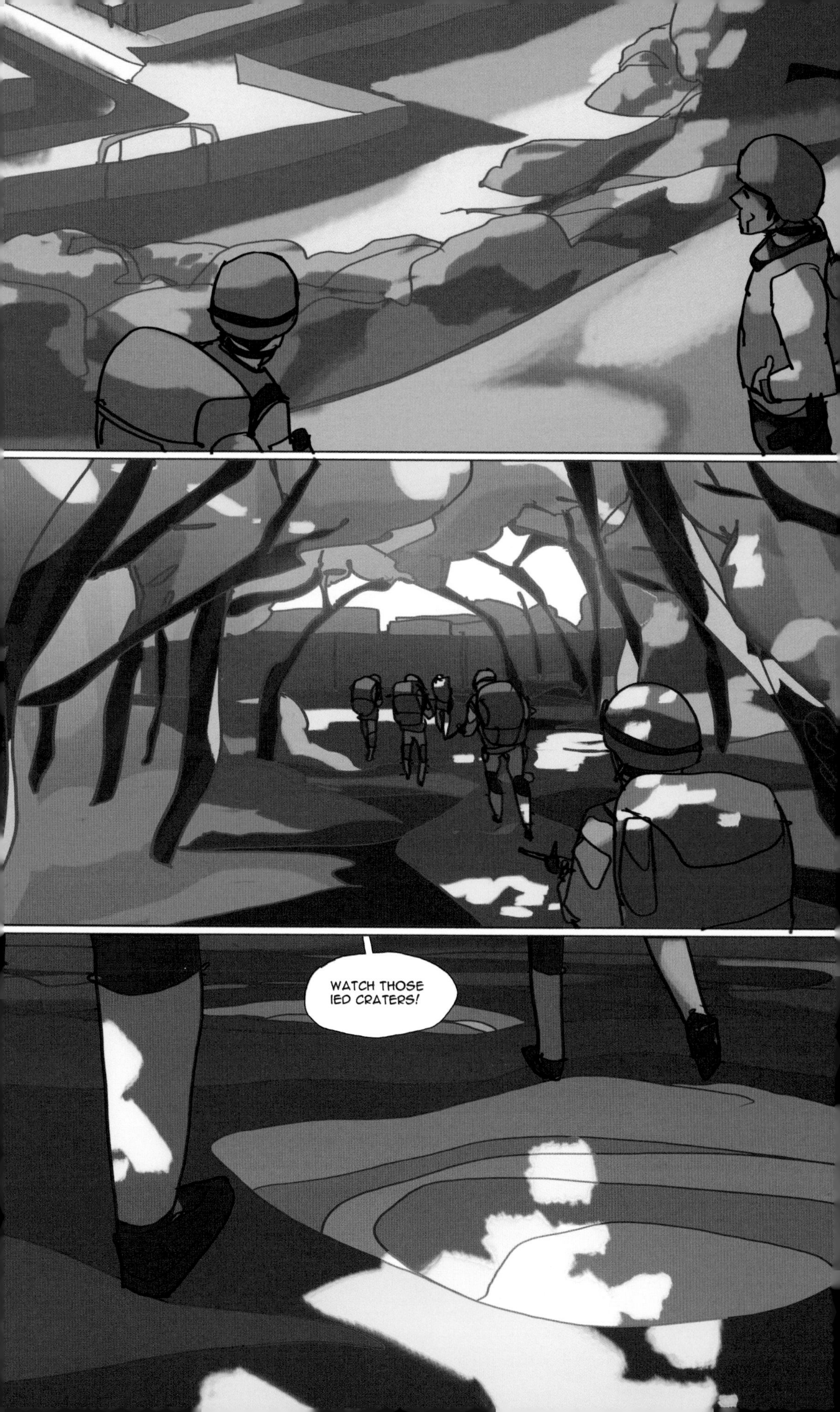
WATCH THOSE IED CRATERS!

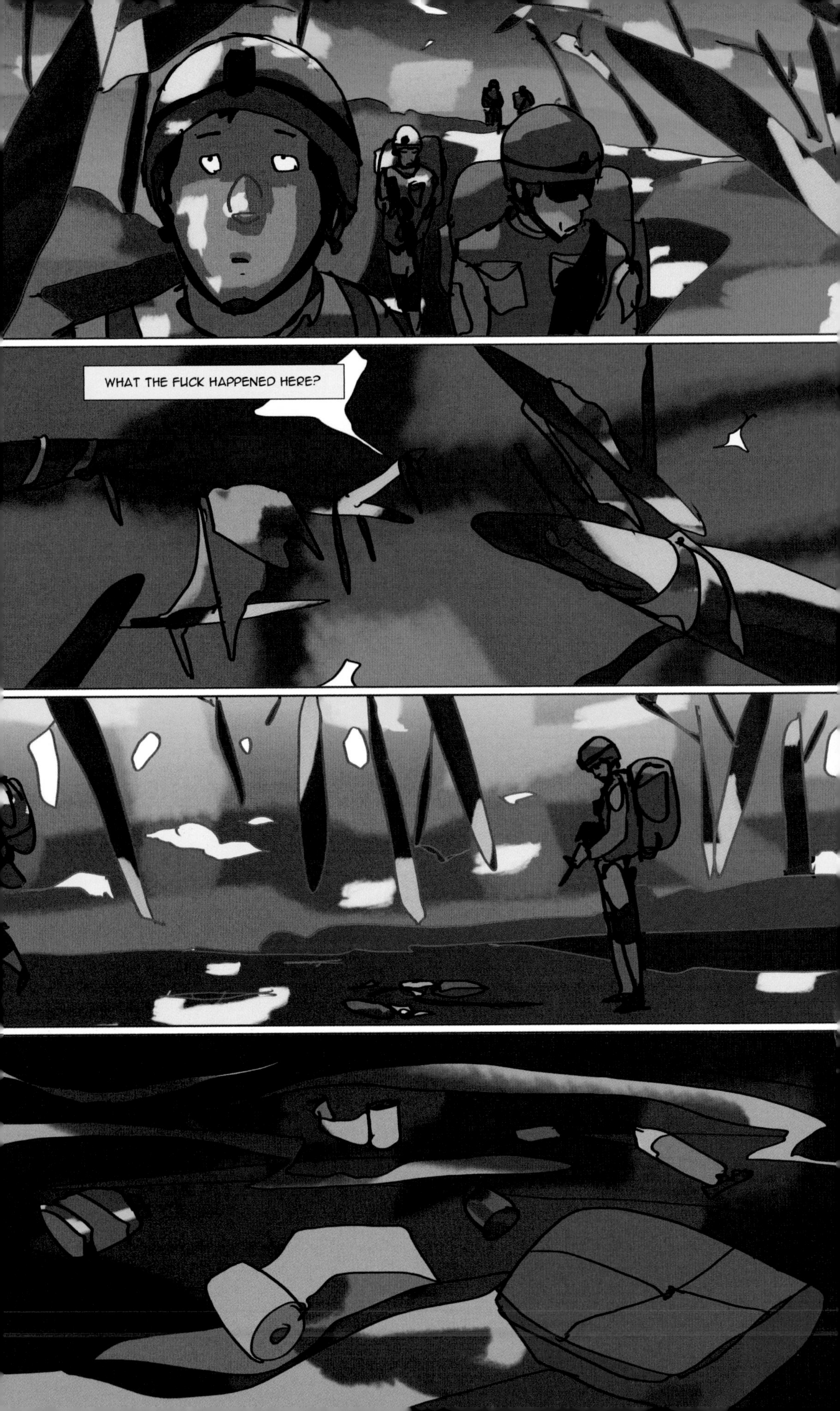
WHAT THE FUCK HAPPENED HERE?

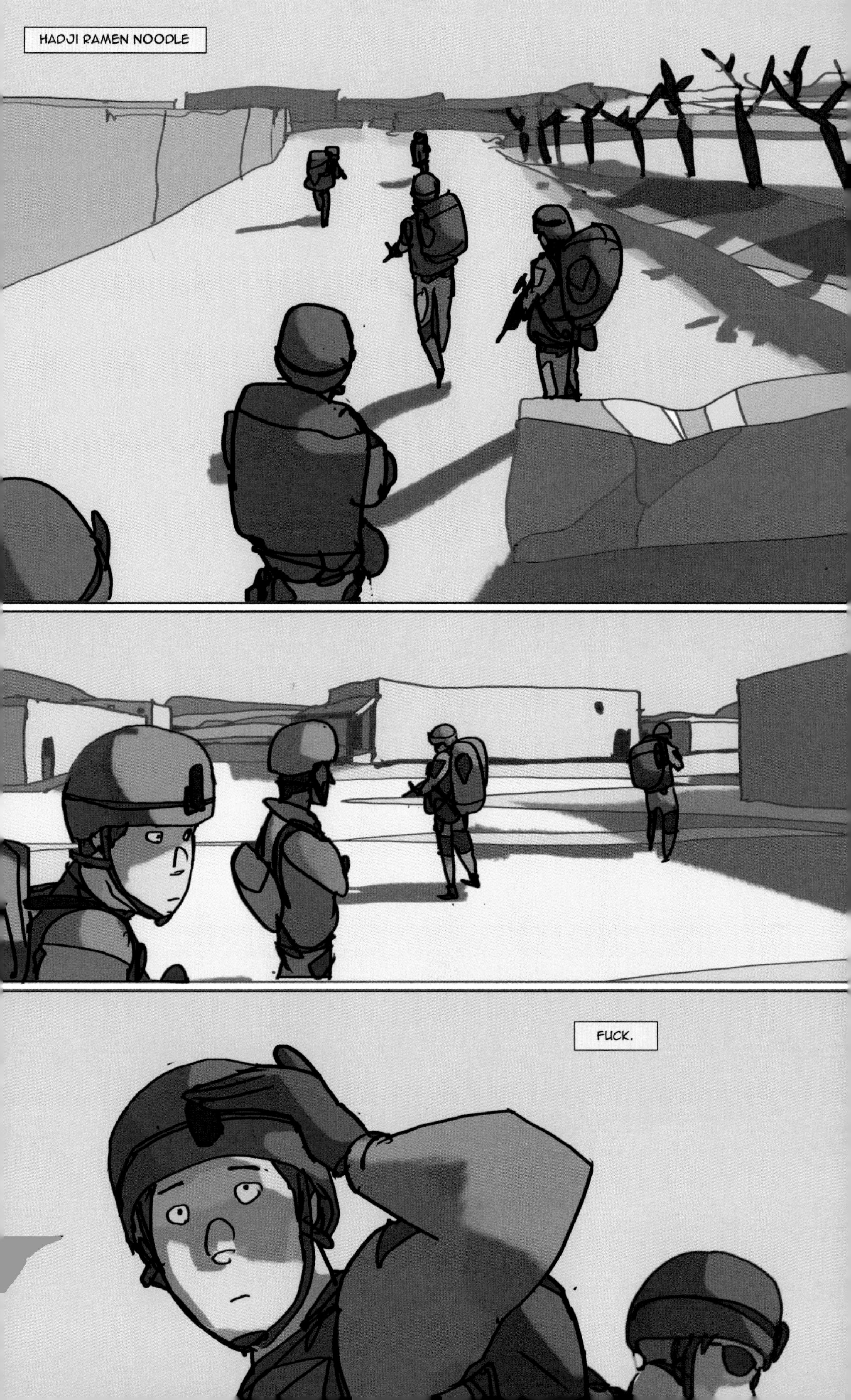
HADJI RAMEN NOODLE
FUCK.

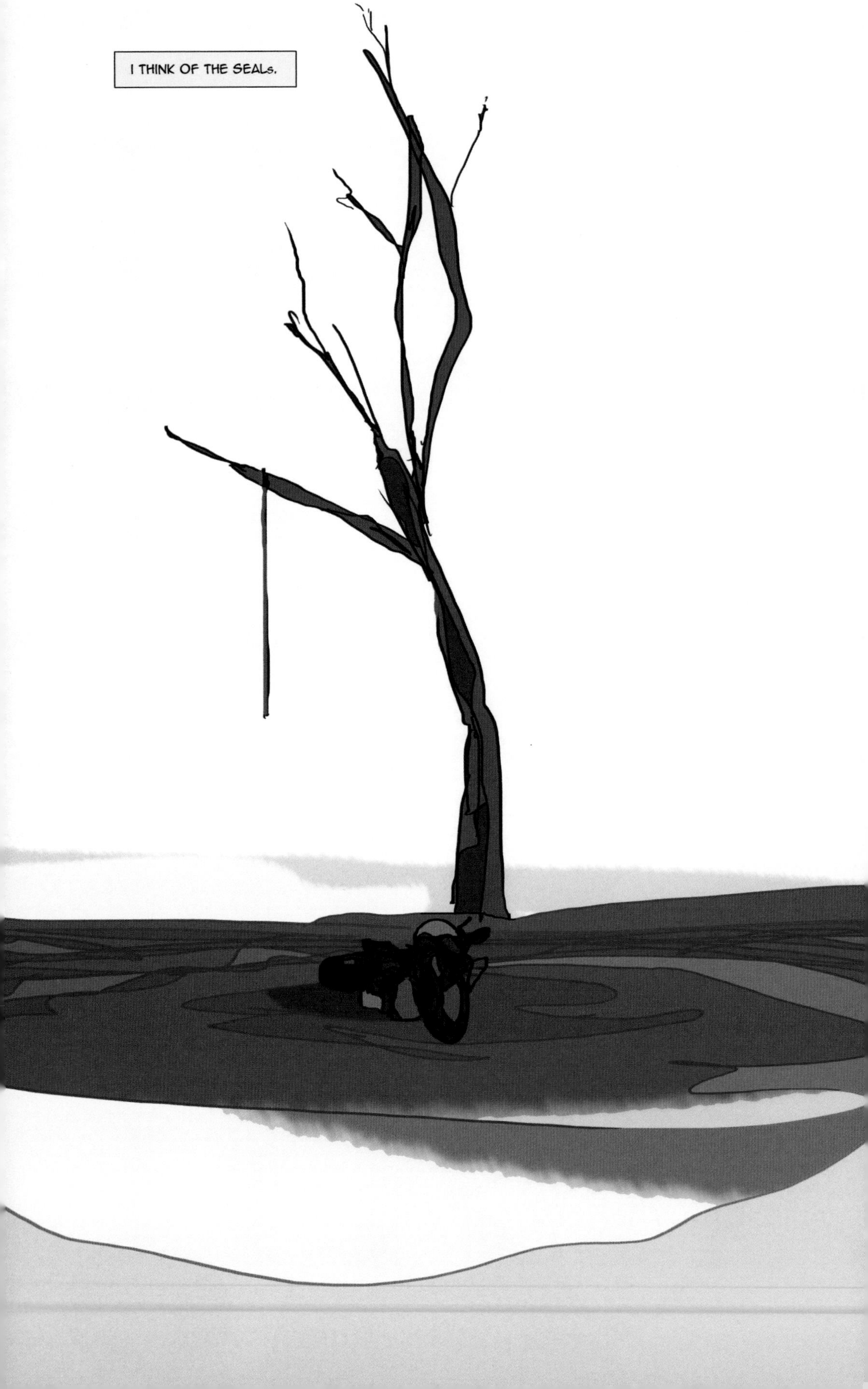
I THINK OF THE SEALs.

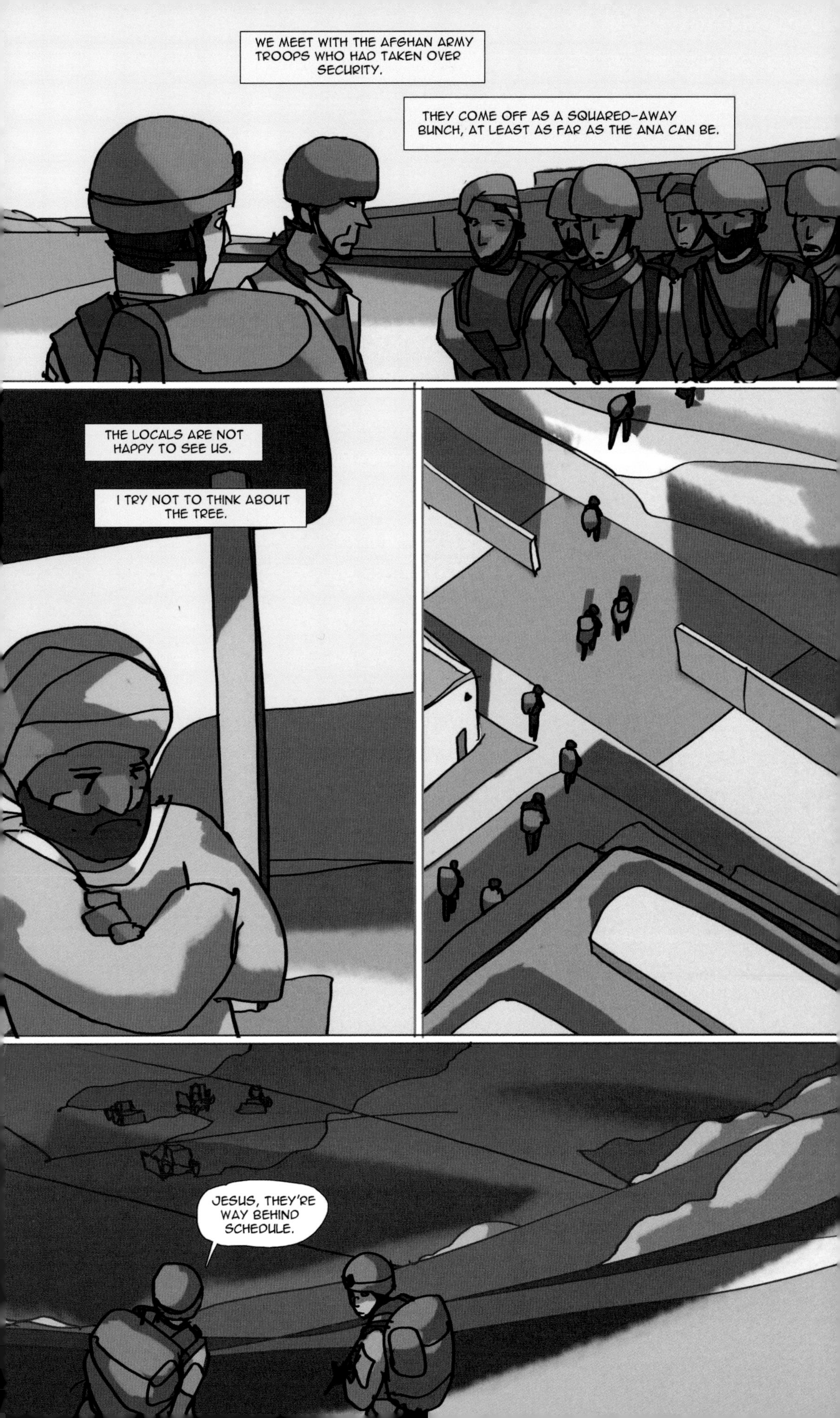
WE MEET WITH THE AFGHAN ARMY TROOPS WHO HAD TAKEN OVER SECURITY.
THEY COME OFF AS A SQUARED-AWAY BUNCH, AT LEAST AS FAR AS THE ANA CAN BE.
THE LOCALS ARE NOT HAPPY TO SEE US.
I TRY NOT TO THINK ABOUT THE TREE.
JESUS, THEY'RE WAY BEHIND SCHEDULE.

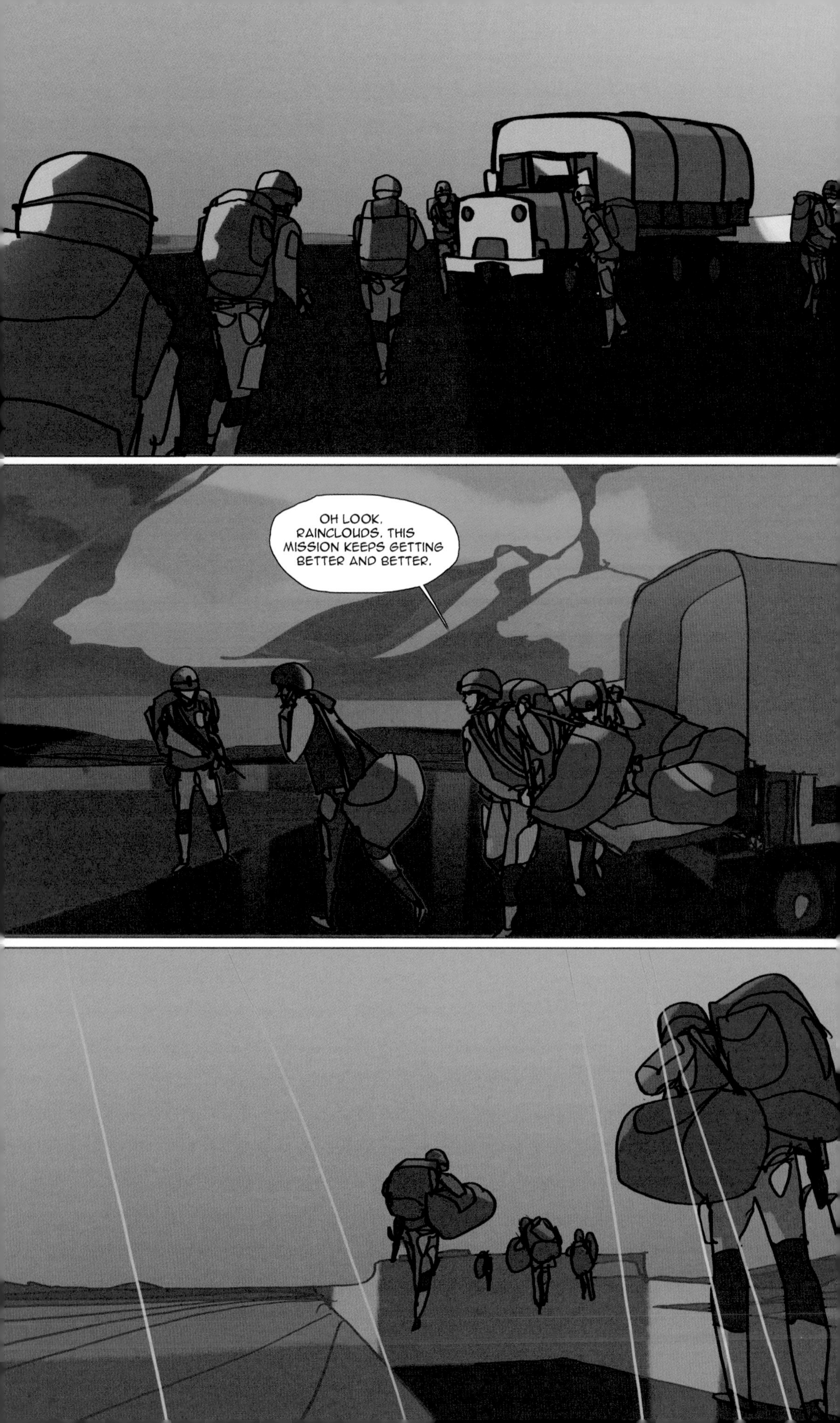
OH LOOK, RAINCLOUDS. THIS MISSION KEEPS GETTING BETTER AND BETTER.

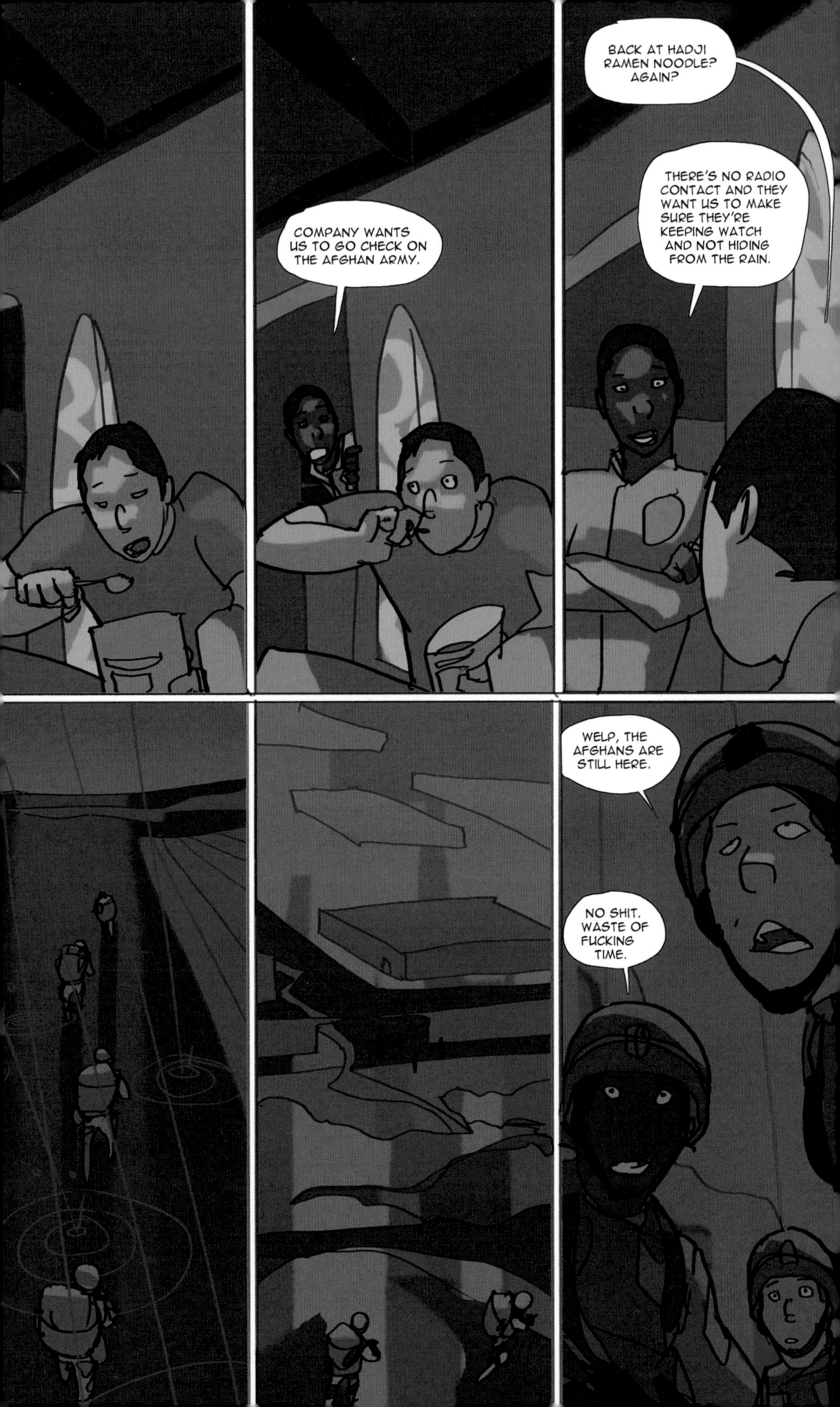
COMPANY WANTS US TO GO CHECK ON THE AFGHAN ARMY.
BACK AT HADJI RAMEN NOODLE? AGAIN?
THERE'S NO RADIO CONTACT AND THEY WANT US TO MAKE SURE THEY'RE KEEPING WATCH AND NOT HIDING FROM THE RAIN.
WELP, THE AFGHANS ARE STILL HERE.
NO SHIT. WASTE OF FUCKING TIME.

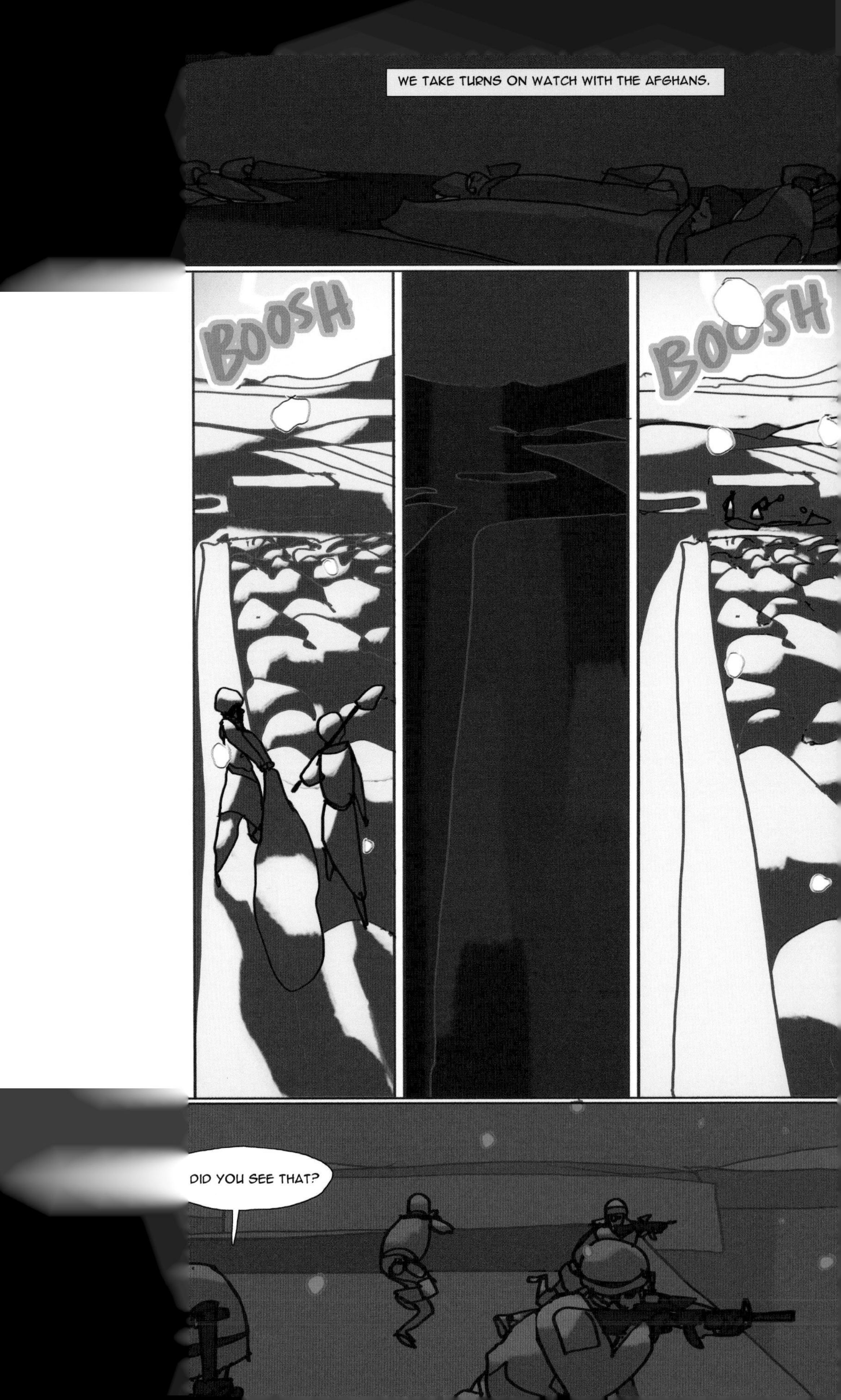
WE TAKE TURNS ON WATCH WITH THE AFGHANS.
BOOSH
BOOSH
DID YOU SEE THAT?

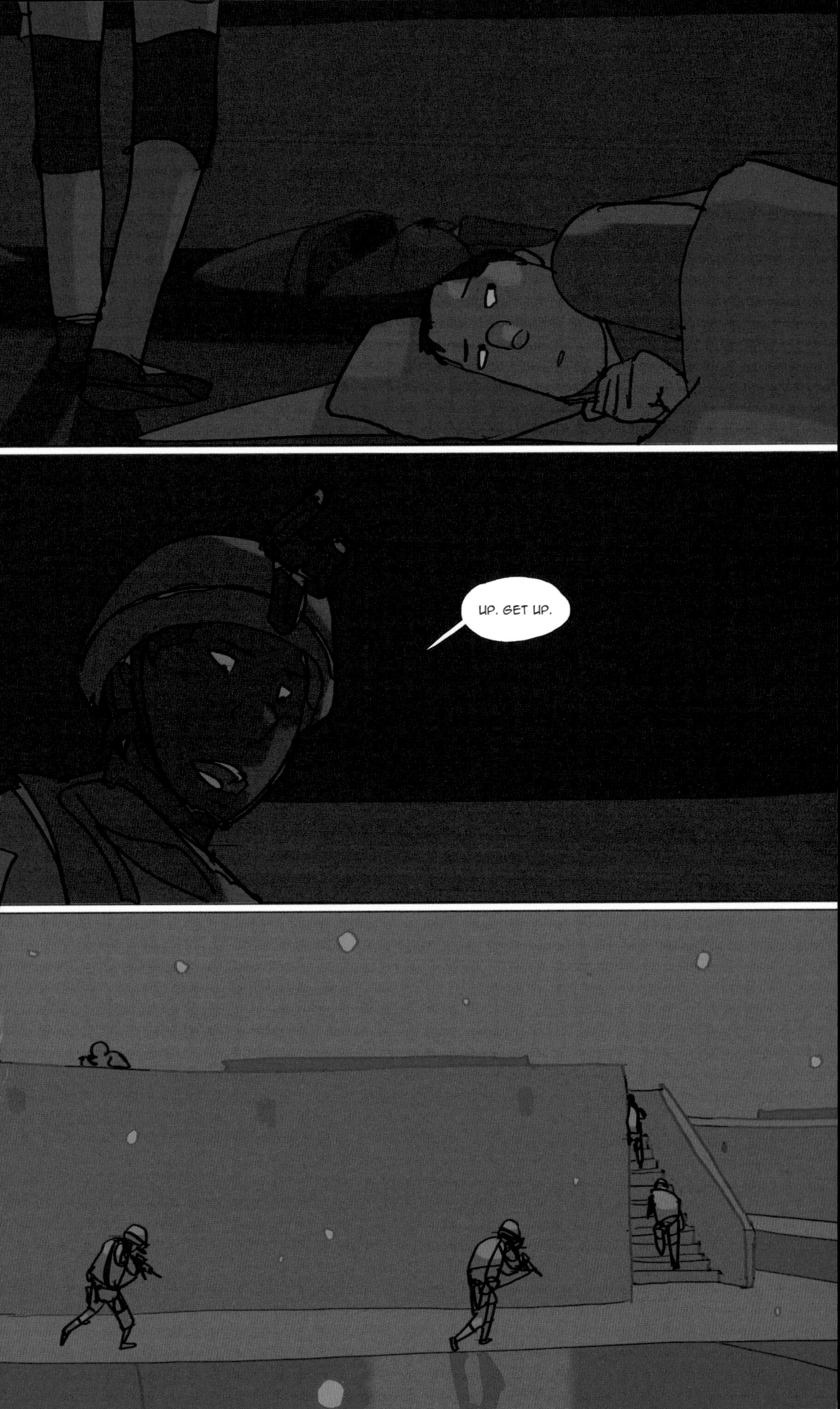
UP. GET UP.

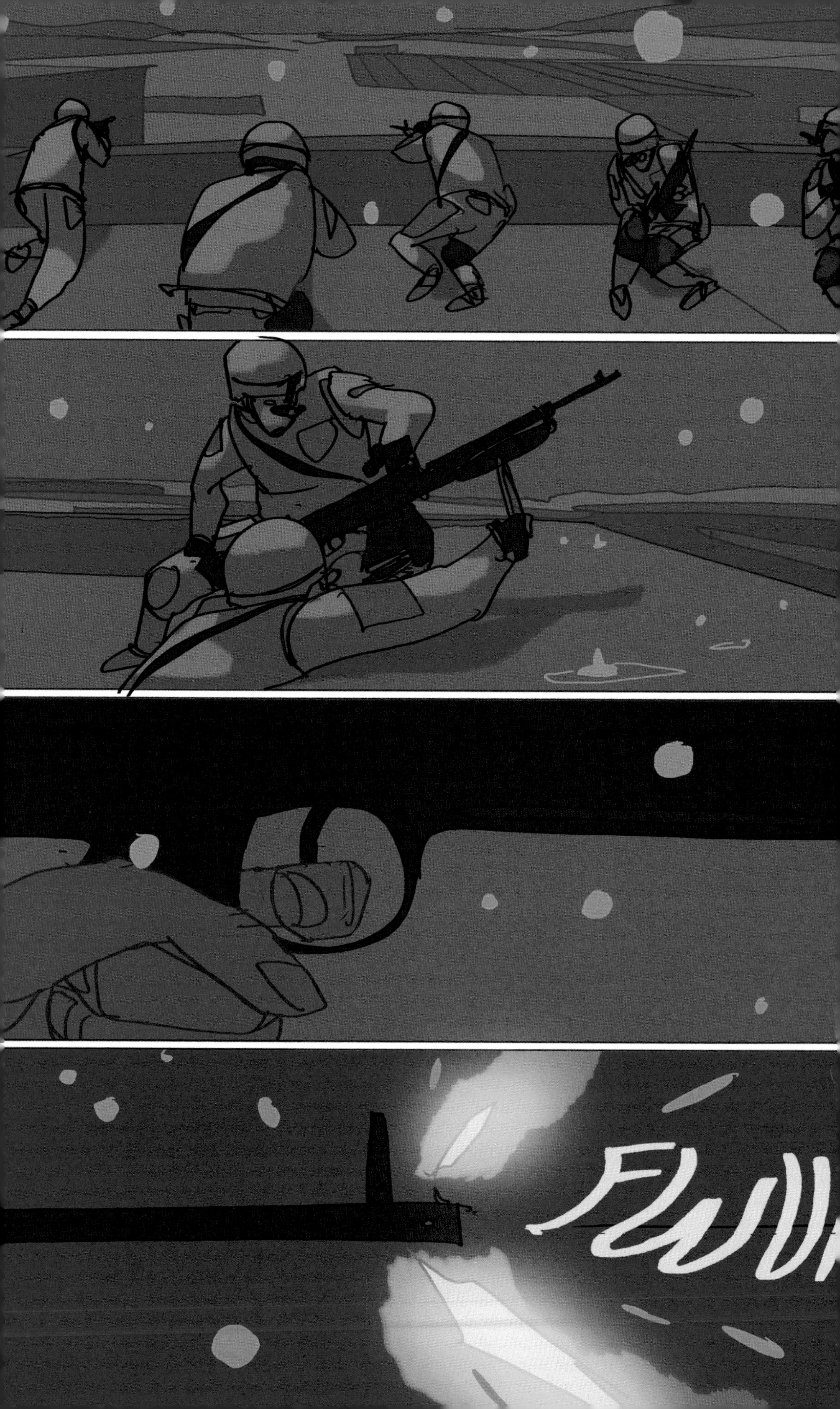
FLW

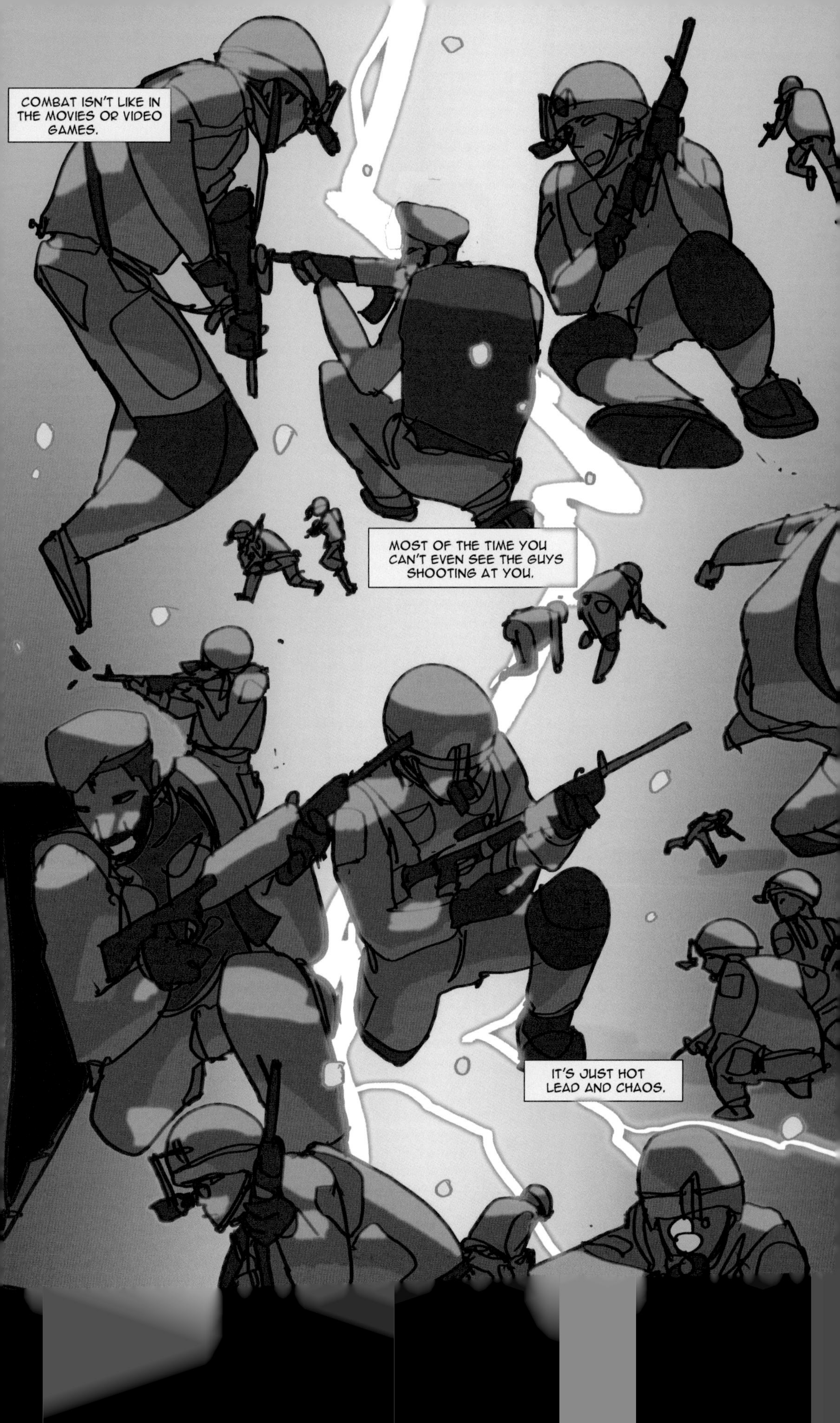
COMBAT ISN'T LIKE IN THE MOVIES OR VIDEO GAMES.
MOST OF THE TIME YOU CAN'T EVEN SEE THE GUYS SHOOTING AT YOU.
IT'S JUST HOT LEAD AND CHAOS.

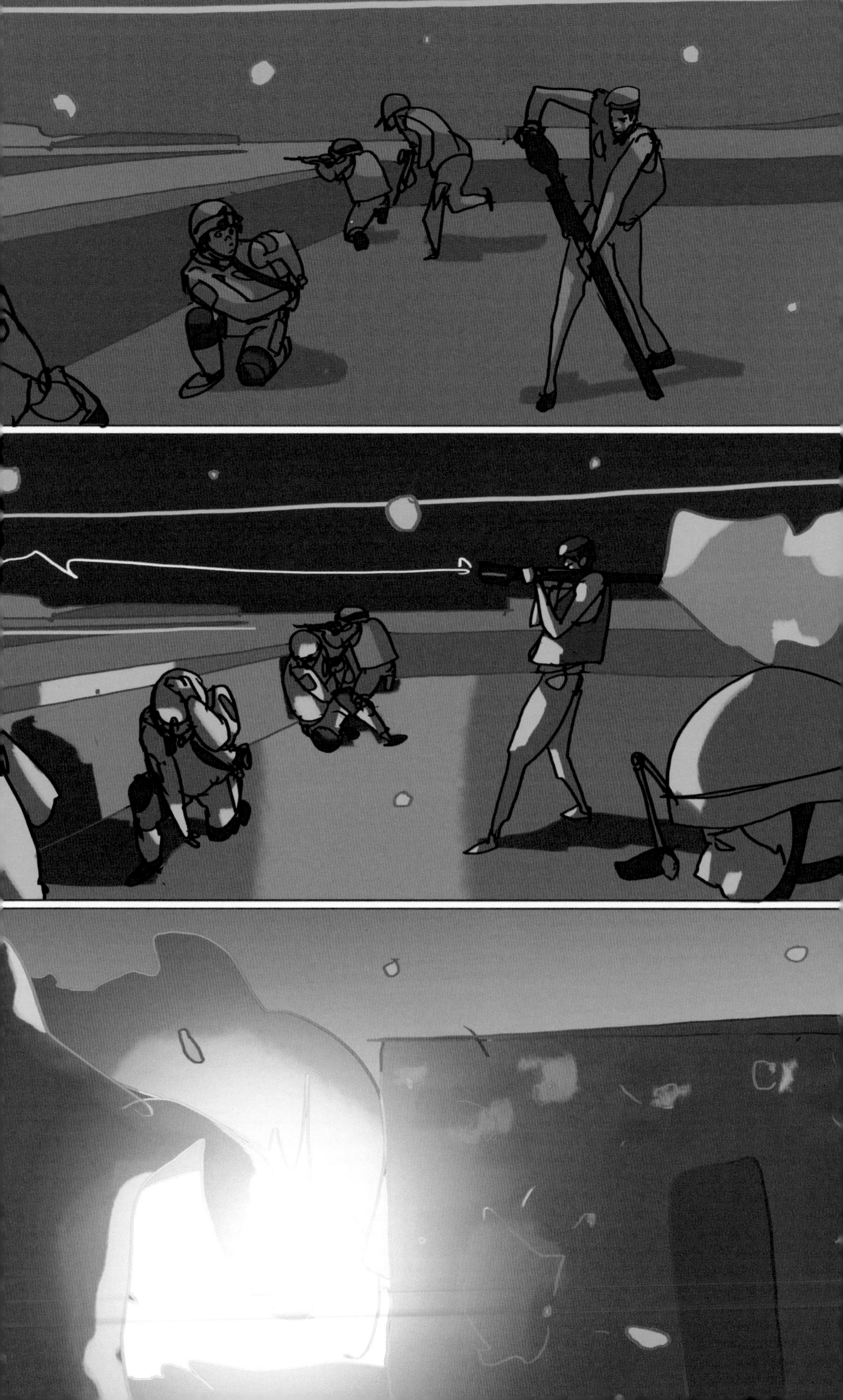

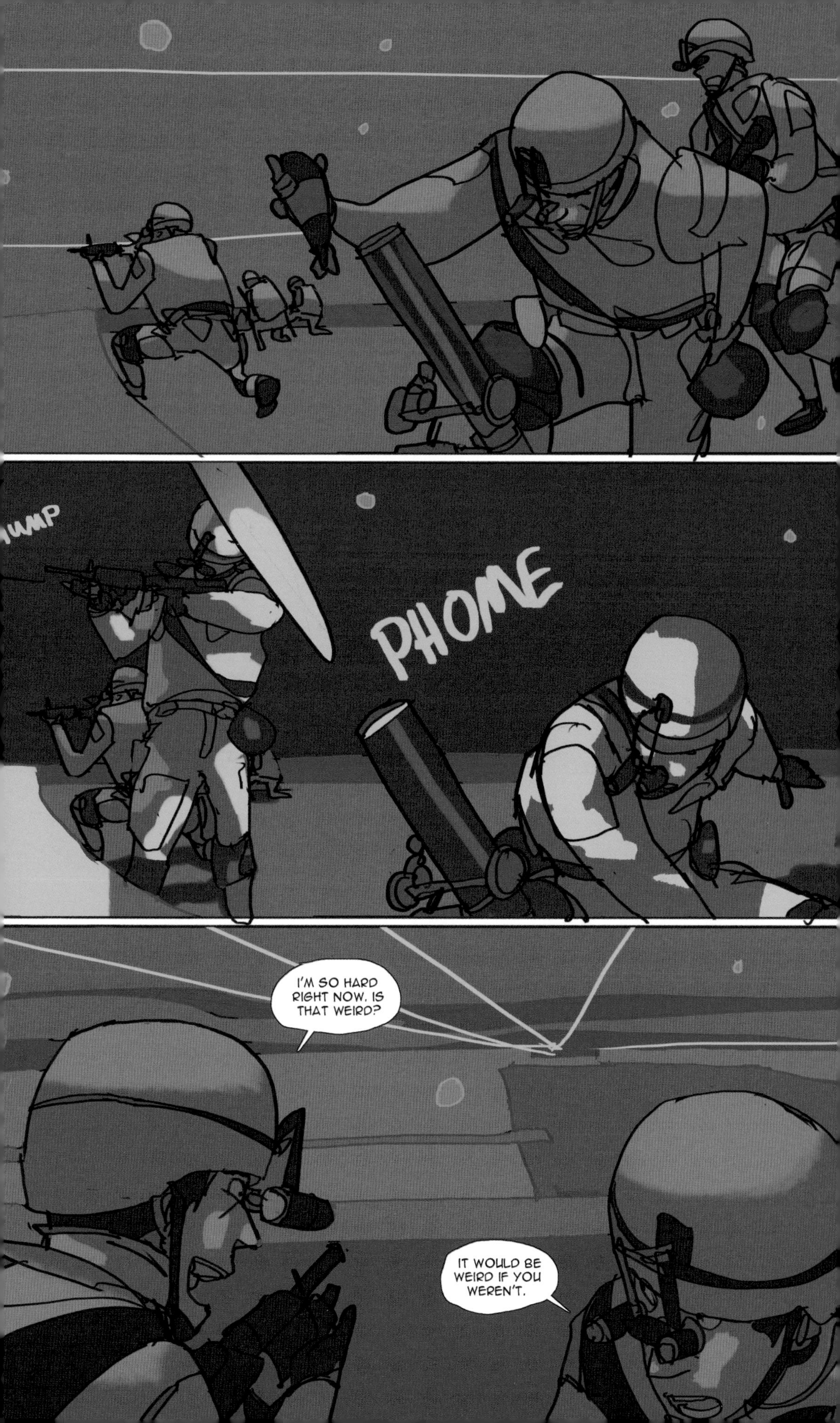

UMP
PHOME
I'M SO HARD RIGHT NOW. IS THAT WEIRD?
IT WOULD BE WEIRD IF YOU WEREN'T.

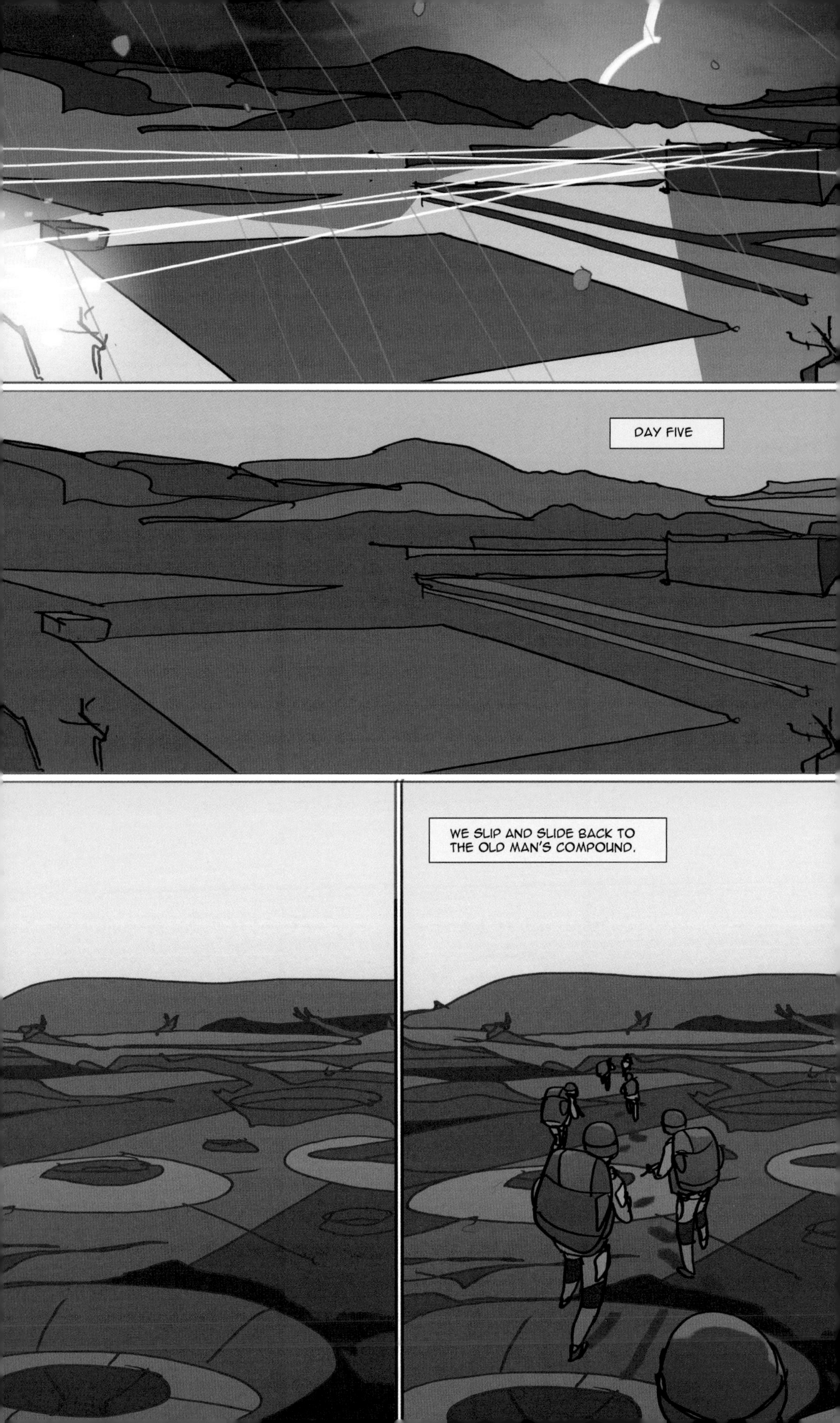
DAY FIVE
WE SLIP AND SLIDE BACK TO THE OLD MAN'S COMPOUND.

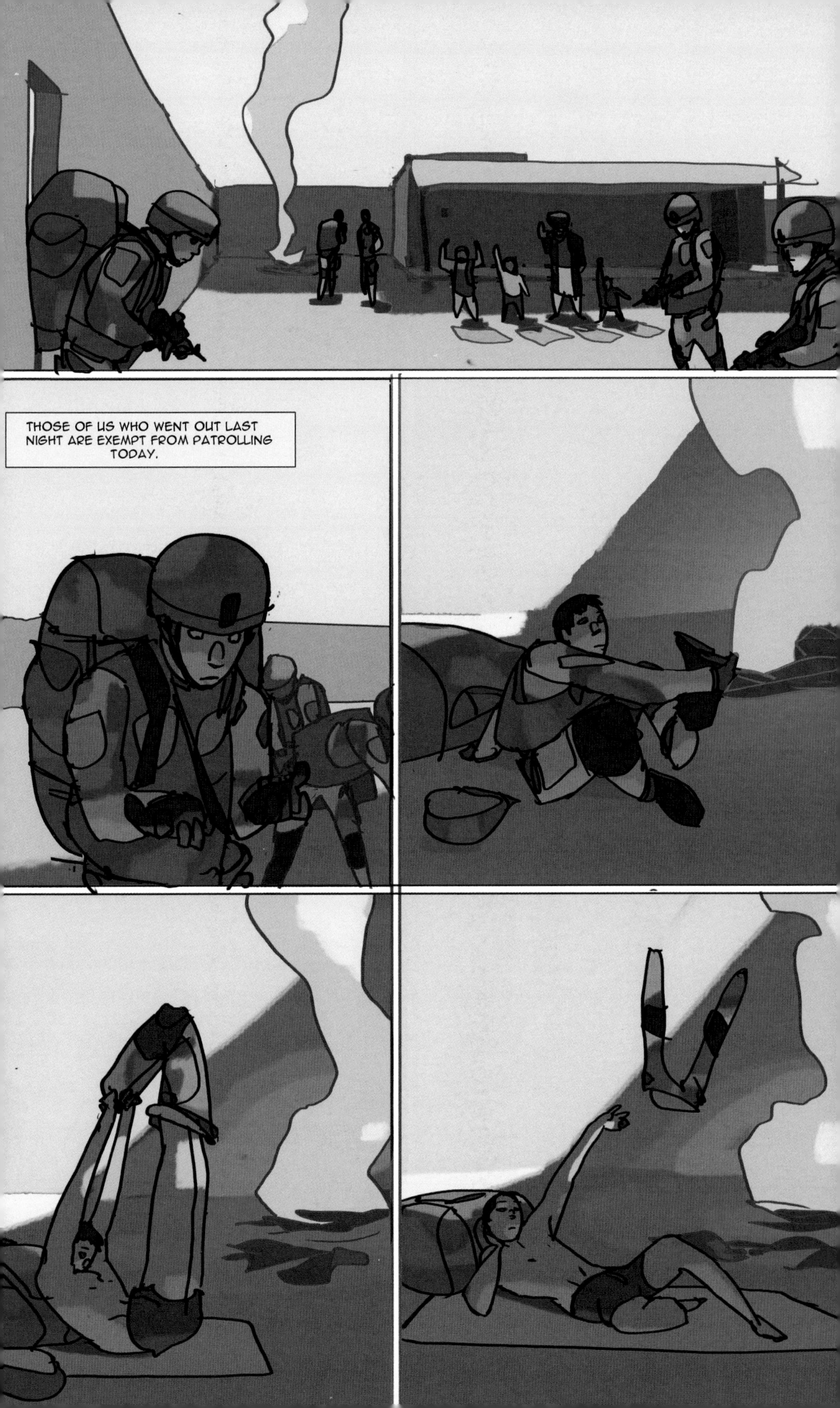
THOSE OF US WHO WENT OUT LAST NIGHT ARE EXEMPT FROM PATROLLING TODAY.

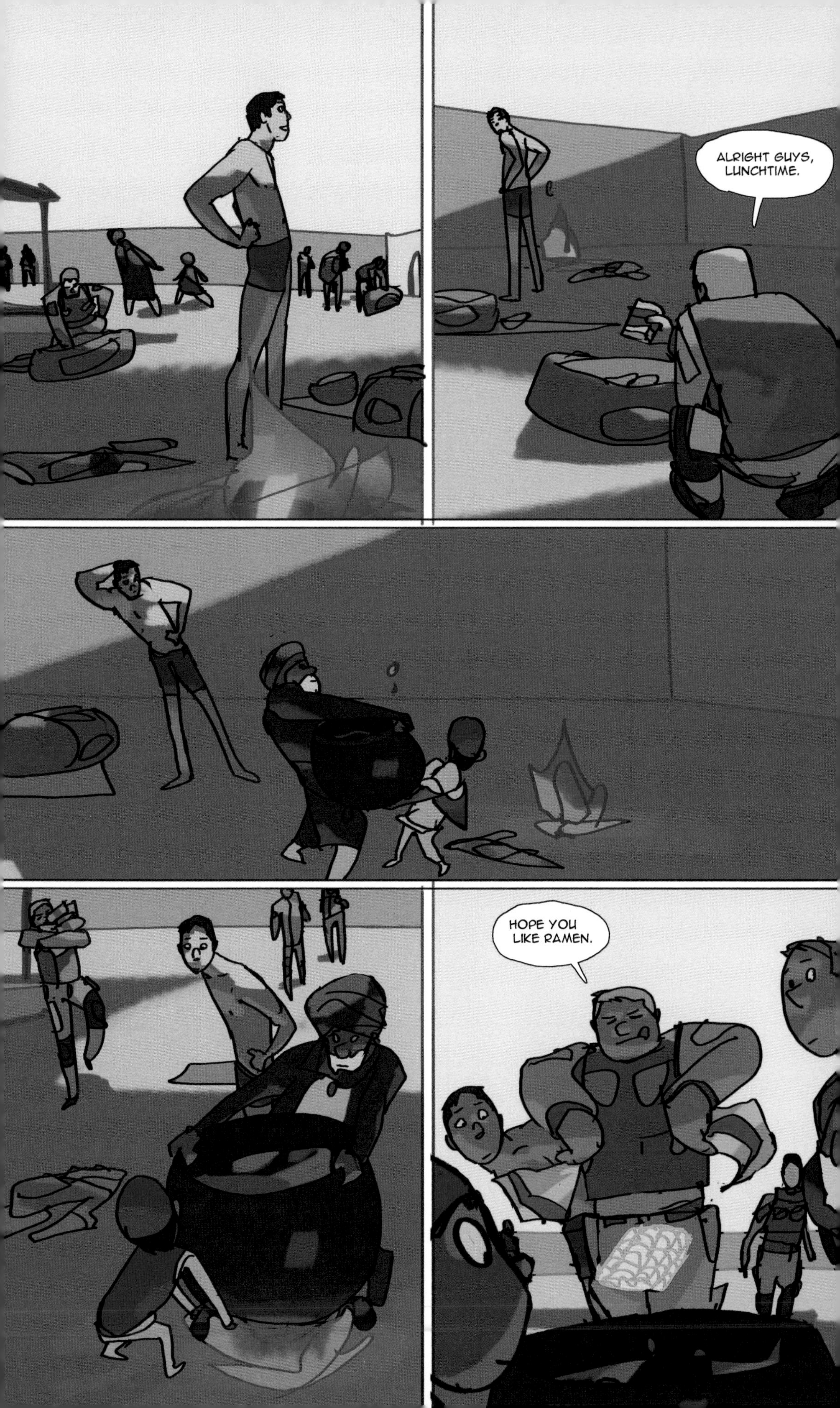
ALRIGHT GUYS, LUNCHTIME.
HOPE YOU LIKE RAMEN.

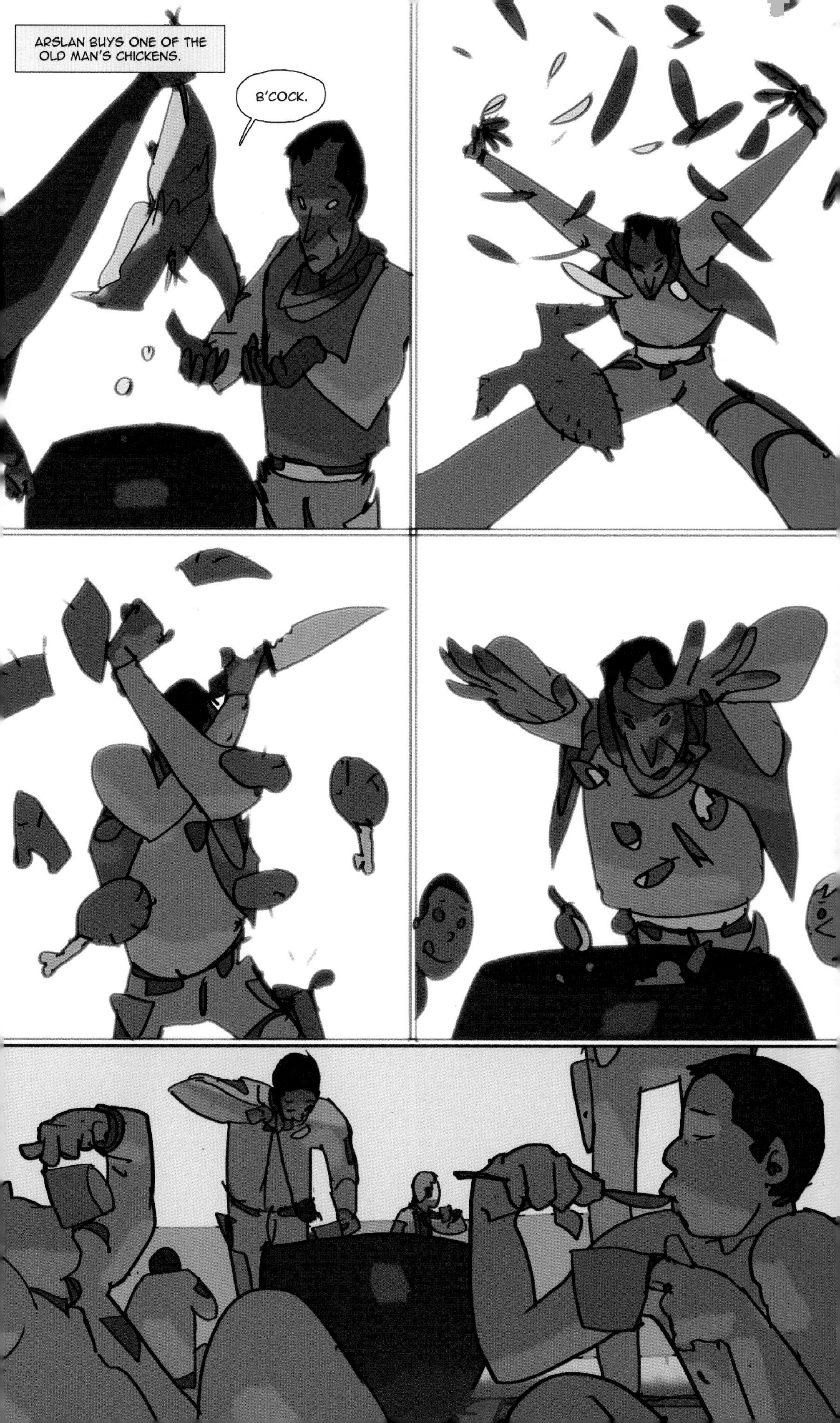
ARSLAN BUYS ONE OF THE OLD MAN'S CHICKENS.
B'COCK.

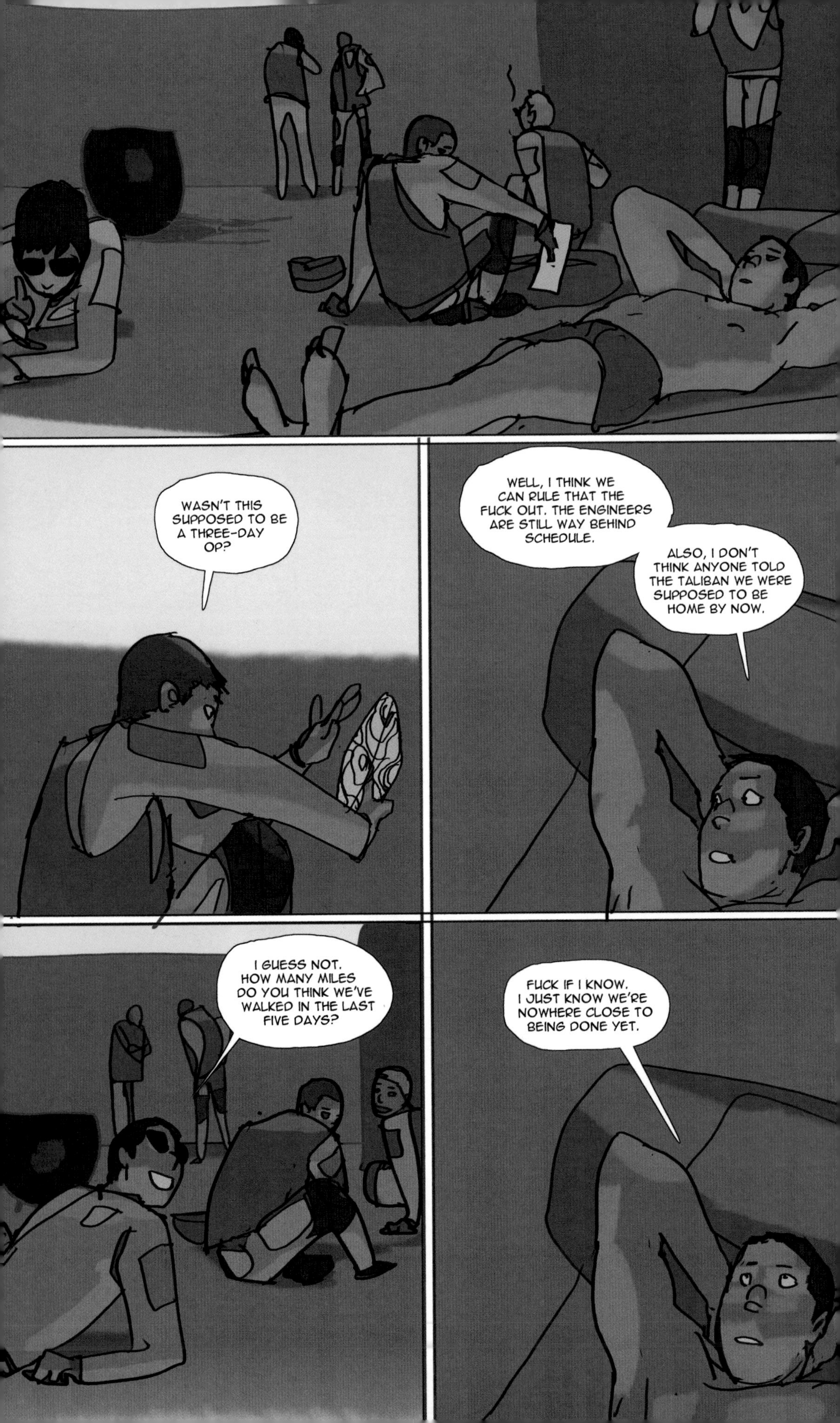
WASN'T THIS SUPPOSED TO BE A THREE-DAY OP?
WELL, I THINK WE CAN RULE THAT THE FUCK OUT. THE ENGINEERS ARE STILL WAY BEHIND SCHEDULE.
ALSO, I DON'T THINK ANYONE TOLD THE TALIBAN WE WERE SUPPOSED TO BE HOME BY NOW.
I GUESS NOT. HOW MANY MILES DO YOU THINK WE'VE WALKED IN THE LAST FIVE DAYS?
FUCK IF I KNOW. I JUST KNOW WE'RE NOWHERE CLOSE TO BEING DONE YET.

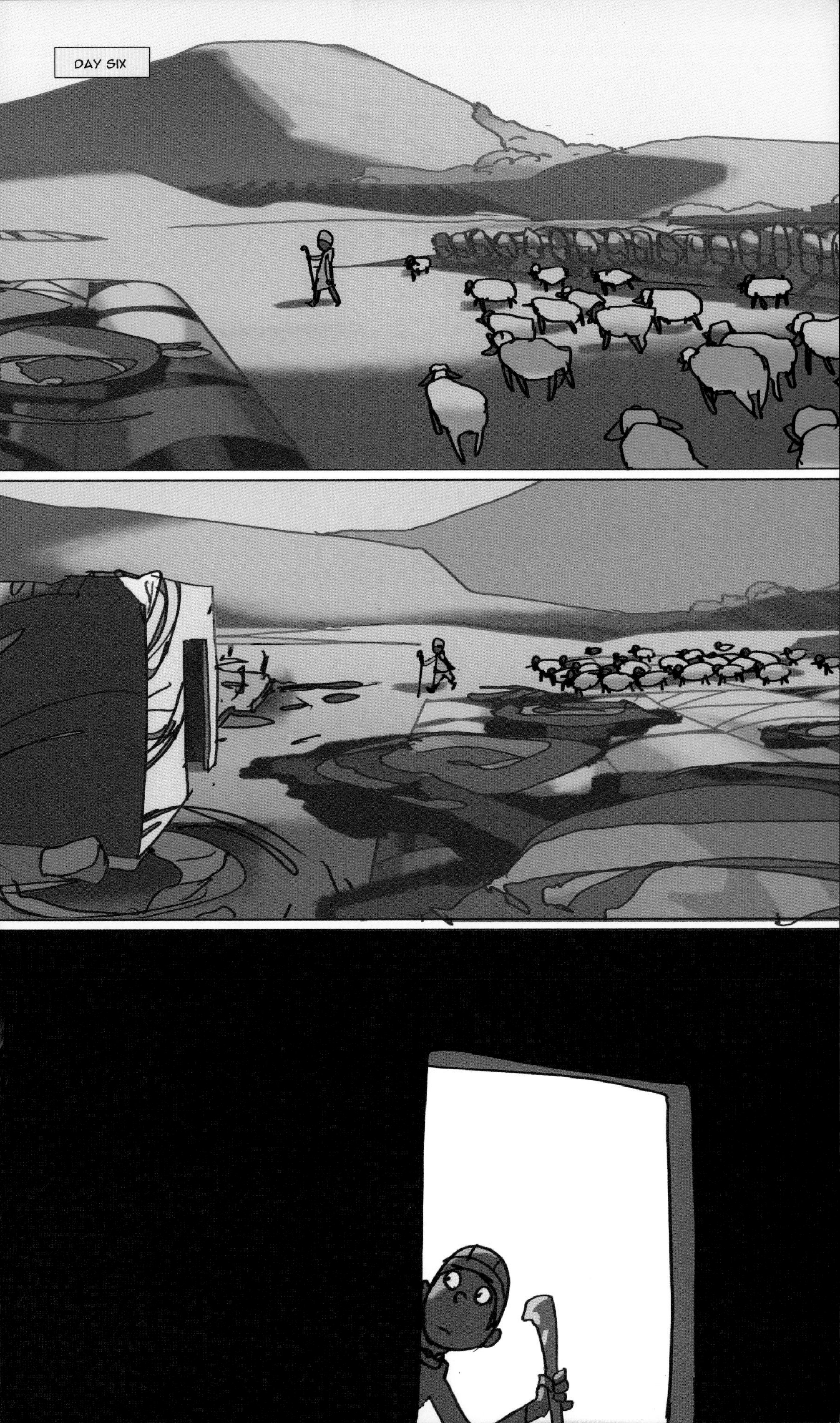
DAY SIX

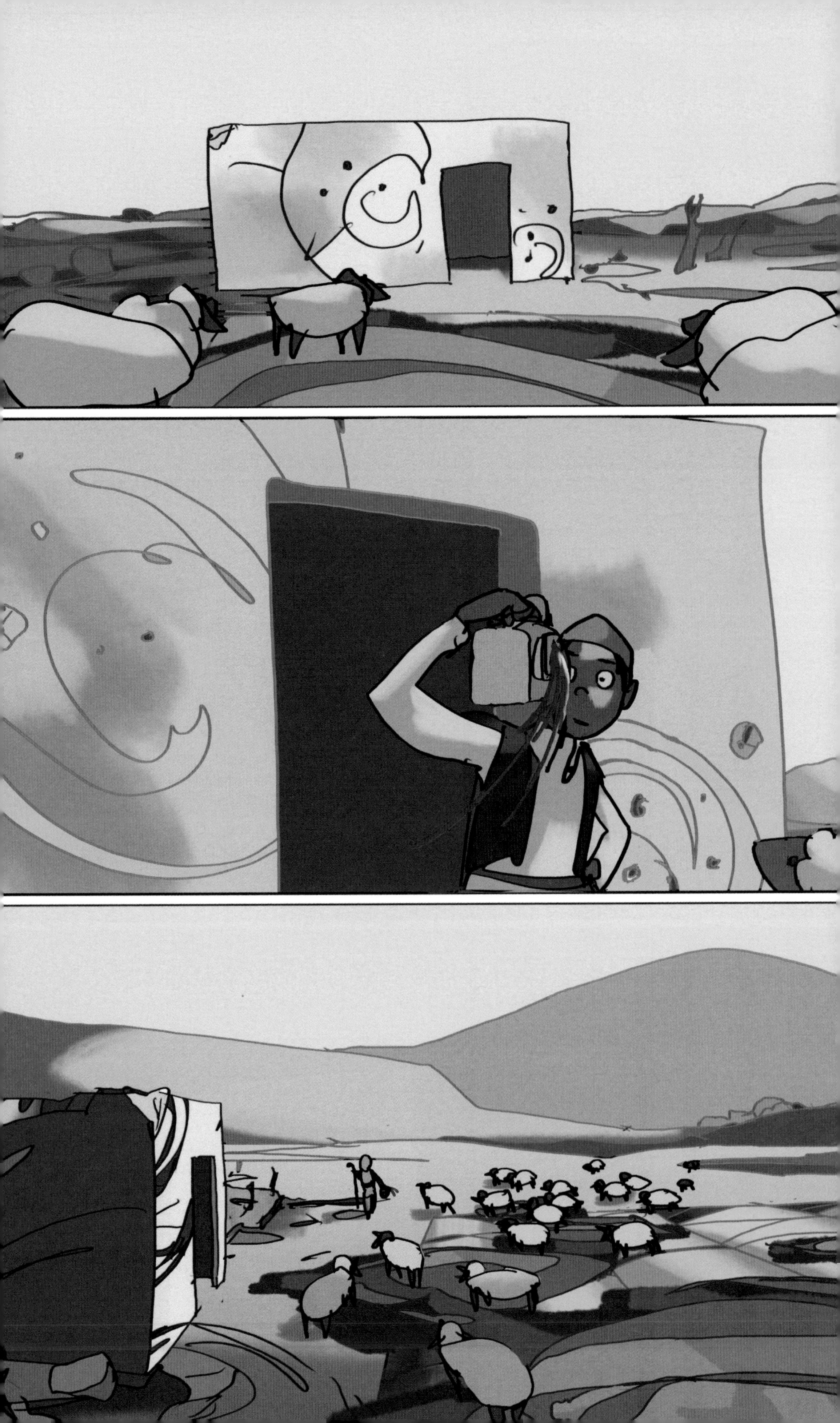

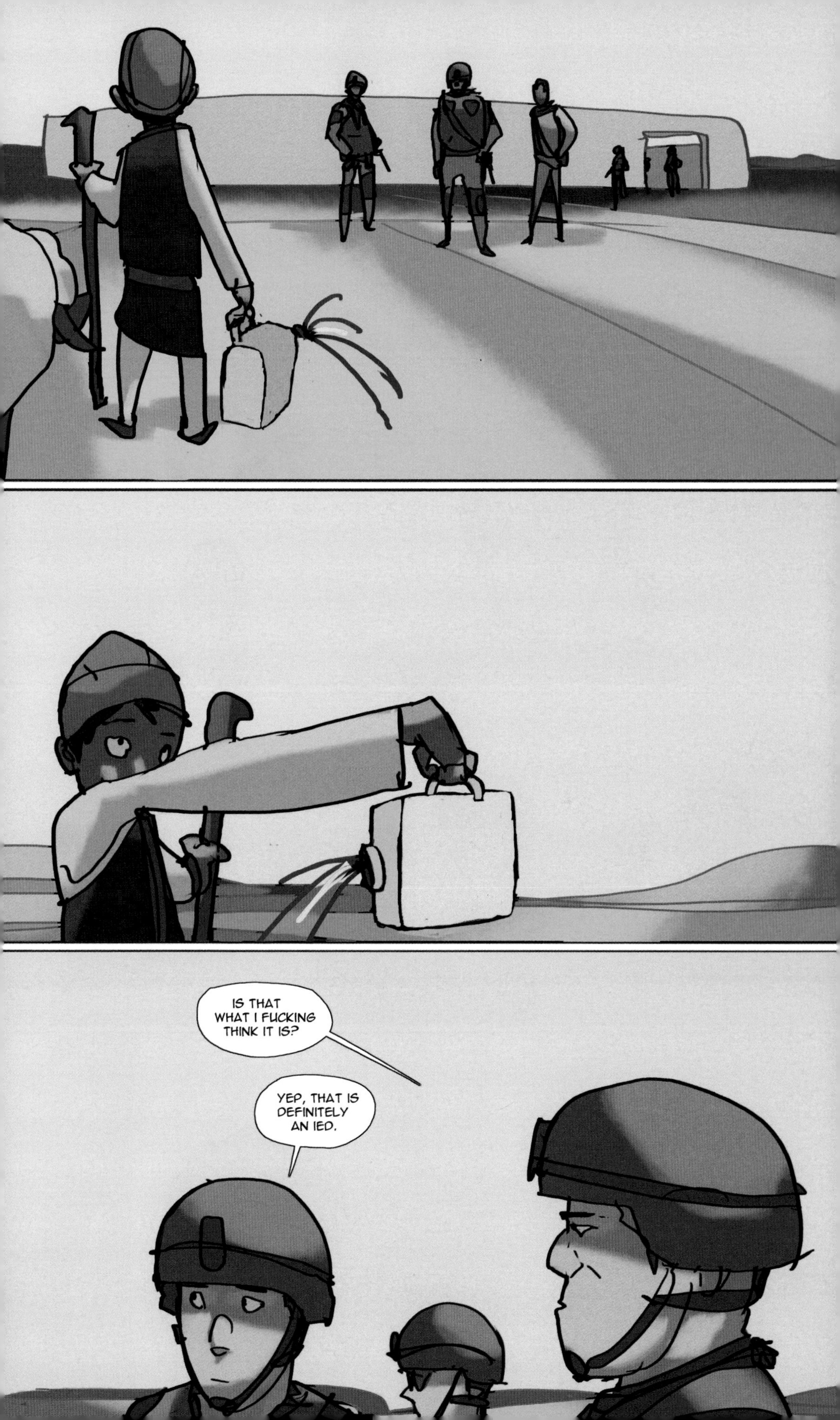
IS THAT WHAT I FUCKING THINK IT IS?
YEP, THAT IS DEFINITELY AN IED.

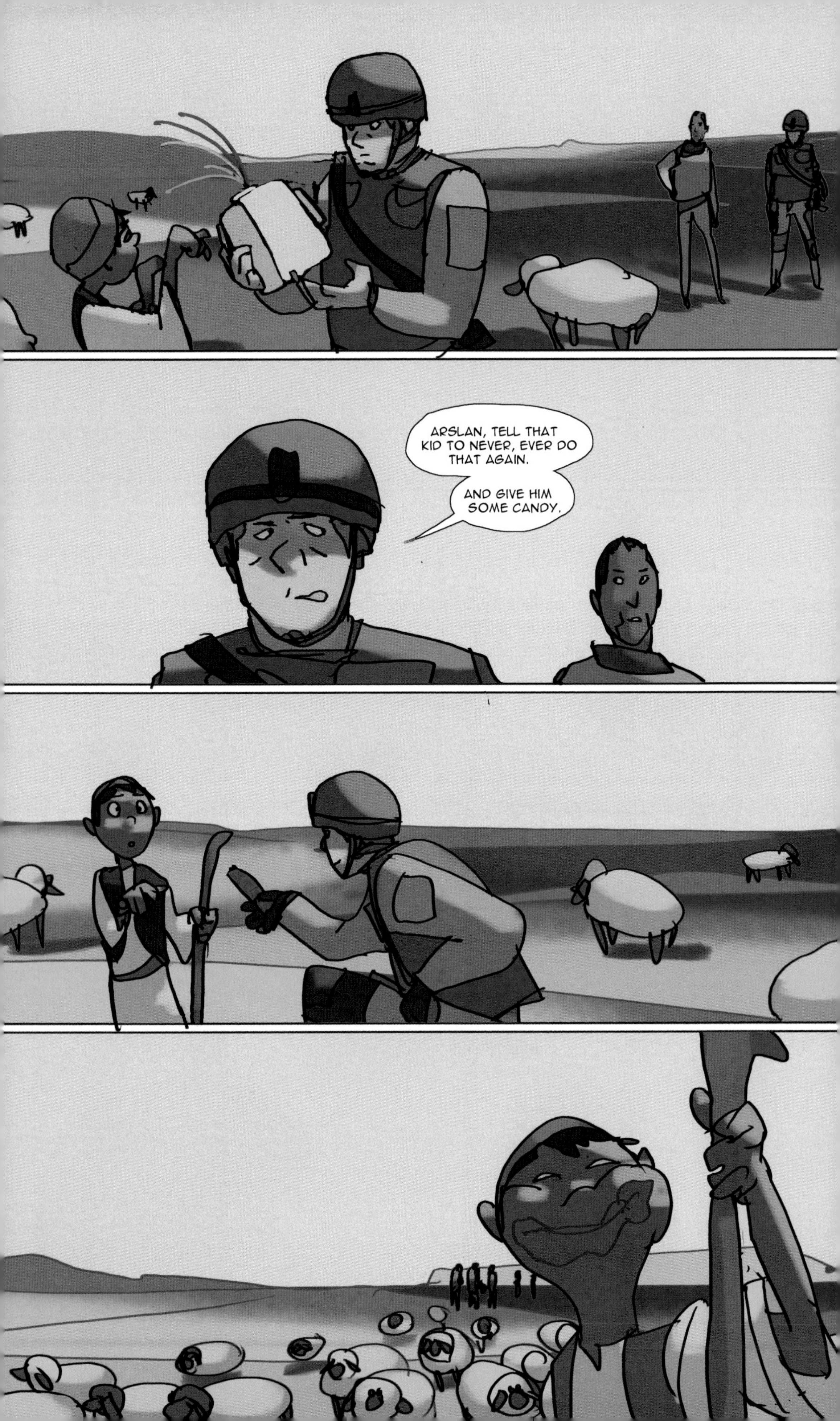
ARSLAN, TELL THAT KID TO NEVER, EVER DO THAT AGAIN.
AND GIVE HIM SOME CANDY.

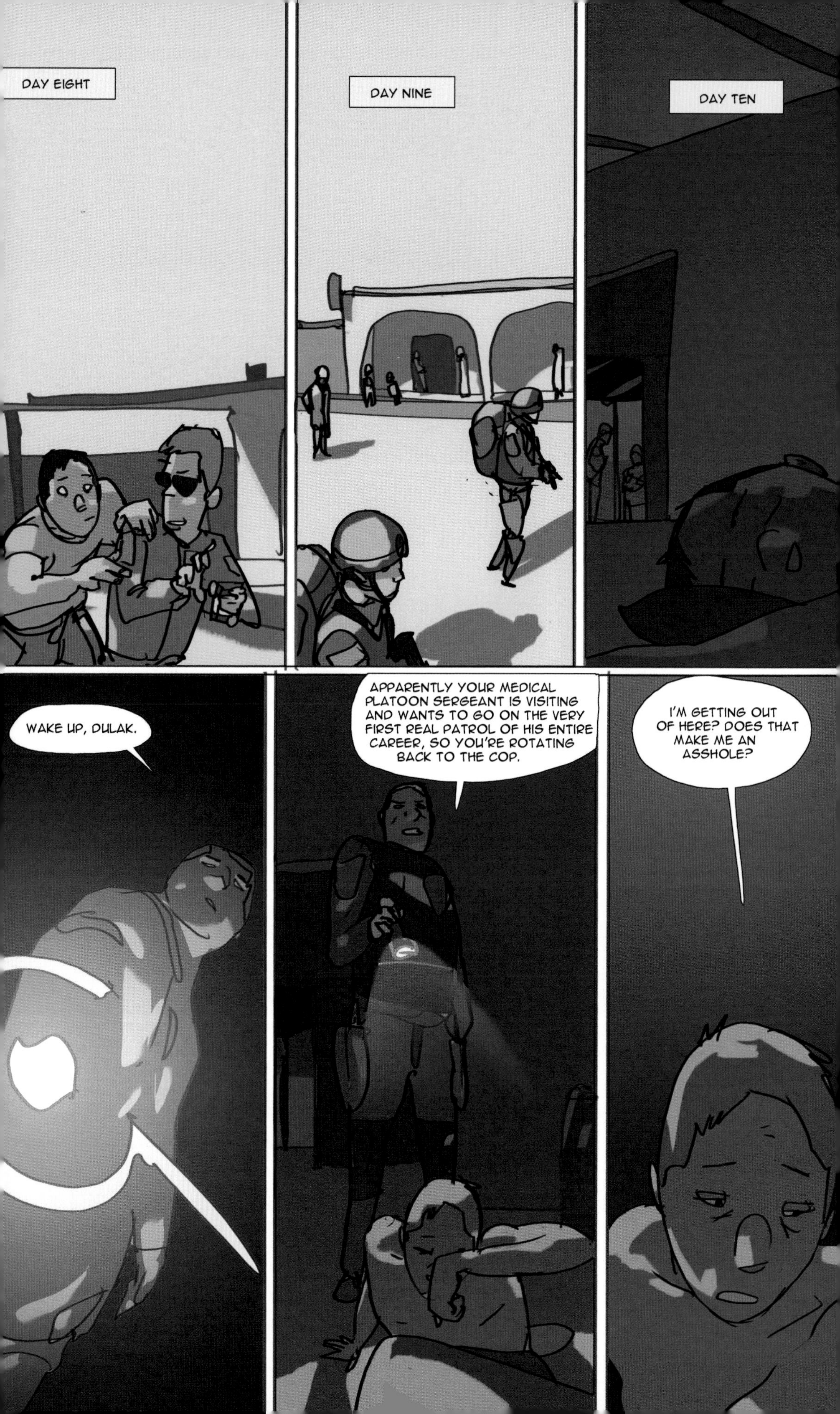
DAY EIGHT
DAY NINE
DAY TEN
WAKE UP, DULAK.
APPARENTLY YOUR MEDICAL PLATOON SERGEANT IS VISITING AND WANTS TO GO ON THE VERY FIRST REAL PATROL OF HIS ENTIRE CAREER, SO YOU'RE ROTATING BACK TO THE COP.
I'M GETTING OUT OF HERE? DOES THAT MAKE ME AN ASSHOLE?

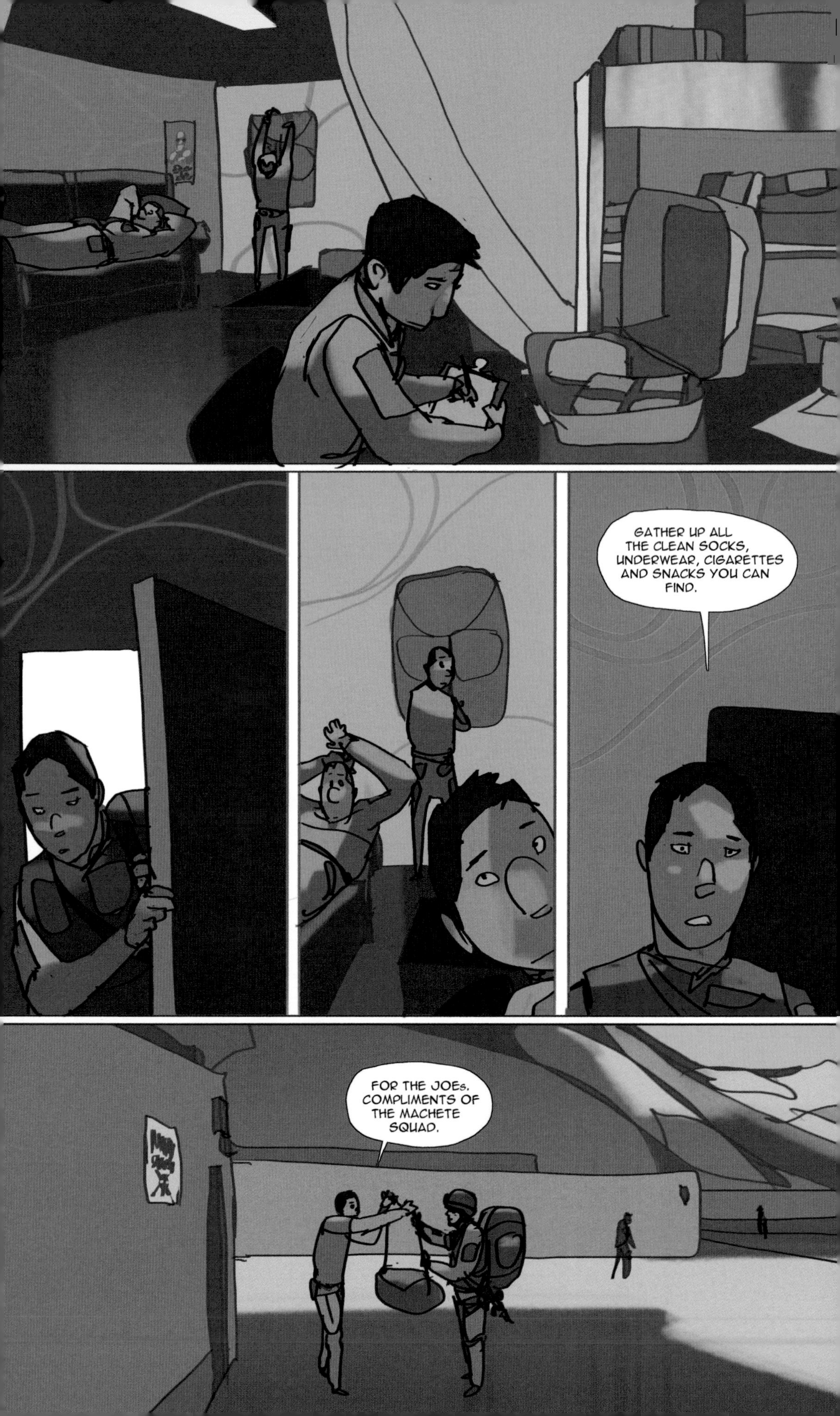
GATHER UP ALL THE CLEAN SOCKS, UNDERWEAR, CIGARETTES AND SNACKS YOU CAN FIND.
FOR THE JOEs. COMPLIMENTS OF THE MACHETE SQUAD.

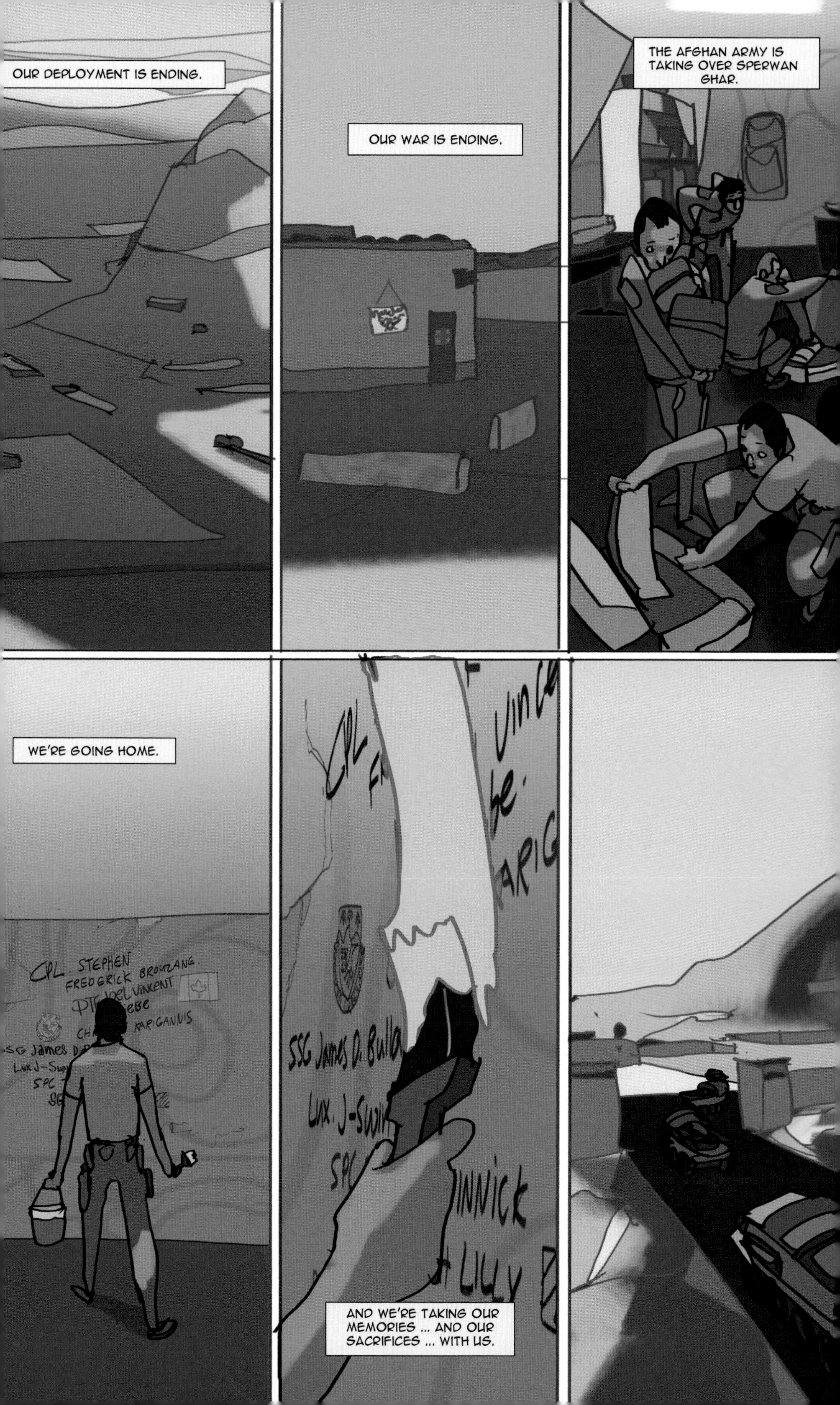
OUR DEPLOYMENT IS ENDING.
OUR WAR IS ENDING.
THE AFGHAN ARMY IS TAKING OVER SPERWAN GHAR.
WE'RE GOING HOME.
AND WE'RE TAKING OUR MEMORIES ... AND OUR SACRIFICES ... WITH US.

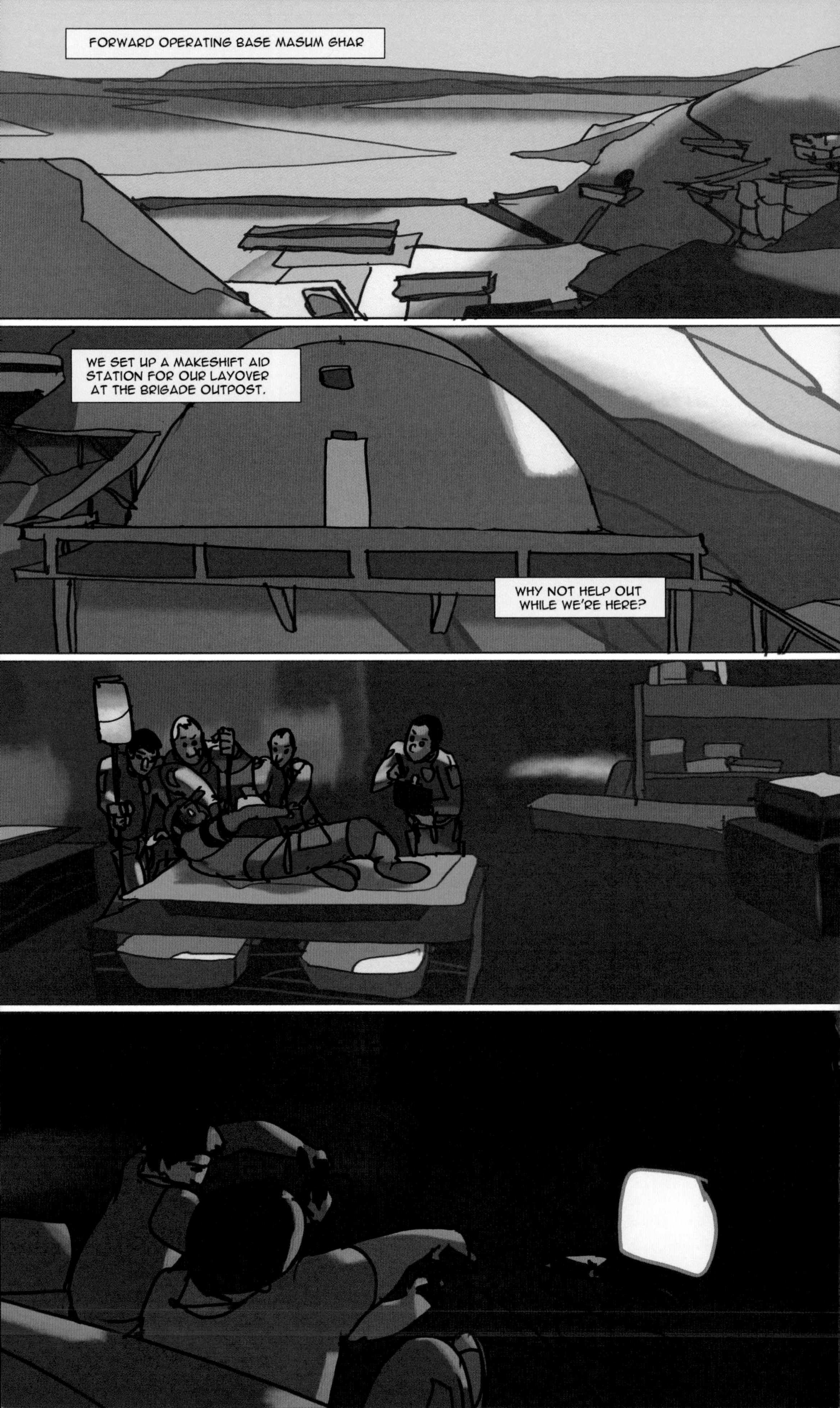
FORWARD OPERATING BASE MASUM GHAR
WE SET UP A MAKESHIFT AID STATION FOR OUR LAYOVER AT THE BRIGADE OUTPOST.
WHY NOT HELP OUT WHILE WE'RE HERE?

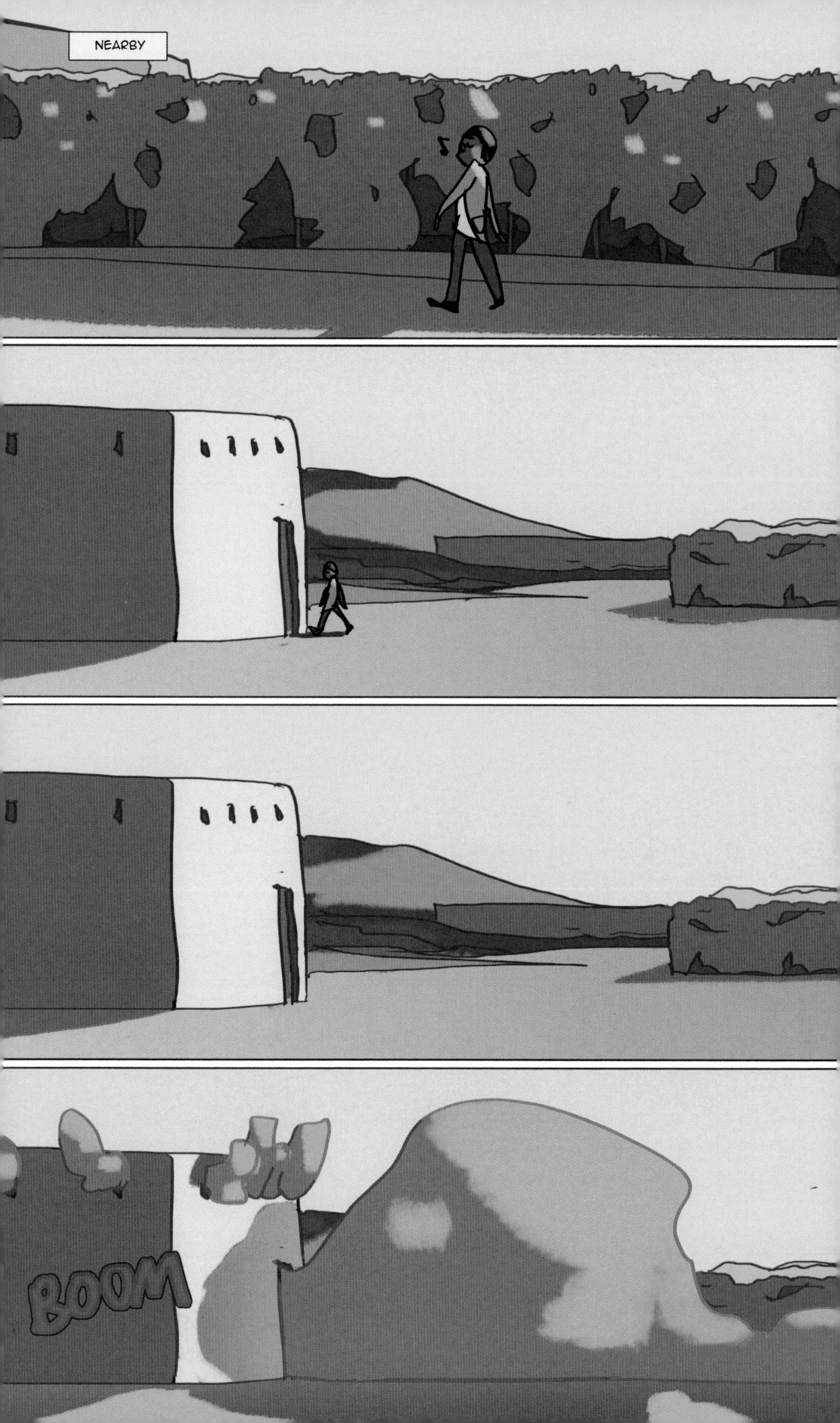
NEARBY
BOOM

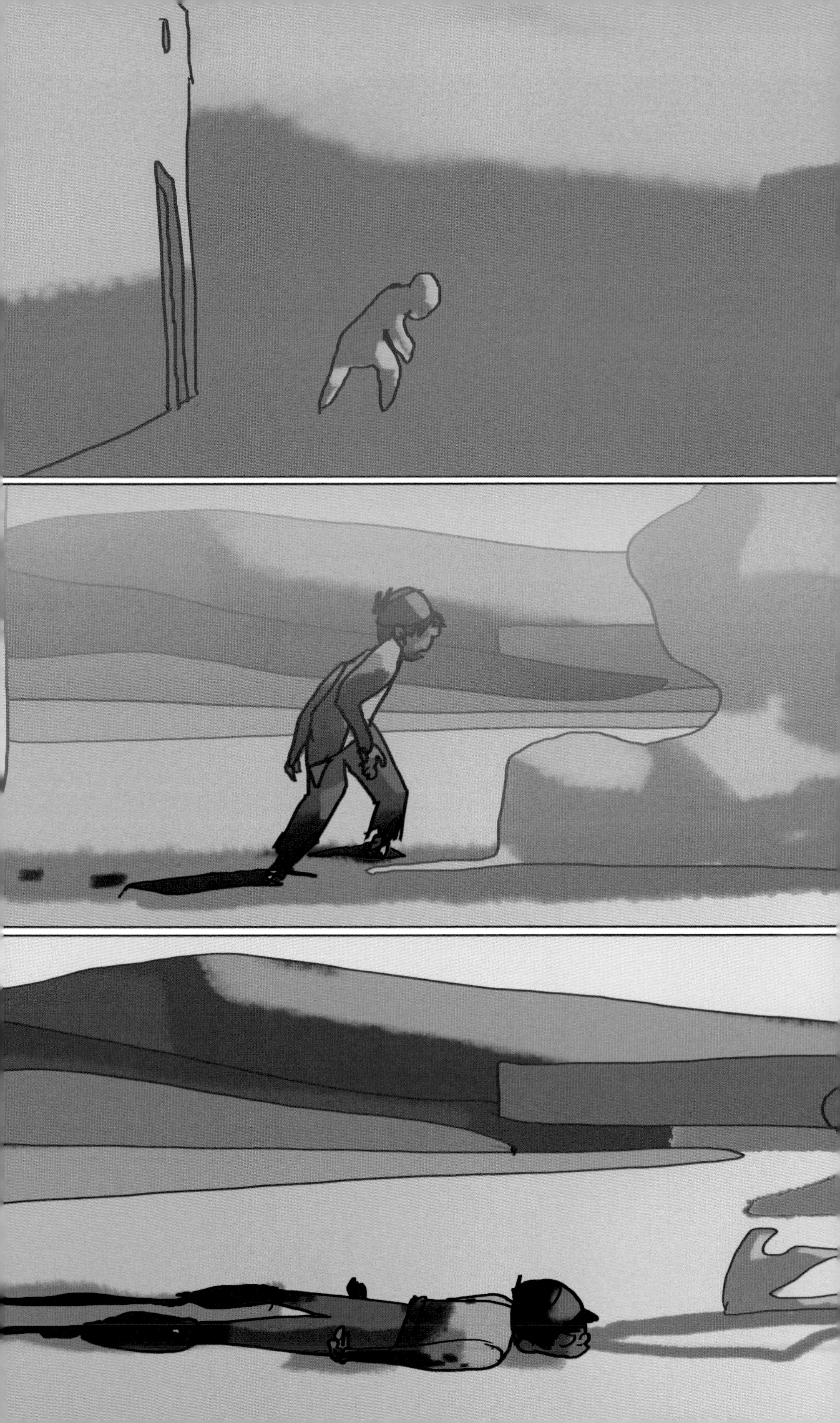

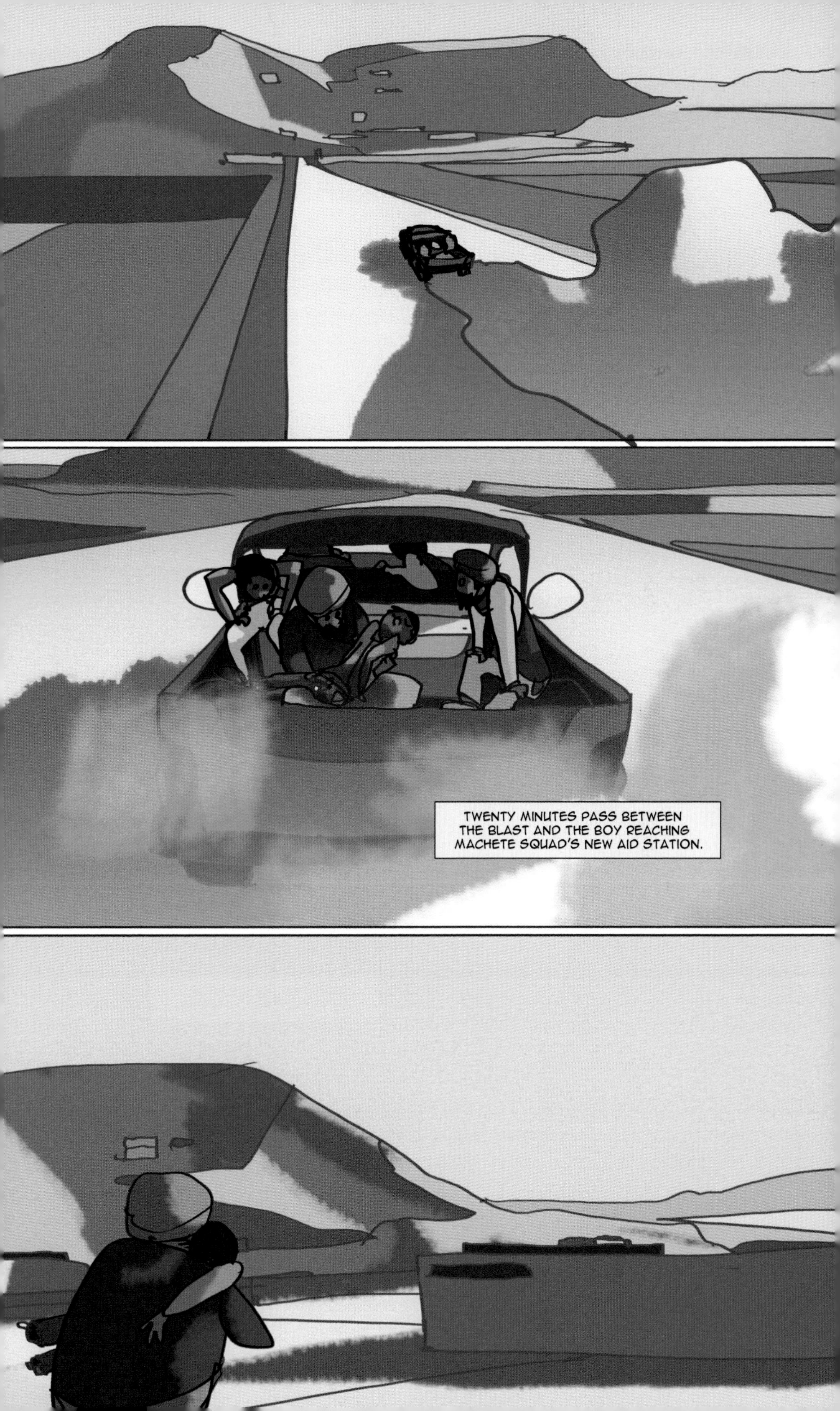
TWENTY MINUTES PASS BETWEEN THE BLAST AND THE BOY REACHING MACHETE SQUAD'S NEW AID STATION.

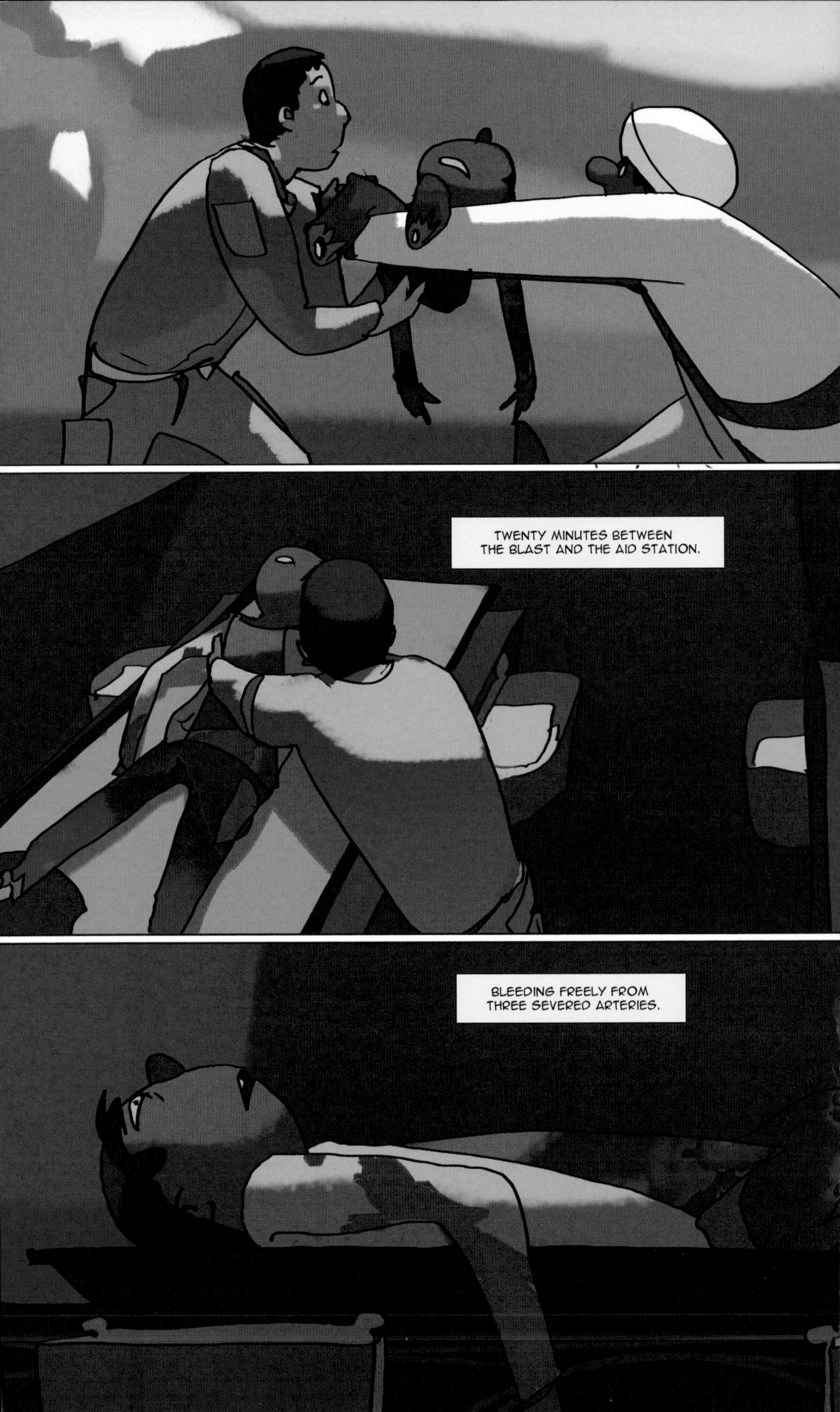
TWENTY MINUTES BETWEEN THE BLAST AND THE AID STATION.
BLEEDING FREELY FROM THREE SEVERED ARTERIES.

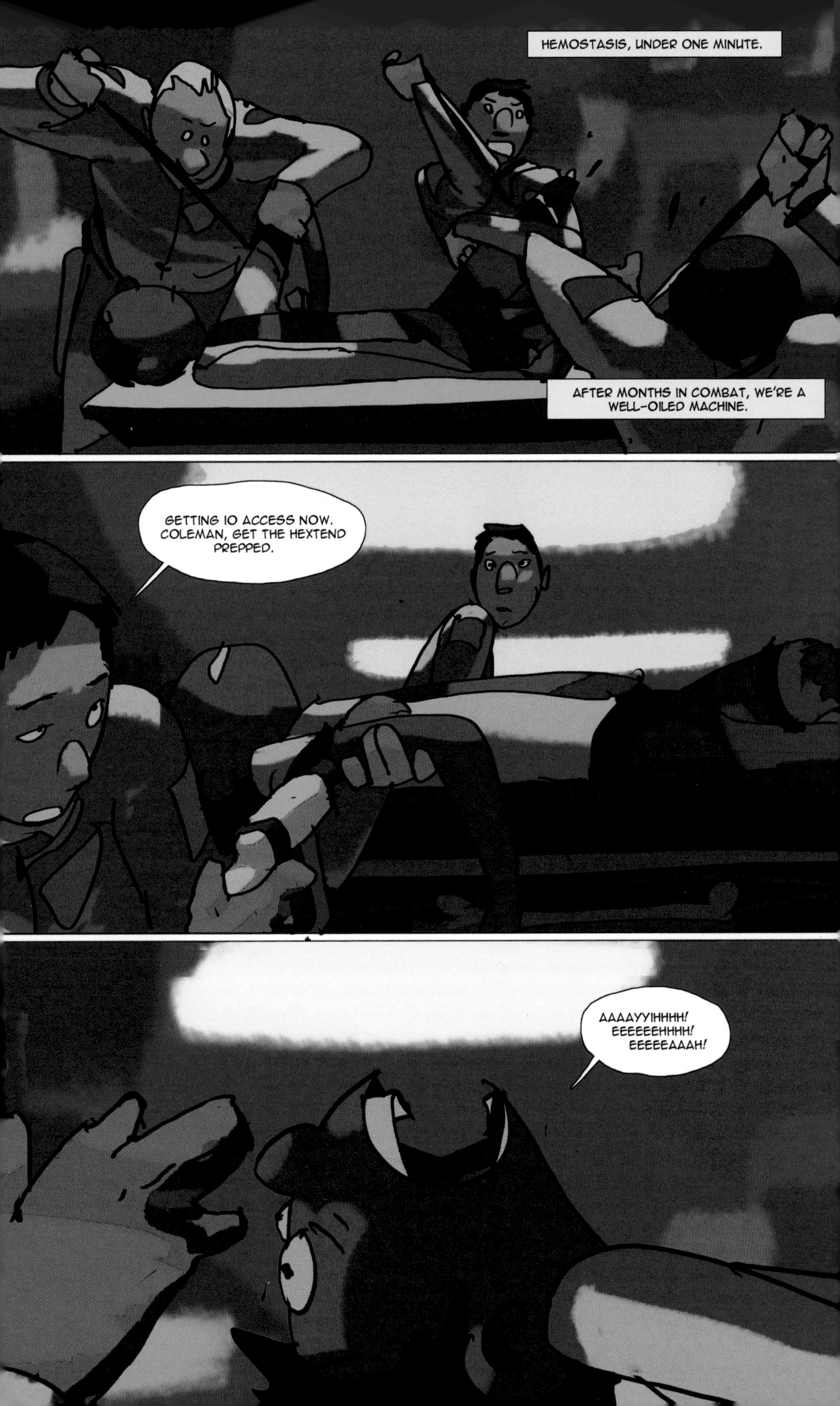
HEMOSTASIS, UNDER ONE MINUTE.
AFTER MONTHS IN COMBAT, WE'RE A WELL-OILED MACHINE.
GETTING IO ACCESS NOW. COLEMAN, GET THE HEXTEND PREPPED.
AAAAYYIHHHH! EEEEEEHHHH! EEEEEAAAH!

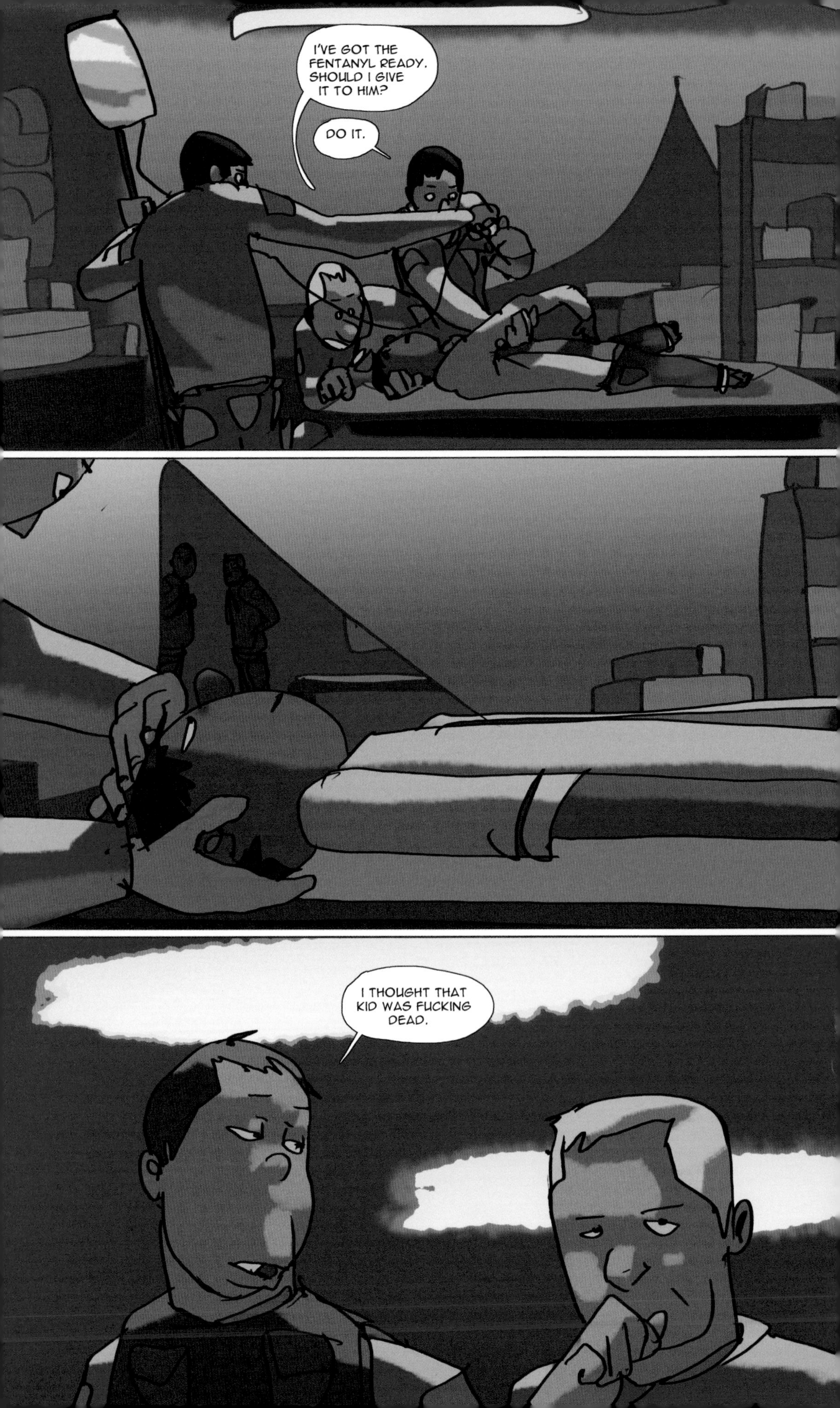
I'VE GOT THE FENTANYL READY. SHOULD I GIVE IT TO HIM?
DO IT.
I THOUGHT THAT KID WAS FUCKING DEAD.

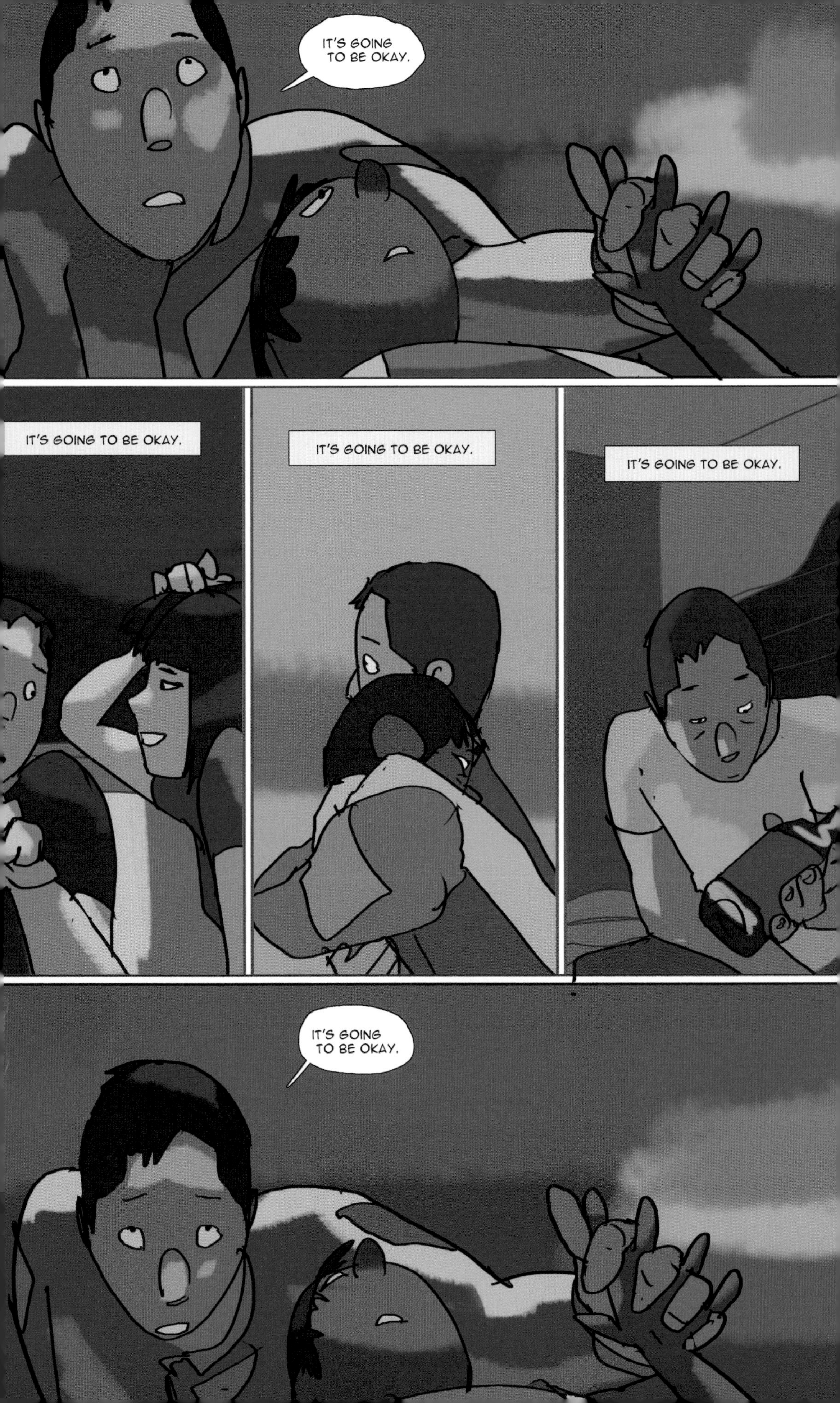
IT'S GOING TO BE OKAY.
IT'S GOING TO BE OKAY.
IT'S GOING TO BE OKAY.
IT'S GOING TO BE OKAY.
IT'S GOING TO BE OKAY.

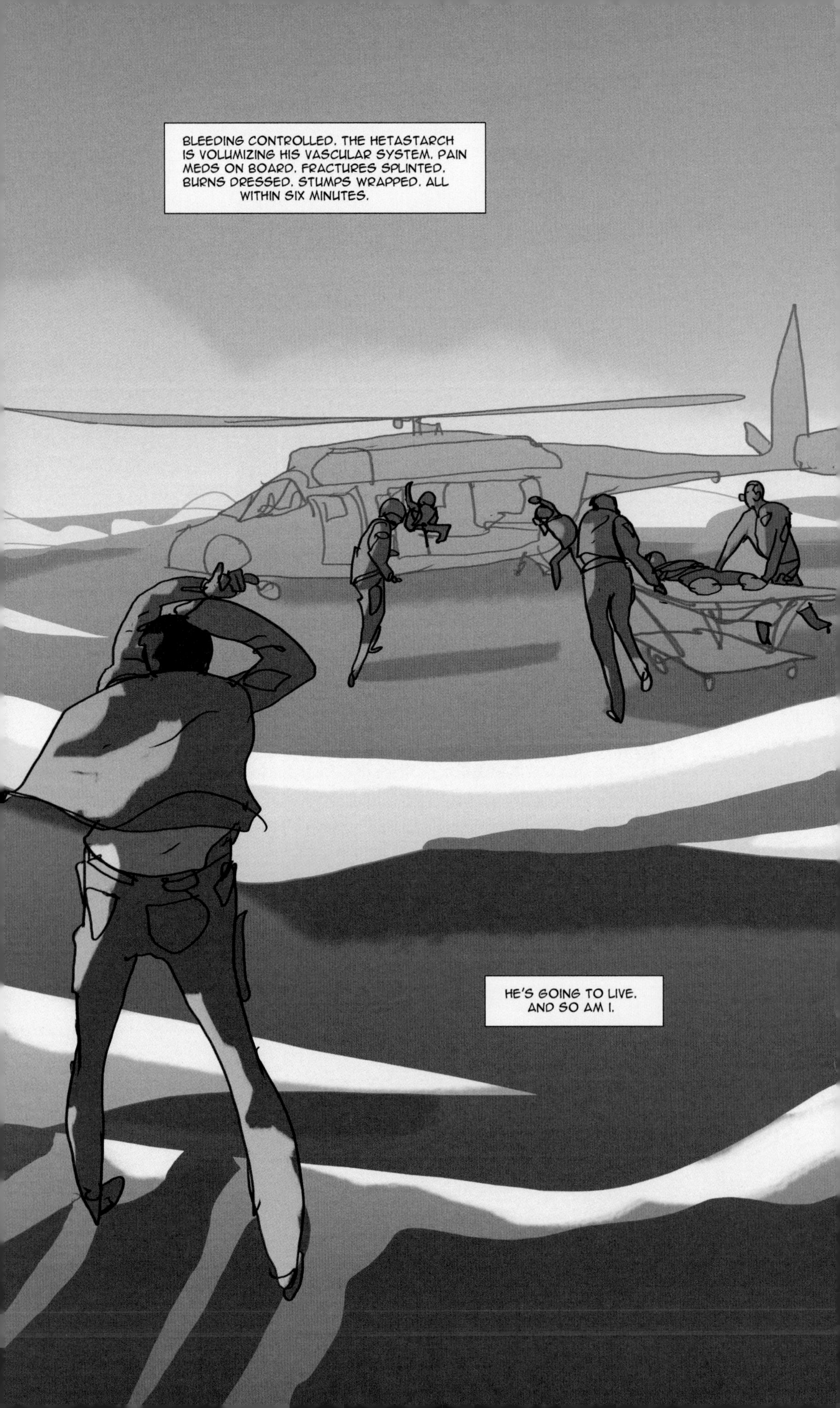
BLEEDING CONTROLLED. THE HETASTARCH IS VOLUMIZING HIS VASCULAR SYSTEM. PAIN MEDS ON BOARD. FRACTURES SPLINTED. BURNS DRESSED. STUMPS WRAPPED. ALL WITHIN SIX MINUTES.
HE'S GOING TO LIVE. AND SO AM I.

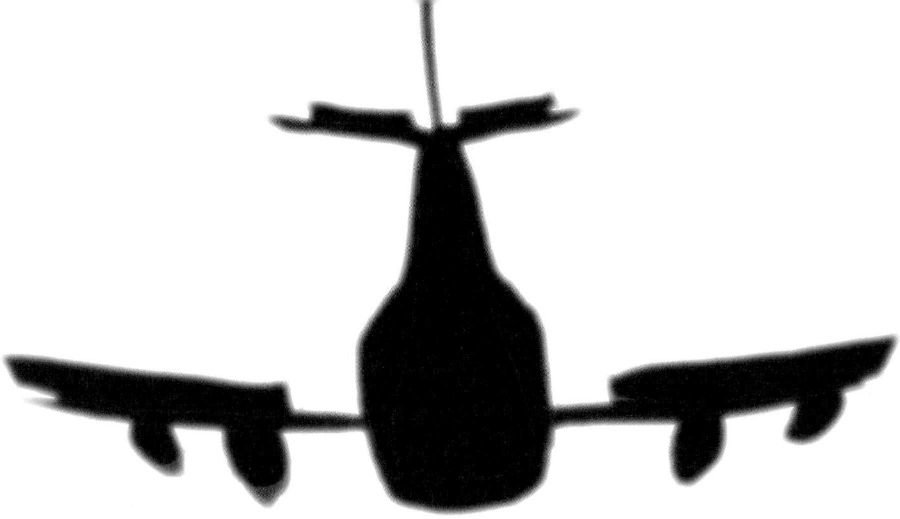

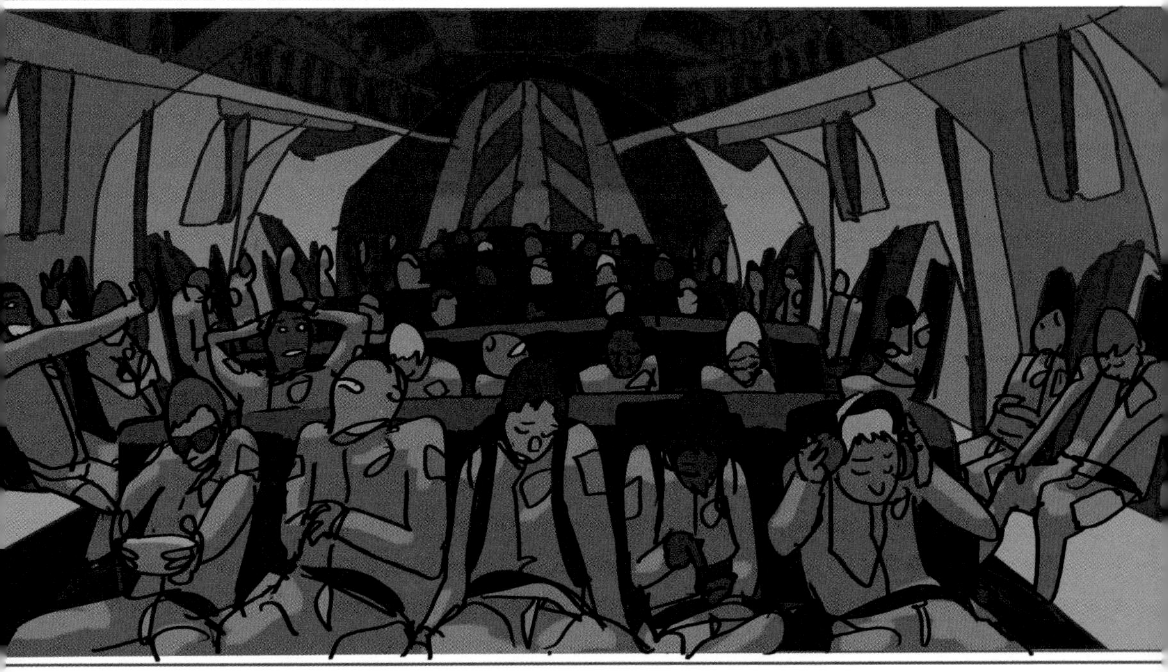

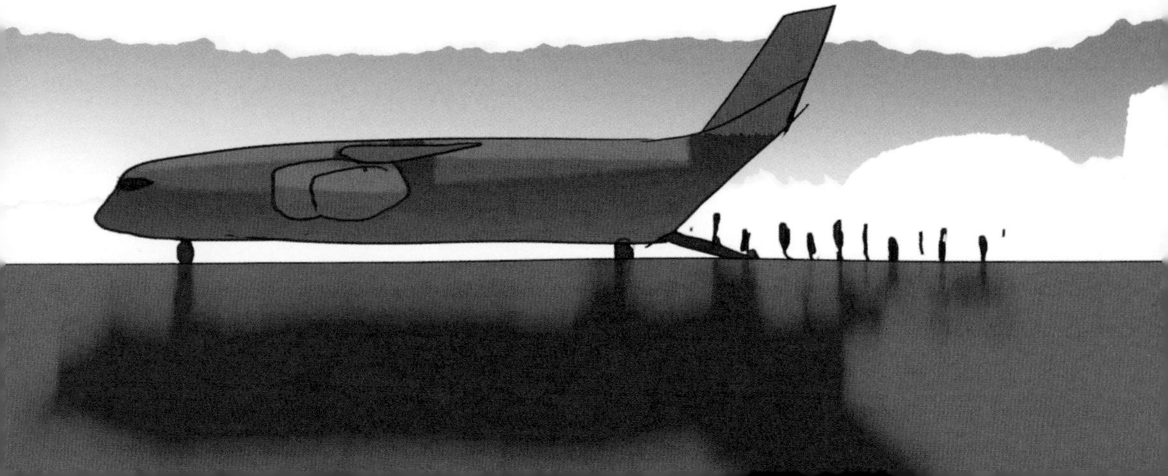

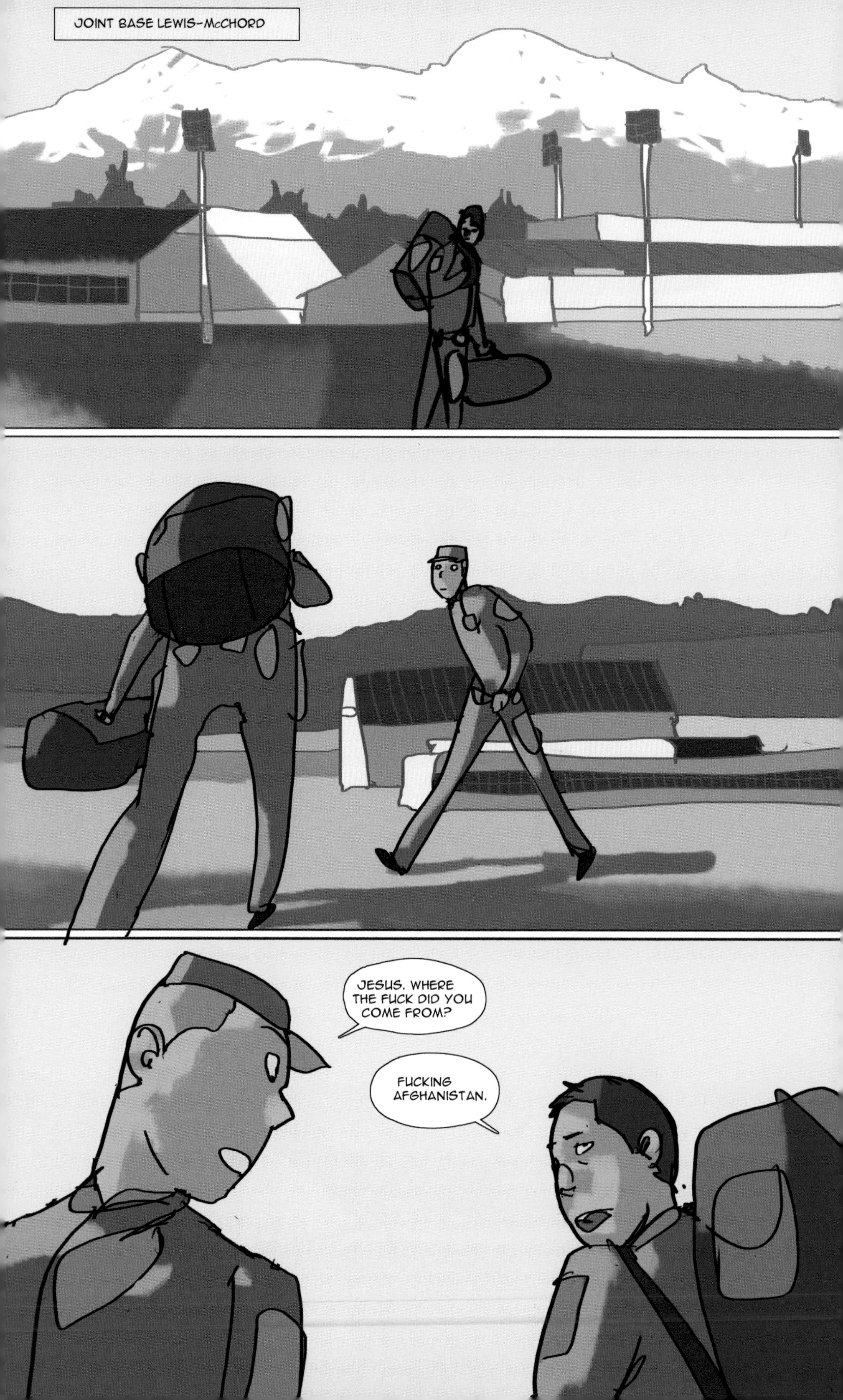
JOINT BASE LEWIS-McCHORD
JESUS. WHERE THE FUCK DID YOU COME FROM?
FUCKING AFGHANISTAN.

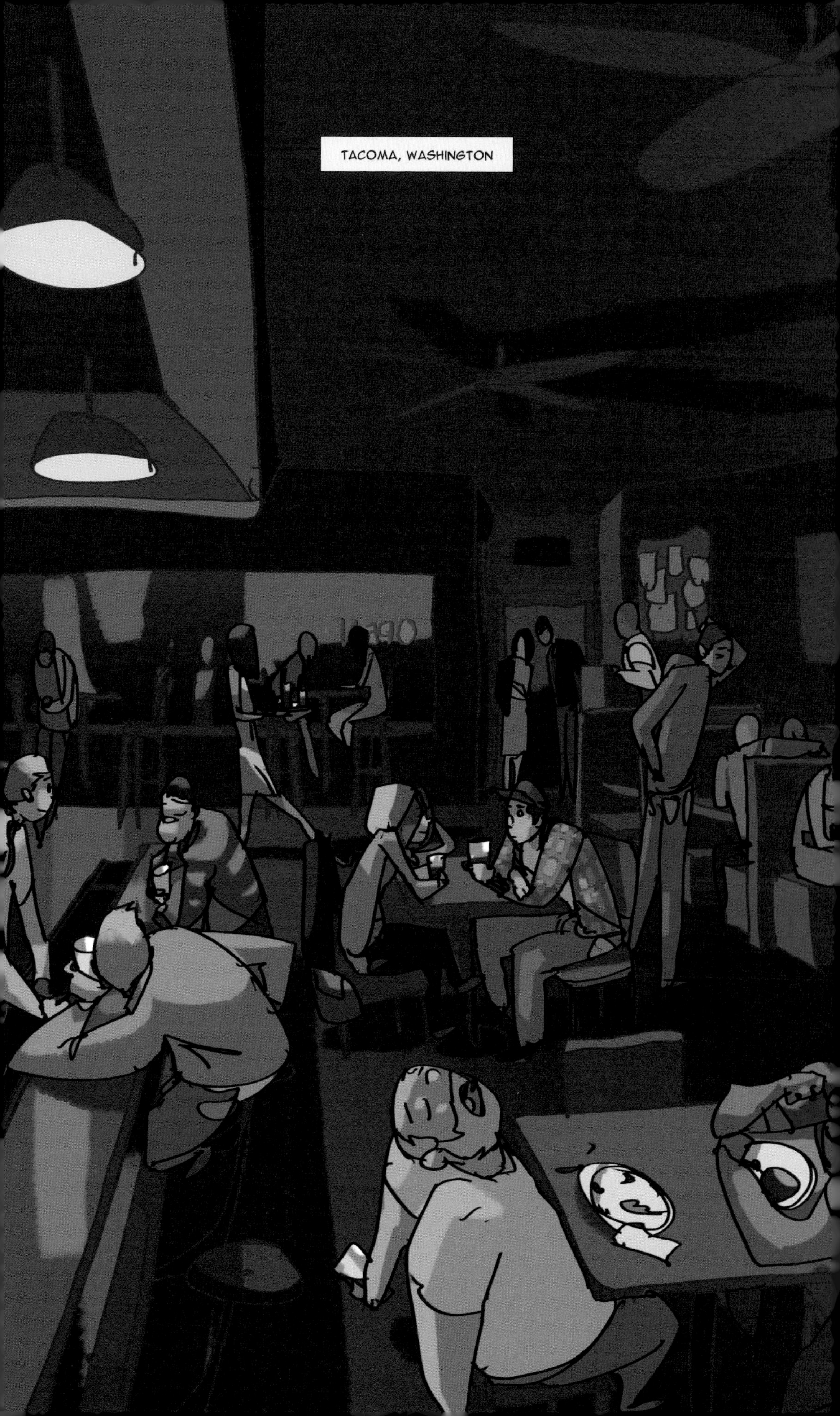
TACOMA, WASHINGTON

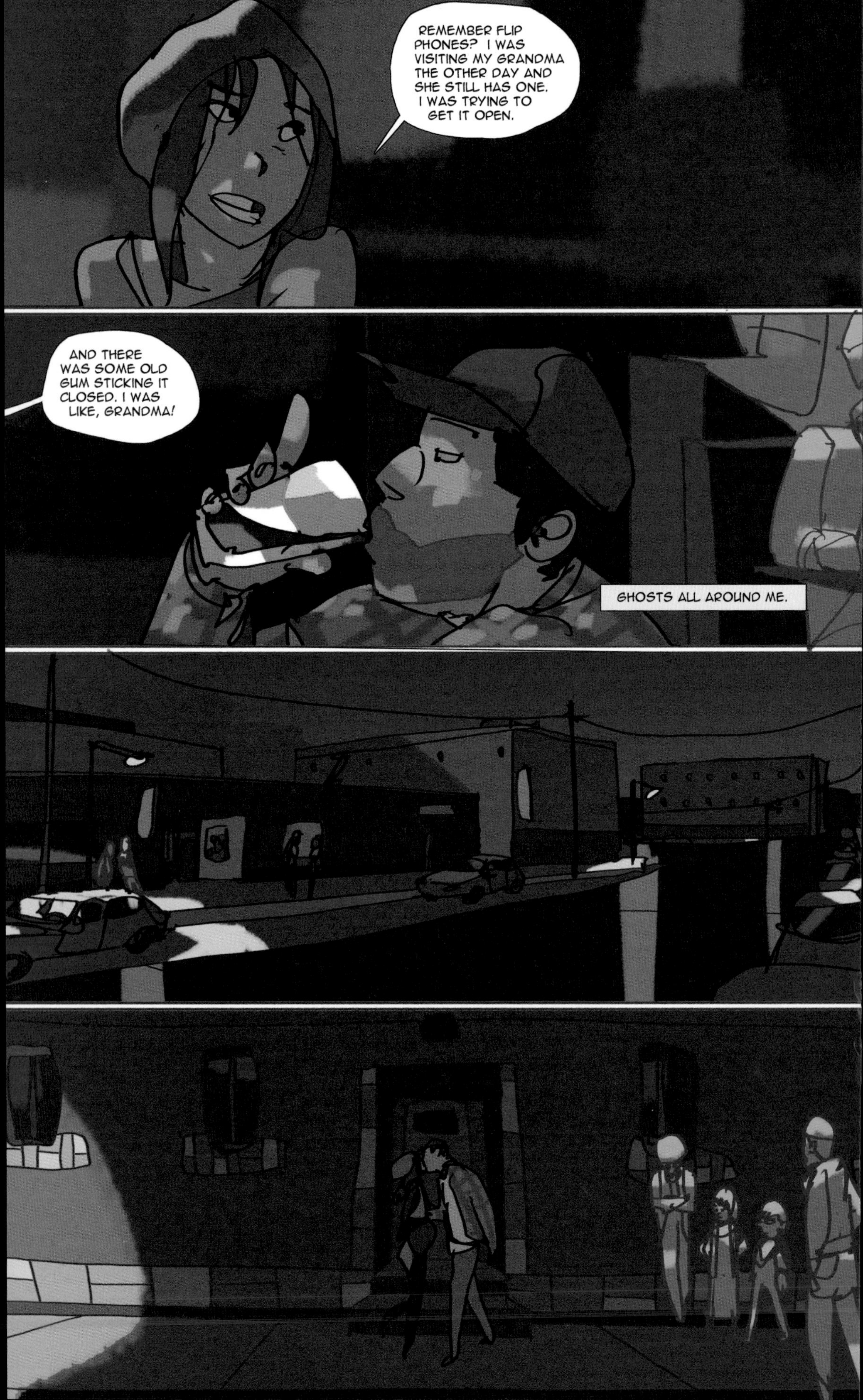
REMEMBER FLIP PHONES? I WAS VISITING MY GRANDMA THE OTHER DAY AND SHE STILL HAS ONE. I WAS TRYING TO GET IT OPEN.
AND THERE WAS SOME OLD GUM STICKING IT CLOSED. I WAS LIKE, GRANDMA!
GHOSTS ALL AROUND ME.

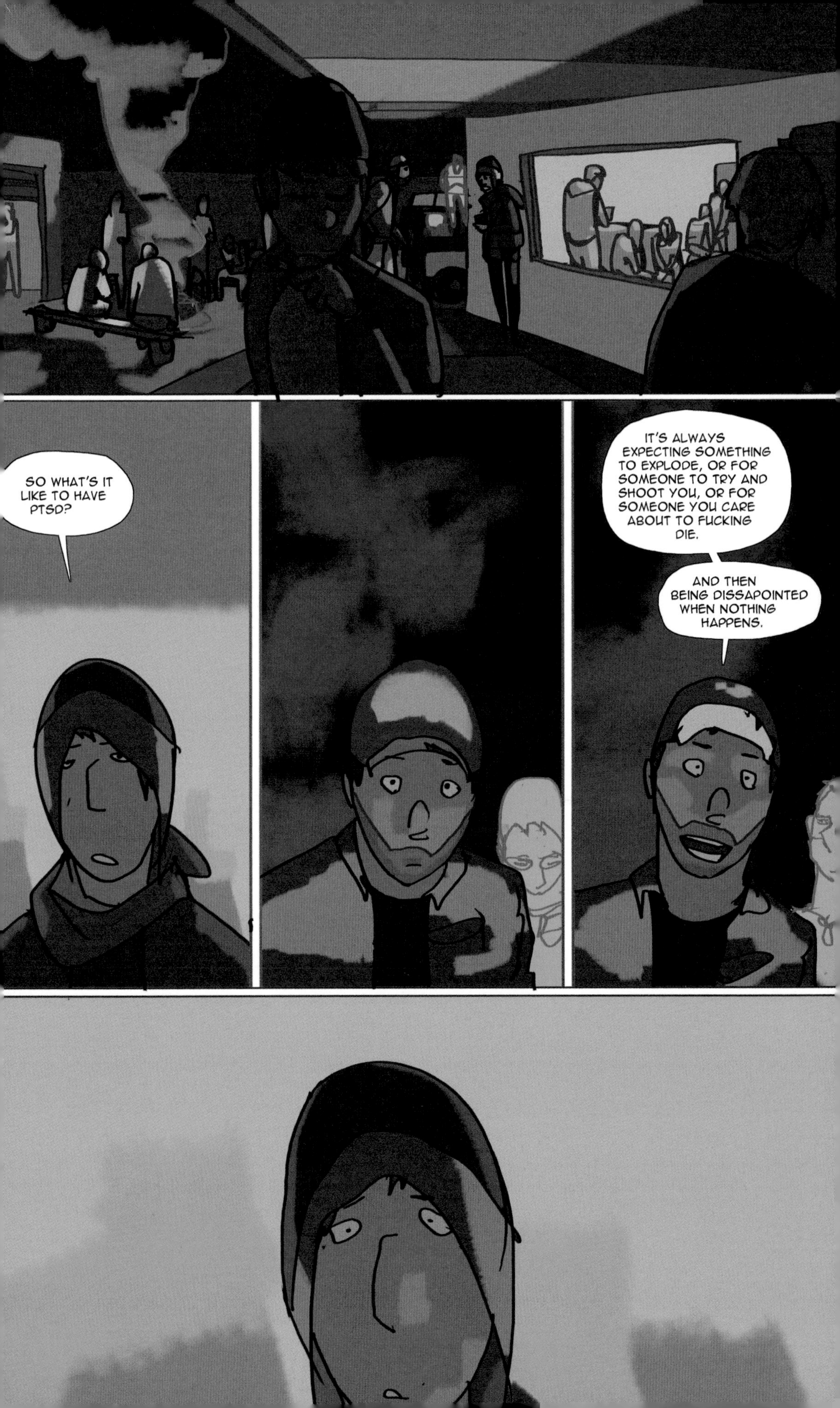
SO WHAT'S IT LIKE TO HAVE PTSD?
IT'S ALWAYS EXPECTING SOMETHING TO EXPLODE, OR FOR SOMEONE TO TRY AND SHOOT YOU, OR FOR SOMEONE YOU CARE ABOUT TO FUCKING DIE.
AND THEN BEING DISSAPOINTED WHEN NOTHING HAPPENS.

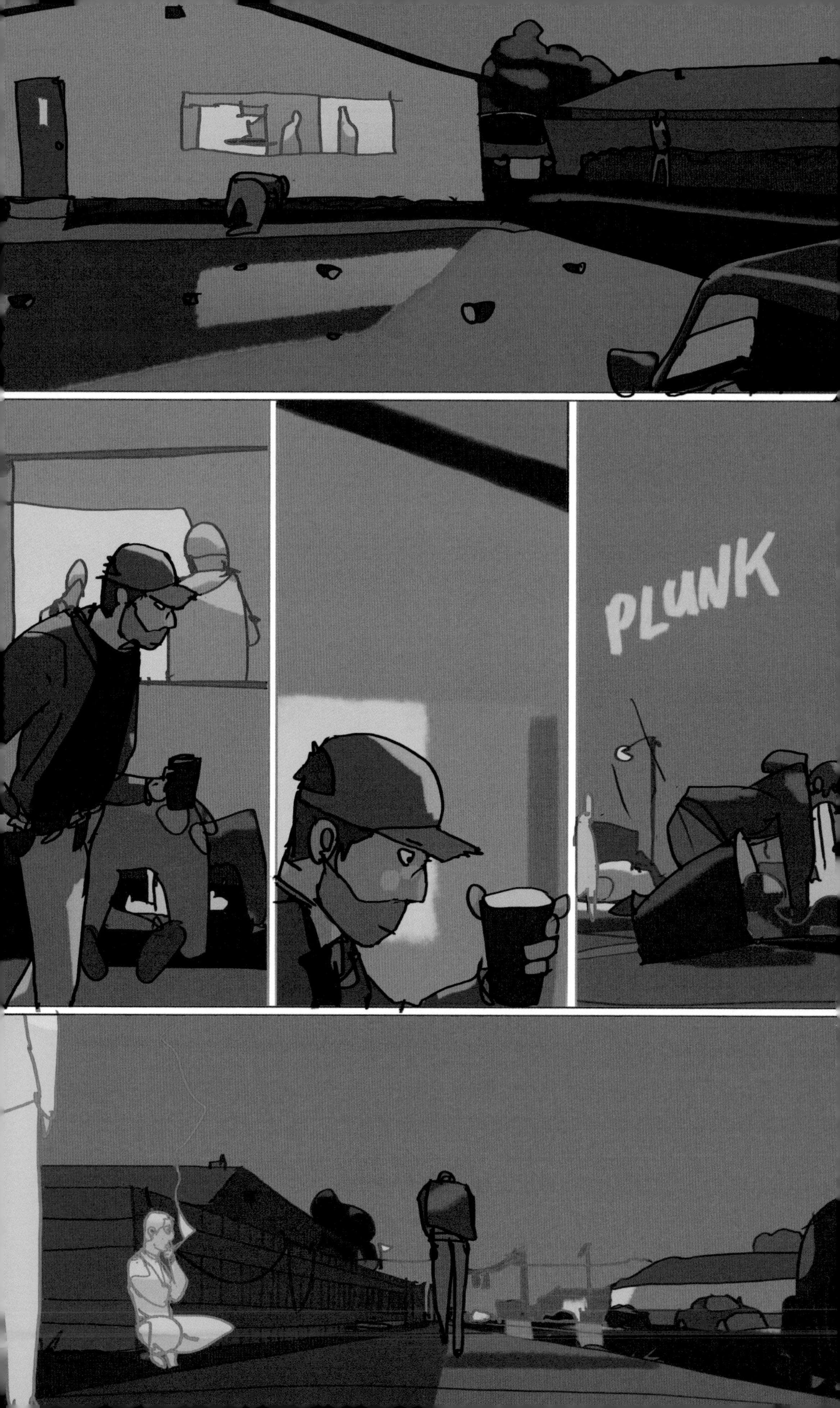
PLUNK

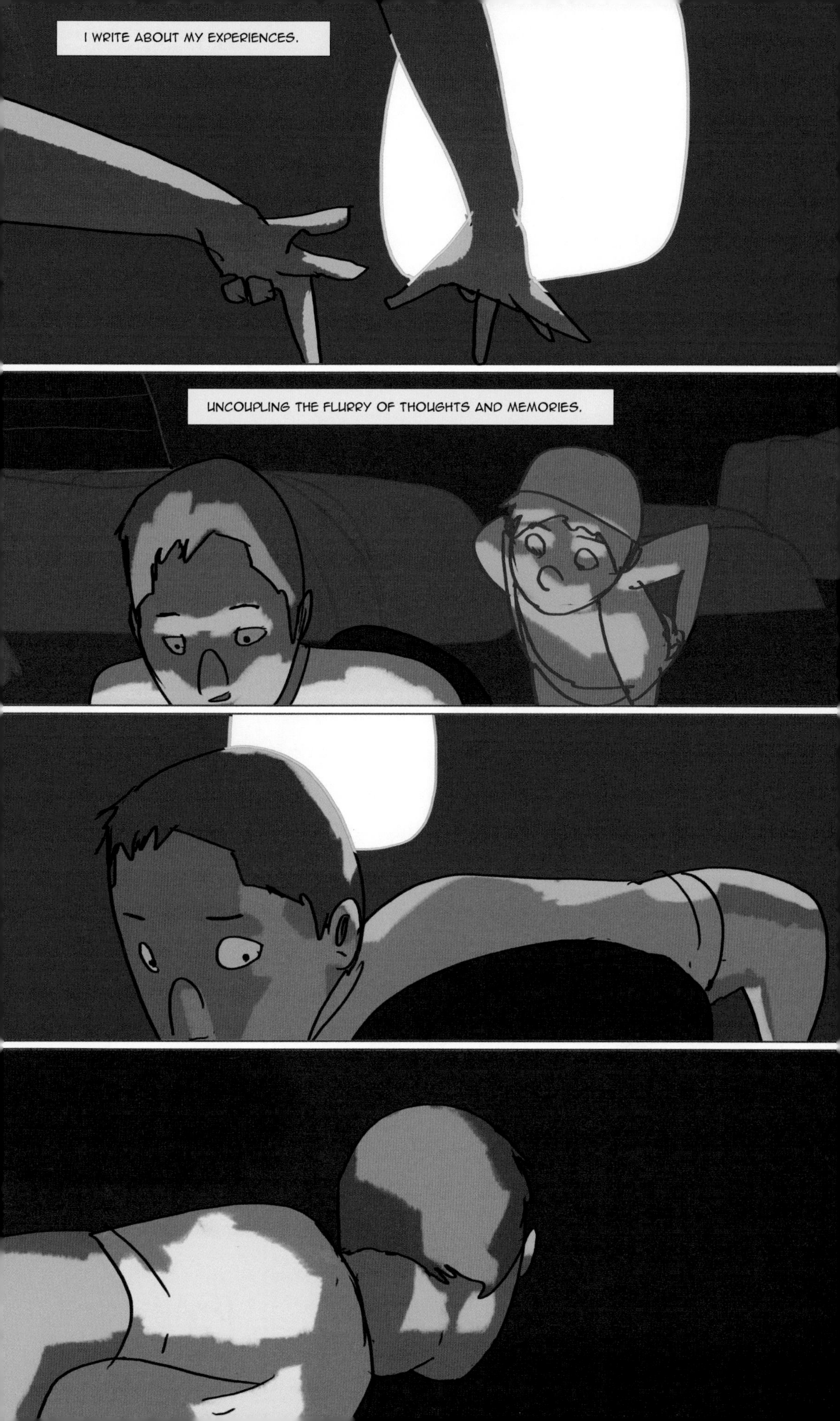
I WRITE ABOUT MY EXPERIENCES.
UNCOUPLING THE FLURRY OF THOUGHTS AND MEMORIES.

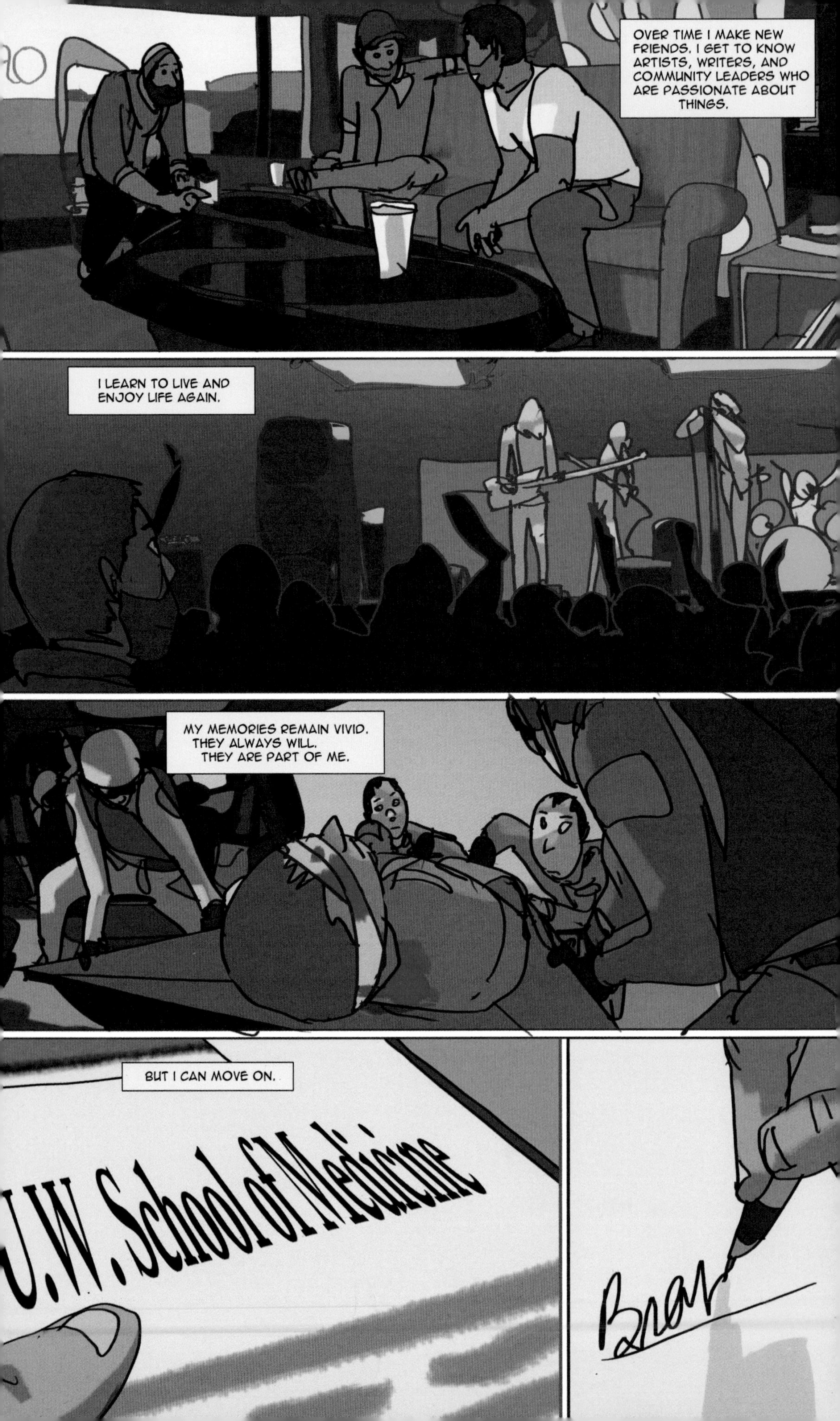
OVER TIME I MAKE NEW FRIENDS. I GET TO KNOW ARTISTS, WRITERS, AND COMMUNITY LEADERS WHO ARE PASSIONATE ABOUT THINGS.
I LEARN TO LIVE AND ENJOY LIFE AGAIN.
MY MEMORIES REMAIN VIVID. THEY ALWAYS WILL. THEY ARE PART OF ME.
BUT I CAN MOVE ON.
U.W. School of Medicine

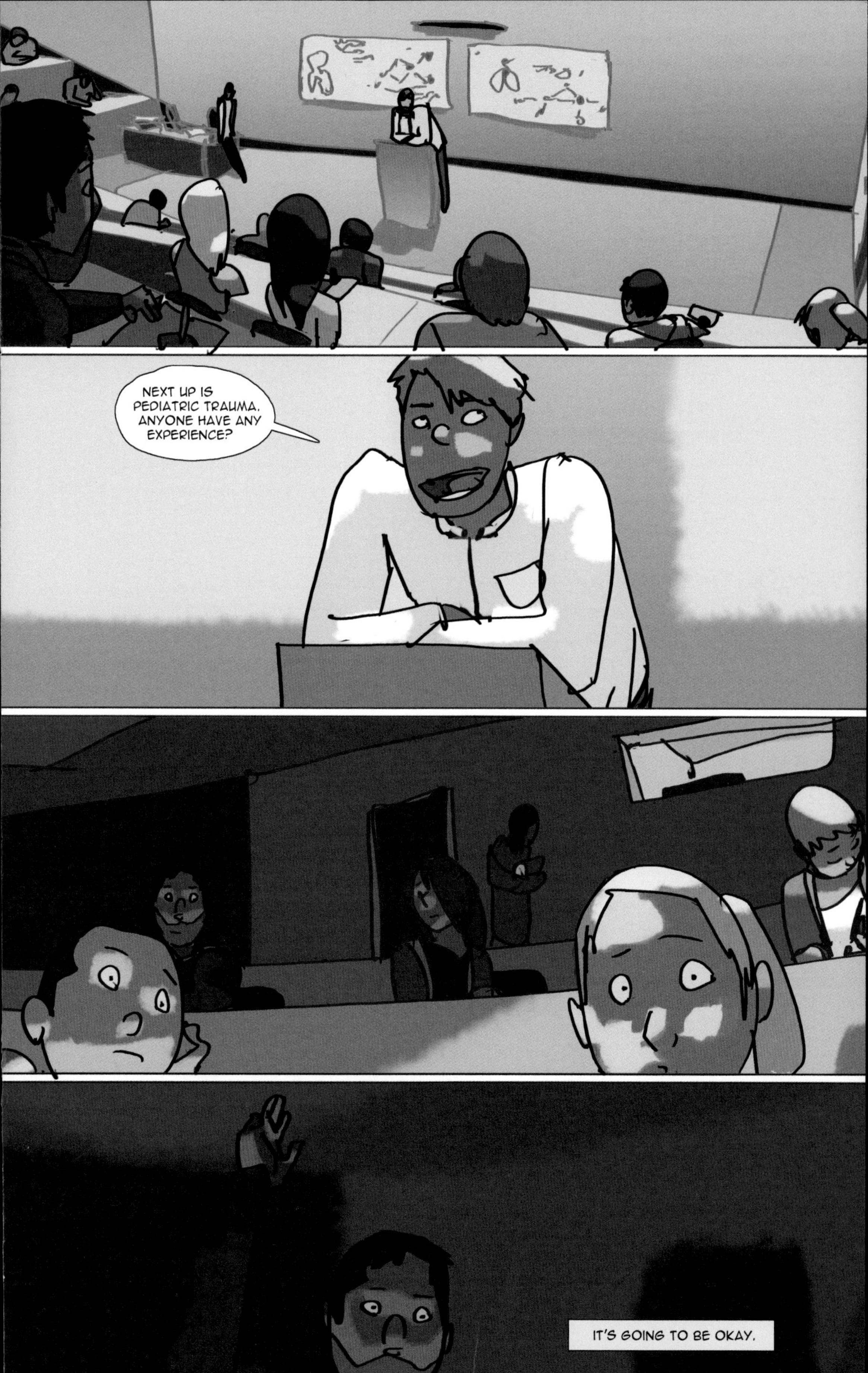
NEXT UP IS PEDIATRIC TRAUMA. ANYONE HAVE ANY EXPERIENCE?
IT'S GOING TO BE OKAY.

AFTERWORD

Well, that's the end of the story, and I want to personally thank you for sticking through to the end. I also want to thank Kevin and Per for everything they did to get this off the ground. This wouldn't have been anything but smeared ink in a waterlogged notebook if it weren't for Kevin. Per, you did an absolutely amazing job bringing Afghanistan and Sperwan Ghar to life on these pages. You absolutely blew my mind.

I had a lot of time between writing all of this out and it actually being published, most of which I spent seriously second-guessing my decision to do this. Right now I'm honestly assuming this won't be read by many people aside from my friends and family, and up until now they have always been really proud of what I did in the military. They had a romanticized view of me, flying off to Afghanistan and being a Real American Hero. Now the truth is out there, though ... I was just a guy who felt overwhelmed and who was struggling to keep his head above water.

A lot of the time I was just on autopilot. You just turn off your brain, turn off your emotions, and keep moving forward. If I didn't process it in the moment, I didn't give myself the opportunity to be scared shitless. If it weren't for the fact that I journaled most days, I probably would have had a breakdown eventually. Writing things down after the fact helped me process all the fucked up things I saw and all the emotions I should have felt at the time. Whether it was the teenager who lost his legs to an IED or listening to the chaos on the radio after a friend on patrol died waiting for medevac, I would just keep working and let it all out onto a notebook at night. And those notebooks are what formed this graphic novel. So this is less a word-by-word account of a deployment to Afghanistan and more of an emotional documentary. Does that make sense? Have I gone full douchebag?

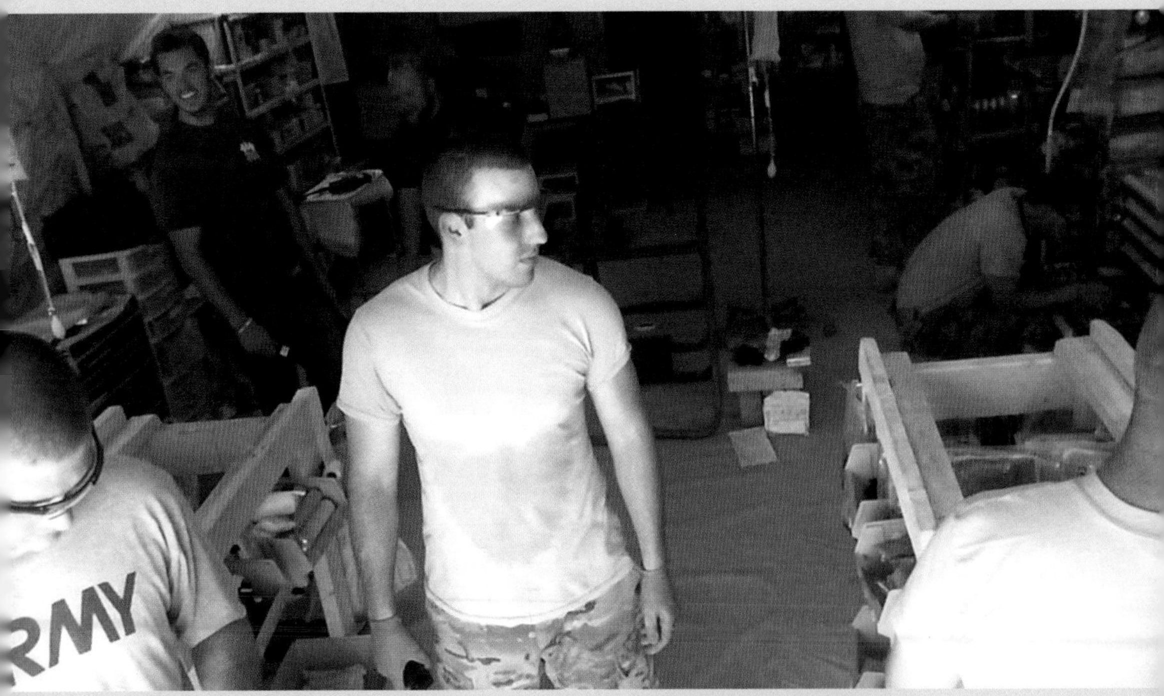
RMY

One thing that I absolutely want to stress is that I have the highest respect for everyone I served with over there. If anyone other than myself has been painted in an ill light, that was absolutely not my intention. The shit we went through bent us all and broke many. None of that means they are lesser or weaker individuals. These are simply experiences that we as humans are not meant to go through. As for Colonel Hendrix, I respect the shit out of him as well. I testified on his behalf during his disciplinary hearing afterward. I said it then, on record, and I will say it again: I would absolutely trust him to provide my medical care. I was pissed in the aftermath of the situation, but it is not hard to understand how the pressures of that deployment can hit someone so hard.

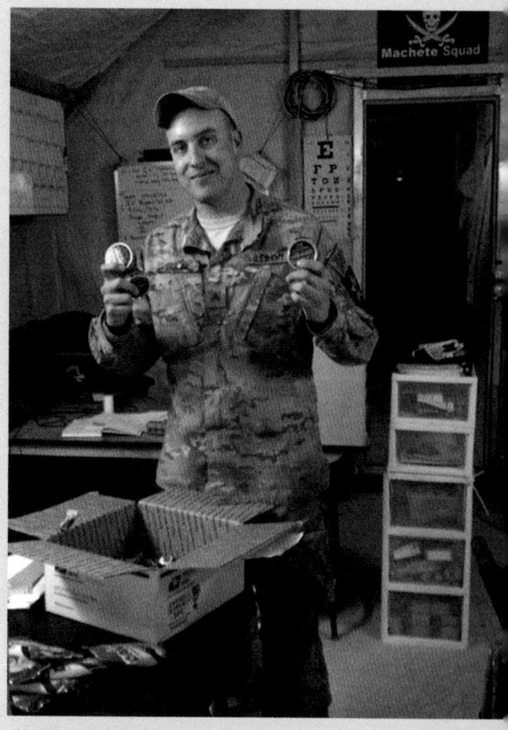
Machete Squad

And now? I'm back in the desert doing emergency medicine, writing this afterword from my condo balcony in Las Vegas after a grueling shift in the ER. The days are long and the nights are warm. Sometimes it feels like I'm back in Afghanistan. If I'm walking around outside at night and I smell cigarette smoke, I'm instantly brought back to the aid station. It's not a bad feeling, it's sort of like thinking about a long-lost ex. Life here is good, I feel great, and I'm back to helping people. Sometimes I still feel lost and unsure, but I don't hide it anymore; I use it as motivation to learn and grow. I wish I had done that a lot more in my earlier days. I think I would have been a lot better off if I had just asked my friends and family for help when I needed it, instead of hiding it in order to be that Real American Hero. I wish some of my friends had asked for help. If you're reading this and you feel that way, well, then I wish you would ask for help, too.

Machete 7, out.

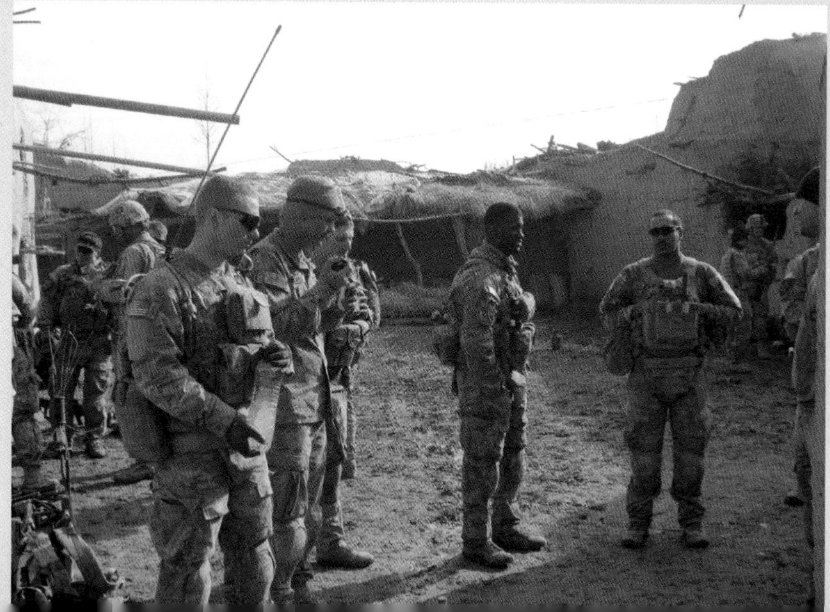

ABOUT THE CREATORS

BRENT DULAK grew up in Wisconsin, where he hated his job and then decided to join the Army. He deployed twice to Iraq and once to Afghanistan. He's a graduate of the University of Washington's School of Medicine and works as an Emergency Medicine Physician Assistant in Las Vegas, Nevada.

KEVIN KNODELL is a journalist who covers conflict, culture, and crime. His work has appeared in *Playboy*, *The Week*, *Vice*, *Soldier of Fortune*, *The News Tribune*, and other publications. He's a former contributing editor at Warisboring.com and writes the *Acts of Valor* comic series for *Naval History Magazine*.

DAVID AXE is a writer, editor, and filmmaker living in Columbia, South Carolina. A former war correspondent, he has written for *Vice*, *The Daily Beast*, *The Village Voice,* and many other publications. He is the writer of the graphic novel *War Is Boring* and the 2017 movie *The Theta Girl*.

PER DARWIN BERG is a comic artist and writer currently working out of Seattle, Washington, in the indy market. He volunteers weekly with the Bureau of Fearless Ideas, a writing center for K–12 students. His favorite hobby is comedy, but he's not that funny.